TAKEN BY SURPRISE

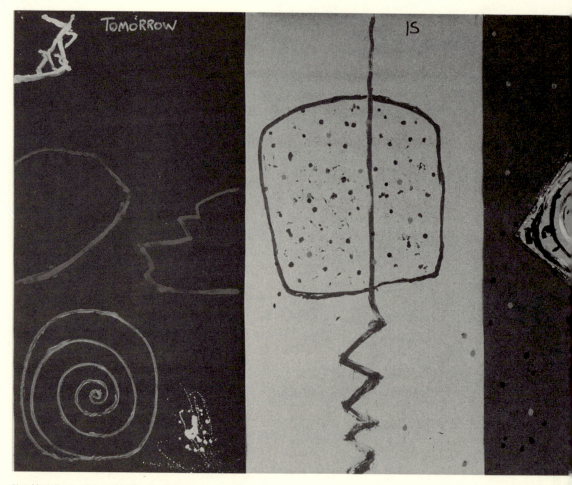

Mural by Mike Henderson. (© Mike Henderson.)

TAKEN BY SURPRISE

A Dance Improvisation Reader

Edited by Ann Cooper Albright and David Gere

Wesleyan University Press
Middletown, Connecticut

Published by Wesleyan University Press, Middletown, CT 06459
© 2003 by Wesleyan University Press

Library of Congress Cataloging-in-Publication
    Taken by surprise : a dance improvisation reader / edited by Ann Cooper
    Albright and David Gere
        p. cm.
    Inclides bibliographical references and index.
        ISBN 0–8195–6647–0 (cloth : alk. paper) —ISBN 0–8195–6648–9
(pbk. : alk. paper)
        1. Improvisation in dance.   I. Albright, Ann Cooper.   II. Gere, David.
    GV1781.2.T35 2003
    792.8—dc21   200312767

For our children

Isabel and Cyrus,

Christopher and Isadora,

Who keep us in the moment.

A.C.A. and D.G.

CONTENTS

ACKNOWLEDGMENTS

The editors would like to acknowledge the contributions of all those who made presentations at the 1994 *Taken By Surprise* conference in Berkeley, California, as well as those who spoke (and danced) at CI25, Oberlin College, in 1997. The funders of these events have contributed to this reader by providing a location for the authors to present early versions of their material and to meet each other for deeper thinking and debate. *Taken By Surprise* funders included the National Endowment for the Arts, Zellerbach Family Fund, Wallace Alexander Gerbode Foundation, Fleishhacker Foundation, and individual contributors to the Talking Dance Project, a project of the Ellen Webb Dance Foundation. CI25 was supported by an infrastructure of volunteers and teachers across the world, as well as Contact Collaborations, *Contact Quarterly,* and Oberlin College.

This volume owes a special debt to the journal *Contact Quarterly (CQ),* the home of so much insightful writing on improvisation and improvisers. Quite a number of the pieces written for this volume previously appeared in print or are reprinted courtesy of *CQ,* which is coedited by Nancy Stark Smith and Lisa Nelson. In addition, we gratefully acknowledge the many writers and photographers who have contributed so generously to this volume; Muriel Topaz for her interest and guidance at an early stage; and UCLA graduate students Laurah Klepinger, Ann Mazzocca, and Norah Zuñiga Shaw for their fine work preparing text and image for publication. Others who have offered their creativity and ideas include Katy Matheson, author of the essay on improvisation in the *International Encyclopedia of Dance* and a presenter at the *Taken By Surprise* conference; Sandy Walker, whose fine eye and activist stance influenced the shape and look of that conference and this book; and Mike Henderson, whose mural created on the spot for that conference serves as the frontispiece of this eponymous volume. We reserve a special acknowledgment for Suzanna Tamminen and her excellent editorial team at Wesleyan University Press. We are grateful to Suzanna not only for recognizing the importance of this collection, but also for serving as an advocate for new dance scholarship that values creativity and experimentation.

From Oberlin College, Ann Cooper Albright writes: Editing this book has given me the opportunity to reflect on the history of my involvement with many different forms of improvisation. Special thanks to my co-editor, David Gere, for being generous and flexible enough to open his Talking Dance Project (co-directed by Ellen Webb) to include many of the improvisational forms arising out of the practice of Contact in the 1980s and '90s. Working with him over the course of dissertations, kids, jobs and various books, has always been fun, a bright spot in the endless to-do lists of my middle life. This project is rooted in my early experiences dancing and watching improvisation in performance at places such as A Cappella Motion in Northhampton, Mass., and at Seminole Works in Philadelphia. Seeing really good improvisers in performance was deeply magical to me; improvisation struck me early on as a form based on a heightened sense of responsiveness, both physical and psychic, and much of my life has been spent encouraging mine and other's abilities to respond to the ever-changing world. For introducing me to the magic of improvisation as an entry into finding one's own style of movement, I would like to acknowledge Francoise de la Morandière. Later, in graduate school, John Gamble taught me to take improvisation seriously as both a method for physical training and for scoring group performances. Over the ensuing years, my work has been greatly influenced by Nancy Stark Smith, who has always been wonderfully generous with her ideas and her dancing. Steve Paxton, Lisa Nelson, Andrew Harwood, Alito Alessi, K. J. Holmes, and Kirstie Simson have also inspired my teaching and dancing. My commitment to dancing spills over into my life in many un-predictable ways. I am especially grateful to Tom Newlin, who taught me long ago how to open the possibility of happiness within my personal life. He has brought the wonder of improvisation into the realities of maintaining a family, and his intelligence and humor has kept me going on many occasions.

From UCLA, David Gere writes: Working with Ann Cooper Albright on this book has been like running alternating legs of a marathon, a lively baton-passing improvisation taking place across phone lines and internet connections, with the occasional face-to-face meeting over good food. Writing this, I am remembering the time many years ago when Ann pulled me onto the floor in a Contact class and assured me she could support my six-foot lanky frame. She's been support-ing me ever since. What a gift. I also want to send an especially big thank you to Ellen Webb, who introduced me to the performance of improvisation in the Bay Area nearly two decades ago and who had a hand in my seeing, and valuing, the work of Ruth Zaporah. Partnering with her in friendship and in the work of the Talking Dance Project has been one of my life's greatest pleasures. At UCLA I am grateful for ongoing intellectual and dance partnerships with colleagues and friends Susan Leigh Foster, Dan Froot, Angelia Leung, Victoria Marks, Judy

Mitoma, Peter Nabokov, Colin Quigley, Allen Roberts, David Rousseve, Marta Savigliano, Peter Sellars, Keith Terry, Christopher Waterman, and Cheng-Chieh Yu. Here's a toast to John Bishop for his last-minute assistance with the photos. The exquisitely professional support of staff members Carol Endo, Muriel Moorhead, Carl Patrick, Silvily Kessler Thomas, and Lilian Wu is also greatly appreciated. Additionally, the University has enabled the completion of this book through numerous Academic Senate grants and Career Development awards. On the homefront, effusive thanks to Peter Carley, my partner in love and life, for waiting.

Finally, a huge explosion of thanks to Simone Forti, whose image graces the front cover of our book, and whose example of dancing and improvising a life that keeps curiosity at the fore inspires us both.

INTRODUCTION

David Gere

Most books about dance improvisation classify as how-to's. They compile exercises. They offer proven tips from previous practitioners. They instruct. This book is different because it does not profess to tell the reader how to improvise; rather, it suggests a range of ways to think and talk about improvisation. It is, after all, a *reader,* its very format making the implicit argument that improvisation is not only something to practice, but to write and speak and read about as well. I do not mean to say that this is a book for the library shelf rather than the studio. Not at all. In fact, the editors of this volume view it as an improviser's intimate companion, not to be tossed on a bedside table or stuck in a locker, but to be literally and figuratively thumbed through and pored over while the dancer works in the studio. In our mind's eye, we see the book poised in the improviser's outstretched hand, its pages unfurling as the improviser wends her way intelligently through the space. This book may not tell a dancer precisely how to move, nor precisely how to think; it may, however, goad a dancer to engage more lucidly in the process of improvisation.

Even as it makes a case for lucidity, this collection of essays presupposes the central position of the element of surprise in improvisation—what Susan Leigh Foster in her opening essay posits as the interface between the "known" and the "unknown." The contrast between verbal articulation and the mysteries of the moment animates every page of this book, even when that contrast seems to point up an impossible conundrum. And no wonder. More than any other aspect of contemporary dance practice, improvisation calls forth images of a state beyond language, where images are plumbed from the depths of the human psyche, and where words do not suffice. C. G. Jung's notion of the collective unconscious, a philosophical touchstone for the early modern dancers who began using improvisation as a rehearsal technique, was co-opted by them in the 1940s and 1950s to suggest that, through improvisation, the dancer/choreographer might gain special access to the realm of the preverbal. In fact, many artists in the modern dance idiom have argued for the importance of improvisation as a primary (read: primal) means of unearthing the subterranean geographies of the self, for turning over the wet rock to reveal its mossy underside. And yet in their day these same artists, ranging from Mary Wigman to Martha Graham, systematically rejected the idea of performing improvisationally on the public stage. Improvisation is for private reflection and discovery, they argued. Composition and the rigors of choreography must follow.[1]

This collection of essays, however, proposes that improvisation is by its very nature among the most rigorous of human endeavors, and that even those who subscribe to improvisation as a preverbal, protomagical activity must admit that it requires the resources both of body and of mind. In fact, if the Cartesian dualism of body as separate from mind is ever to be surmounted—as seems to be the major thrust of current dance scholarship—dance improvisation provides the perfect paradigm. For it is while improvising that the body's intelligence manifests itself most ineluctably, and that the fast-moving, agile mind becomes a necessity. The body thinks. The mind dances. Thought and movement, words and momentum, spiral about one another. It is the project of this volume, then, to suggest that improvisation, rather than being swathed in mystery, is in fact susceptible to careful articulation. Furthermore, the shared principle animating these essays is that the careful articulation of the improvisational moment by no means renders it any less valuable, or any less capable of surprise.

As the reader will find on his or her journey through these pages, surprise is everywhere. And mystery too. Improviser Ruth Zaporah recounts a performance in which she spontaneously created a character named Alice out of a doll prop. Afterward, three anonymous women sitting in the audience came to her, shaken, to explain that they had joined together that evening to celebrate the memory of a dead friend named Alice. Not surprisingly, these women felt that their friend had been manifested in Zaporah's doll, and in the story she wove around it. T. Balasaraswati, the great improviser in the Bharatanatyam tradition of South India, has been described as an oracle of the divine for her exceptional ability to improvise on sacred song texts. How else might one explain her remarkable fluidity and prescient poeticism? Indeed, the rhetoric of magic runs throughout the discussion of improvisation: to theorize about improvisation is to theorize about consciousness, and to theorize about consciousness is to push the boundaries of physical discourse toward consideration of the spirit, the divine, the unfathomable, and the unimaginable.

Improvisation may, in some respects, verge on the unimaginable, but it seems significant that neither Zaporah nor the late Balasaraswati emerged as great improvisers out of nowhere. They did not simply appear in public one day, like idiots savants, to perform at the apex of improvisational accomplishment. Quite the contrary, they prepared themselves by making improvisation a regular practice, a daily practice even, in the course of which they were forced to confront such questions as how to proceed when a lapse in concentration occurs, or what to do at a moment of choice (to repeat a phrase, say, or to move on) or what resources to draw upon if nothing particularly innovative animates the body, or how to attend to the energies in a room, to the people who are sitting and watching. This is to say that virtually all improvisation takes place upon a firm foundation of training and practice—think of J. S. Bach's public improvisations on the organ—through which a vocabulary of conventions and possible variations is committed to movement memory and deeply explored. Call it magic, or spirit, or skill, as you wish, but the spark that sets improvisation in motion comes on top of committed labor. Without the fuel of training, the spark would have nothing to burn.

Nonetheless it is worth noting that, at the beginning of the twenty-first century in the United States, the pleasures of dance improvisation remain stigmatized. To improvise, it is held, is to engage in aimless, even talentless, noodling. Though elements of improvisation were surely present even in nineteenth-century classical ballet (where ballerinas interpolated variations on the spot)[2] as well as in all West African–influenced social and theatrical forms (which arguably means every dance form in the United States since slavery),[3] the word "improvisation" did not come into common usage with regard to dance in the West until the 1960s, at the time of the Judson Dance Theater. Anna Halprin, an influential teacher and performer on the West Coast (and a student of Margaret H'Doubler's from the University of Wisconsin), was central in establishing an interest in improvisation based upon the model of child's play, as opposed to monolithic choreography. The Grand Union, formed in 1970 by a consortium of dancers including Barbara Dilley, Steve Paxton, Yvonne Rainer, and Trisha Brown, popularized the term "improvisation" on its extended tours from college campus to college campus, offering madcap theater-dance performances composed on the spot.[4] But even as the excitement of improvisational performance was catching fire, Bessie Schönberg, perhaps the greatest choreographic mentor of the second half of the twentieth century and a committed modernist, instructed her pupils that improvisation was fine in the studio but never in performance.[5] Control of one's materials has been held by many to be paramount. And improvisation connotes lack of control.

As will be argued in this volume, however, improvisation ought not to be conceived in such terms. Quite the contrary, it should be recognized for the great demands it places upon a performer, including the demand for nearly instantaneous responsiveness to a broad palette of sensation and perception. Choices concerning such formal issues as repetition and variation, for example, cannot be arrived at with the leisure of the studio, over the period of hours or days, months or years. These decisions must be made now. This moment. While it is true that virtually all artmaking demands decisiveness, in improvisation choices must be arrived at without creative block or procrastination. There is not time for delay in improvisational performance. There is simply no time.

The thought of improvising in public may sound frightening to many of us, yet there is not a studio, theater, or university dance department in the world where improvisation is not being practiced every day of the week. For example, you can see improvisation in the release technique class when a dancer feels her way toward mastery of the morning's phrase and then extends and embellishes it in her own way. You can see it in the flamenco studio when a battery of footwork takes on a new life, a variation in rhythm, or a double-time flurry. You can even see it in the choreography studio in the five minutes before class, when students are devising studies that in just a few moments must be ready to show. (The urgency of the deadline can serve as a potent prod to improvisation.) You can see it most directly, of course, in the improvisation classroom, as a master teacher such as Simone Forti teaches her students, by example, to seek new and resonant combinations of words and movement. You can see it at night in the theater in the expression of the professional performer who lingers an extra split second in a choreographed one-legged balance and is forced to catch up the lost time by squeezing the next few steps into a nanosecond. And I can feel it now in my fingers on the keys as I send an impulse—a thought, an idea, a rhetorical device—onto the computer screen and then pause to see how it will complete itself. Improvisation is everywhere in dance and, I would argue, everywhere, every moment, in the world. It is present in every action and in every pregnant moment between.

My coeditor, Ann Cooper Albright, who has penned the concluding essay in this collection, has devoted much of her career to improvisation, both as a performer and as a thinker. I, on the other hand, am a rather unlikely scholar to be focussing his attention on this subject. I am, by nature, a planner. At the start of every day, I make a list of tasks to accomplish and I take great pleasure in checking off the completed activities. I am inclined to write my lectures rather than to deliver them spontaneously. If I am in charge of an event, I like to think through all the exigencies, from the arrangement of chairs to the details of the personal introductions. In the parlance of dance practice, I am—in my scholarly work and in my life—more like a choreographer than an improviser. I do not like to leave things to chance. And yet, even with my pronounced proclivities for planning, I have come to recognize and appreciate the myriad ways in which improvisation operates in my life. In the midst of my prior work as a journalist and critic in the Bay Area, from the mid-1980s to the mid-1990s, I began actively to nurture the traces of improvisation then emerging in my writing process, and I have sought to deepen my understanding of improvisation ever since.

In my early years as a critic, writing was a frankly laborious process in which I painstakingly transferred ideas and observations into prose. This process was more like translation than writing, really, and to shape a single paragraph might take me hours. In fact, it was not unusual for me to stay up all night after a performance in order to produce three pages of text for the next morning's 10 A.M. deadline. Partly from experience and partly from necessity—how many all-nighters in a row can one pull?—I realized I had to devise a new approach. So I began to write deadline reviews with nothing more than an opening line and a few scrawled notes to jump-start the process. I still clung to my notes and took time at the outset of each writing session to establish a sense of direction; I felt I couldn't start with the gas tank on empty. But I began fashioning an approach that would require me to let go of complete control. In so doing, I began to enjoy a new perspective on the process of writing, as exactly that, a process. A few words typed onto the computer screen created an opening for new ruminations and, significantly, for new wordplay. By holding on less rigidly to a fore-ordained outline or overworked phraseology, the writing began to flow at a steadier rate, to become a form of pleasure even, rather than forced labor.

In retrospect, I believe I was learning to replace an impacted and deep-seated fear of the unknown with a new sense of joy in the moment of discovery, and a basic trust in the mental and physical processes that are necessary to render dancing into language. My critical capacities were still hard at work but in a different way. I was learning to see myself as a reliably responsive intelligence and as a flexibly physical instrument. With that personal revelation in my pocket, I began to consider all the other ways in which improvisation operates in my life, our lives. And given the new pleasure I was experiencing, it should not be surprising that I began to want to incorporate more improvisation, more of the time, even in the simplest of my daily actions.

You might want to as well. For example: You are reading the morning paper and decide to skip the lead story and go straight to the horoscopes. You get to decide. Your kid, or kid sister, interrupts you while working and next thing you know you are bouncing a toddler on your knee. Some of this is just fun. It transforms life's drudgeries into light work. But I'm also inclined to see these mundane improvisations as a form of what the French theorist Michel de Certeau has termed "tactical" action. Such action offers a way to coalesce and channel traces of personal power in a world where the "strategic" powers that govern us can seem overwhelming, even crushing. As we make our way through the morning paper in our own way, or weave down the straight-and-narrow sidewalk on an irregular trajectory, or improvise against the grain of Doris Humphrey's rules for good choreography, we become what de Certeau has termed "poets of [our] own acts."[6] We reject established pathways and forge our own. In this sense, the box that holds improvisation can be seen to be very large indeed. It contains virtually every aspect of our lives.

The impulse for the creation of this reader arrived over a meal—a favored site for improvisation, what with the twin glories of conversation and food. My friend Ann Cooper Albright and I were sharing a long lunch in midtown Manhattan and playing hooky from sessions of a national dance conference at Lincoln Center. While swapping ideas for upcoming projects, I mentioned that Ellen Webb, a choreographer and my collaborator in the Talking Dance Project, and I were organizing a conference in Berkeley on improvisation, and that we were striving to convey its importance as extending beyond dancing to life itself. We hoped a group of publishable essays might grow out of it. Albright, a long-time Contact improviser, immediately confessed that she had harbored a similar idea. Why not work together?

So it is that this volume draws upon talks delivered at the Berkeley conference—"Taken By Surprise: Improvisation in Dance and Mind," presented by the Talking Dance Project in June 1994 at the Julia Morgan Theater. It also includes material generated from Albright's CI25 event, a celebration on the occasion of Contact Improvisation's twenty-fifth anniversary, held at Oberlin College in June 1997. These two gatherings and the writings emerging from them reflect the range and eclecticism of our various interests, Ellen Webb's and mine in contemporary improvisation, Zen practice, the history and theory of improvisation, and the dance forms of Asia and Africa; Ann Cooper Albright's in all of the above plus a determined focus on Contact Improvisation. It was only after the majority of these essays was gathered together that we realized that, with a few additions and some judicious reprinting of existing articles, we could shape a volume of larger significance than we had first imagined. What has evolved, then, is a broad-based reader that deals with dance improvisation from theoretical, historical, and ethnographic perspectives, and that makes the case for a dramatically expanded notion of improvisation in our daily lives.

The opening section of the reader, "Improvising Body, Improvising Mind," explores the nature of improvisation from theoretical and philosophical perspectives. What do we know about improvisation as a movement activity? And how might that knowledge illuminate our human predicament as beings who live in bodies and through minds? Susan Leigh Foster's keynote performance at the Berkeley conference—a scholarly tour de force that included overturning the lecturn, running up and down the aisles, and pressing her body hard against, and almost through, the projection screen—sets the framework for this broad consideration. Foster's parsing of the interface between the known and unknown takes on particular resonance with the addition of a new section in her essay considering the work of her late colleagues and friends Cynthia Novack and Richard Bull. Bruce Curtis's essay on gravity, meanwhile, is an exploration of the physical forces that bind us to the earth. Curtis, a quadriplegic, also manages in his contribution to denaturalize customary references to "organic" or "authentic" dancing by writing from the perspective of a person whose body "looks different and moves differently" from others, thus forcing a re-visioning of improvisation's clichés. Ruth Zaporah, a leading dance improviser with strong links to theater, describes the importance played by the audience in performance situations, especially when characters such as Alice emerge. And Kent De Spain provides a vertiginous view inside the improviser's mind and body by literally "reporting" on his own experience and that of six allied improvisers as they dance alone in a black-box studio. Taken as a whole, these essays outline large-scale issues concerning consciousness and physicality in relation to improvisation.

"A Duet with Postmodern Dance" deepens what, heretofore, has been the main emphasis of writing on improvisation in the United States: the history of the form in relation to postmodern dance. The historical roots of contemporary improvisational performance in New York and California in the 1960s are addressed here by a quartet of writers. Janice Ross, an expert on Anna Halprin's work, delves for the first time into the significance of Halprin's work with children. Simone Forti, a central player in postmodern dance and improvisation since the 1960s, offers a career retrospective, while Carmela Hermann, a Forti protégé, explains firsthand what she has learned from her mentor. Sally Banes, a scholar whose work has served to contextualize the postmodern moment, offers a sweeping view of the three decades of improvisation in postmodern dance. Together, these essays illuminate the practice of postmodern improvisation in the United States, in some cases rewriting and contesting previously accepted histories.

The third section, "Expanding the Canon," explores considerations of improvisation along another axis by pushing the cultural boundaries of this volume beyond the artificial limits of American postmodernism. Here we have contributions from Constance Valis Hill on tap dance, Michelle Heffner Hayes on flamenco (and, as it turns out, postmodernism as well), Margaret Thompson Drewal on dances of the Yoruba in Africa, and Avanthi Meduri on *Bharatanatyam*, one of India's classical dance forms. The argument here is that improvisation is not the sole property of U.S. postmodernists; in fact, improvisation is practiced to varying degrees and in a myriad of contexts in dances all around the world. By rights, there should be a dozen essays in this section, but we have found that the scholarship in this area remains largely nascent. These four essays, then, are intended to encourage scholars in new directions and to elicit future writings especially on improvisation in social dance forms, from salsa to goth. To aovid reifying the false divide between concert dance in the United States and every other movement practice in the world, we have also tucked in this section an essay by Victoria Marks, a postmodern choreographer who expands the canon of writings on improvisation by arguing *against* improvisation in favor of choreography as a performance form.

"Reconsidering Contact" comprises a set of essays that take a fresh look at Contact Improvisation. First conceived by Steve Paxton and a small group of like-minded movers in 1972, Contact is everywhere now, from contemporary ballet to the dramatic-theater world to the flamenco classroom. An early practitioner of the form, Nancy Stark Smith jump-starts this section with a compilation of Editor Notes from the movement journal *Contact Quarterly* chronicling major developments in the history and aesthetics of Contact over a twenty-five-year period. Paxton, among the most articulate practitioners of any dance form, has spent his entire career working to understand the principles that animate improvisational dancing, principles he lays out here. Following Paxton's lead, Ray Gibbs, a linguist, and Karen Schaffman, a dancer and dance theorist, take Contact Improvisation as the starting point for a he-said/she-said dialogue on the question of meaning in movement. In twin essays, they write their way through an improvised performance by Julyen Hamilton and Alito Alessi. Ann Cooper Albright caps off this section by taking readers inside the 1997 celebration marking the silver anniversary of Contact Improvisation. By deemphasizing hierarchy, embracing differently abled bodies, and endorsing disorientation and awkwardness, Contact has much to teach us, she suggests, even after a quarter century. Moreover, it remains enormous, even exhilarating, fun.

The final section of this reader, "Improvisation in Everyday Life," addresses the point proposed earlier in this introduction by de Certeau, that we are all poets of our own acts, and that virtually every activity of daily life can be seen as a kind of intention-filled improvisation. Rachel Kaplan's essay on her travels abroad and their inherent improvisational aspects offers a view into the processes of mind that coalesce as a dancer and improviser encounters the world. Maura Keefe paints a vivid verbal portrait of baseball as structured improvisation. Ellen Webb applies the lessons and insights garnered in her practice of Zen Buddhism to her other life, as a dancer, choreographer, and improviser. And Nancy Stark Smith, in a second, more modest compilation of Editor Notes from *Contact Quarterly*, brings this section to a close by offering up writings on subjects that connect dance to the world. Readers of this volume may imagine their own experiences filling out this section, on subjects ranging from the trajectory of a normal day to the problem of overplanning.

Taken By Surprise concludes with an epilogue by Albright, my coeditor, that argues for the importance of improvisation in the twenty-first century—especially at a moment dominated by global terror and instability. By allowing ourselves to dwell in the perceptual "gap" (as Nancy Stark Smith calls it) created by contemplation and emptiness, Albright suggests that we can open up our access to the power of the imagination. To begin, all we need is curiosity.

The necessary partner of curiosity, of course, is surprise. A curious frame of mind makes it possible for improvisers of all stripes to be surprised at what emerges from within themselves, from the material of the cogitating body. The same is true for those who watch. And for those who read. As you flip through these pages—in the studio, or at home, or in the library, wherever— see what the writings in these pages might open up for you. Allow yourself to be taken by surprise.

NOTES

1. See Agnes de Mille, *Martha: The Life and Work of Martha Graham* (New York: Random House, 1991), 107, 123, 254, 376, for anecdotal references to Graham's use of improvisation; and Susan A. Manning, *Ecstasy and the Demon: Feminism and Nationalism in the Dances of Mary Wigman* (Berkeley and Los Angeles: University of California Press, 1993), 54, 91–92, for a discussion of Wigman's use of improvisation and her debt to Rudolf Laban. Regarding Wigman's use of improvisation, see also Erika Thimey and Dianne Hunt, *A Life of Dance, A Dance of Life* (Washington, D.C.: Erika Thimey Dance & Theater Company, 1999) as excerpted in *Dance Magazine* (April 2000): 58–59.

2. See Katy Matheson, "Improvisation," in the *International Encyclopedia of Dance*, ed. Selma Jeanne Cohen (New York: Oxford University Press, 1998). Matheson provides commentary on early balletic examples of improvisation as well as a comprehensive history of improvisation in the United States.

3. For a strong argument that West African aesthetics come to all Americans "as electricity

through the wires," see Brenda Dixon Gottschild, *Digging the Africanist Presence in American Performance: Dance and Other Contexts* (Westport, Conn.: Praeger, 1996).

4. For the history of the Grand Union see Sally Banes, *Terpsichore in Sneakers: Post-Modern Dance,* 2d ed. (Middletown, Conn.: Wesleyan University Press, 1987); Susan Leigh Foster, *Reading Dancing: Bodies and Subjects in Contemporary American Dance* (Berkeley and Los Angeles: University of California Press, 1986); and Margaret Hupp Ramsay, *The Grand Union, 1970–1976: An Improvisational Performance Group* (New York: Peter Lang, 1991).

5. According to Meredith Monk, one of Schönberg's most famous pupils, in Schönberg's classes "You could never present an improvisation as a piece. *Never.* Not with Bessie." See David Gere, "Swallowing Technology: An Ethnomusicological Analysis of Meredith Monk's *Quarry*" (master's thesis, University of Hawaii at Manoa, 1991), 39.

6. Michel de Certeau, *The Practice of Everyday Life* (Berkeley and Los Angeles: University of California Press, 1984), xviii.

**IMPROVISING BODY,
IMPROVISING MIND**

TAKEN BY SURPRISE

Improvisation in Dance and Mind

Susan Leigh Foster

taken: 1. past tense, passive tense of the verb "to take" (*the dancer clutches the podium's microphone and twists it backward*) 2. to get into one's hands or into one's possession, power, or control (*she scoops space, getting it into her hands, then suddenly grabs the podium's edges*) 3. to catch, to copulate with, to assume, to secure, to adopt, accommodate, or apprehend (*guiding it with commanding then solicitous attention, she lowers it to the floor, then steps to the side of the now toppled support for her lecture*)
by: bye (*she waves good-bye and disappears off the edge of the stage*)
surprise: 1. to impress forcibly through unexpectedness (*she pops out from below, behind, in the midst of*) 2. to astonish, astound, amaze, or flabbergast (*she shrugs her shoulders*)
taken by surprise: the unexpected seizes control, resulting in a sexy, vertiginous encounter with the unknown, an encounter that raises issues around the workings of desire and power (*did the unexpected seize control? well, sort of. was it vertiginous? who can say? did it raise issues? whenever a body is crawling, gliding, leaping, crouching, wiggling, and kicking, all the while reading aloud from a sheaf of papers that it is clutching earnestly, issues are raised*)
improvisation: that which is *composed* extemporaneously, on the spur of the moment

Fig. A1. Susan Foster improvising the delivery of her keynote paper at the *Taken by Surprise* conference, Julia Morgan Theater, Berkeley, California, 1994. (© Sandy Walker. Courtesy the Talking Dance Project. Printed with permission.)

MANIFESTO (*PHENOMENOLOGICALLY*)

The improvising dancer tacks back and forth between the *known* and the *unknown,* between the familiar/reliable and the unanticipated/unpredictable.

The *known* includes the set of behavioral conventions established by the context in which the performance occurs, such as those of a street corner, a proscenium theater, or a lecture. The known includes any predetermined over-arching structural guidelines that delimit the improvising body's choices, such as a score for the performance, or any set of rules determined in advance: for ex-ample, consecutive solos by different members of a group. The known also in-cludes an individual body's predisposition to move in patterns of impulses estab-lished and made routine through training in a particular dance tradition as well as the body's predilection for making certain kinds of selections from a vocabu-lary or a sequence of movements. The known includes any allied medium with which the performance is in collaboration, such as an improvisation among musicians and dancers or an improvisation that addresses the space in which the performance occurs as an active participant. The known includes that which has already occurred previously in the performance of improvising.

The *unknown* is precisely that and more. It is that which was previously unimaginable, that which we could not have thought of doing next. Improvisa-tion presses us to extend into, expand beyond, extricate ourselves from that which was known. It encourages us or even forces us to be "taken by surprise." Yet we could never accomplish this encounter with the unknown without engag-ing the known.

MANIFESTO (*HISTORICALLY*)

The improvised is that which eludes history. The performance of any action, re-gardless of how predetermined it is in the minds of those who perform it and those who witness it, contains an element of improvisation. That moment of wavering while contemplating how, exactly, to execute an action already deeply known, belies the presence of improvised action. It is this suspense-filled pleni-tude of the not-quite-known that gives live performance its special brilliance.

History, however, keeps track almost exclusively of the known. It focuses on those human actions reiterated frequently enough to become patterns of beha-vior. From among this multitude of patterns, it chooses those actions that leave behind some permanent residue documenting their effects. And from among this plethora of documentation, it seizes upon those traces that lend themselves to translation into written discourse.

Histories typically suppress the improvisation that occurs consistently in all human actions. They also deny the improvisation of the historian who selects and interacts with all documentation of the past in an attempt to decipher change over time. Historical inquiry has neglected to question how certain ac-tions slide easily across representational fields into the historical record and others are persistently unnoticed. It has tried to ignore actions resistant to writ-ten description. What would history look like if it were to acknowledge the fact of improvisation? What would a history of improvised dancing look like?

History informs us that the choreographer and dancer Marie Sallé presented her radical rendition of the Pygmalion story in London in 1734, radical because she appeared without corset or wig and because she used pantomime to tell the story without the aid of spoken or sung lyrics. According to a spectator whose description of the ballet was published,[1] she came to life as Galatea and danced an exchange with her sculptor/maker in which he demonstrated simple phrases she not only mastered immediately but also ornamented and improved upon, thereby stimulating him to present the next phrase. Imagine if this danced dialogue were improvised. Imagine the aplomb that Pygmalion would necessarily exhibit as Sallé performed a surprising response, one that required him quite suddenly to think on his feet. Imagine the suspense and involvement that viewers would have felt as they sensed the unpredictability of the exchange. Perhaps the two dancers agreed in advance to improvise their duet. Perhaps Sallé, carried away by the obvious success of her production, introduced improvised elements on opening night. Perhaps her audacious initiative escalated over subsequent performances into a full-scale improvised repartee. Perhaps none of this happened. But perhaps it did.

History informs us that Richard Bull, Cynthia Novack, and Peentz Dubble, members of the Richard Bull Dance Theatre, participated in the performance of *Making and Doing* in New York City in 1985. According to the reviewer this piece was "an exercise in inventing movement and then recalling it precisely."[2] But what does this mean and how did it work? As someone who saw the concert and also participated in an earlier version of the piece, I offer this analysis: Guided by Richard Bull's score, the dancing choreographers, as though conducting a rehearsal, perform warm-up exercises, talk about their preparations, and then run through part of a "dance," each taking a solo and joining in a unison finale. This first section of the dance, seven or eight minutes in length, is then repeated to music. The dancers no longer speak, but they do perform their entire interaction, including casual conversational gestures and facial expressions. They then launch into a third repetition of the "rehearsal-dance" without music but with the original talking as the lights slowly fade to end the dance. By leading viewers through a presumed rehearsal and then re-presenting that rehearsal to music, *Making and Doing* purposefully frames all movements—the stretches of a warm-up, offhand remarks and gestures, the virtuoso execution of rhythmically complex phrases—as dance. It jostles viewers' expectations in part 1 by presenting a rehearsal onstage and in part 2 by delineating the expressivity of each minute gesture as it is performed to the music. Faithfully executing the original timing of the rehearsal, the dancers create suspenseful congruences and dissonances with the musical structure as they work to transform both pedestrian and vituoso movement into dance.

Although the three-part structure of rehearsal, repetition to music, and second repetition guides each performance, the specific movements are always improvised. All three dancers co-choreographing the piece generate new sequences in each performance, innovating in relation to the score, to the unpredictable actions of the other dancers, and to their aesthetic judgment concerning the overall needs of the dance as it is evolving. And all this is done while attempting to remember everything they are doing in part 1 in order to repeat it in parts 2 and 3. Improvisation is also required in these sections as dancers forget portions of the material or differ in their timing of the already performed. Throughout, the dancing choreographers respond to the known and the unknown in one another and to the known and unknown about what makes a good dance. On the night I viewed the performance, the tension among what was happening, what might happen next, and how that choice would influence the overall shape of the piece electrified the performance. Viewers could watch the performance both of a dance being presented and of a dance being made at the same time.

Making and Doing, like Sallé's *Pygmalion,* comments reflexively on dancing and artmaking. Yet whereas Sallé as Galatea embodied an artistic creation whose maker watched her come to life, Bull, Novack, and Dubble each inhabited the roles of choreographer and dance. Sallé's dialogue with the sculptor entailed the introduction of movement phrases, repetition of those phrases, and variation on the steps and phrases that might lead toward the generation of yet more new movement. *Making and Doing* also involved repetition, but of a single, lengthy section of the dance. Sallé and her partner were guided in their improvisation by the codes for graceful dancing, the phrase structure and meter of the music, and the need to respond with wit and agility to one another's initiatives. They selected and combined steps from within a highly delimited vocabulary of dance steps. Bull, Novack, and Dubble, guided by an overall scenario but no specific metric specifications, attempted to choreograph an eight-minute dance, full of innovative movement drawn from the repertoires of everyday gesture and preparatory exercises as well as modern dance movement. They worked to create a trio of dynamic range, intriguing interactions, and structural integrity that could stand the test of re-viewing twice. Neither of these dances announced in advance that parts would be improvised. Viewers slowly deduced the fact of spontaneous composition from the particular quality of alertness that the dancers manifested while they were making as well as doing the dance.

What do these examples tell us? Can the fact of improvisation be informative? Are there ways to compare different blendings and assess the unique effects of the known and the unknown used in various approaches to improvisation? How could the attempt to include the improvised alter the course of historical inquiry? Are there ways to write about improvisation that establish its significance and impact without leaching from it the wonderment and critical awareness that its unexpectedness produces?

MANIFESTO (*DISCURSIVELY*)

Within the meager discourses describing the experience of improvisation that history has left us, the terms *mind* and *body* often stand in for the known and the unknown. We read of improvisation as the process of letting go of the mind's thinking so that the body can do its moving in its own unpredictable way. But this description is an obfuscation, as unhelpful as it is inaccurate; surely, *all* bodily articulation is mindful. Each body segment's sweep across space, whether direct or meandering, is thought-filled. Each corporeal modulation in effort thinks; each swelling into tension thinks; each erratic burst or undulation in energy thinks. Each accented phrasing or accelerating torque or momentary stillness is an instance of thought. Conceptualized in this way, bodily action constitutes a genre of discourse.

If, then, bodily articulation is mindful, what quality of mindfulness does improvisation hope to transcend? The capacity to evaluate and censor? Even these faculties remain active during improvisation. Improvisation involves moments where one thinks in advance of what one is going to do, other moments where actions seem to move faster than they can be registered in full analytic consciousness of them, and still other moments where one thinks the idea of what is to come at exactly the same moment that one performs that idea. Still, both the changing of the course of things and the riding of that course through its course are mindful *and* bodyful. Rather than suppress any functions of mind, improvisation's bodily mindfulness summons up a kind of hyperawareness of the relation between immediate action and overall shape, between that which is about to take place or is taking place and that which has and will take place.

We also read in the discourses on improvisation allegations that improvisation, because of its bodily spontaneity, requires no technique. This, too, is a muddled and wrongly cast charge. Improvisation makes rigorous technical demands on the performer. It assumes an articulateness in the body through which the known and the unknown will find expression. It entails a vigilant porousness toward the unknown, a stance that can only be acquired through intensive practice. It depends upon the performer's lucid familiarity with the principles of composition. (After all, to improvise is to compose extemporaneously and composition is an arrangement into proper proportion or relation.)

Improvisation also demands a reflexive awareness of when the known is becoming a stereotype, a rut instead of a path, and it insists upon the courage and wit (also acquired talents), to recalibrate known and unknown as the performance unfolds.

Improvisation does not, therefore, entail a silencing of the mind in order for the body "to speak." Rather, improvisation pivots both mind and body into a new apprehension of relationalities.

MANIFESTO (*ANALYTICALLY*)

In the form of its function, improvisation most closely resembles a grammatical category found in the verb forms of many languages (including classical Greek) known as the middle voice. With this particular kind of verb—and verbs are the closest of all linguistic elements to dancing—events occur neither in the active nor passive voice. The subject does not act nor is the subject acted upon. A close equivalent in the English language (which does not have middle voice) to this nonactive/nonpassive voicing is the phrase "shit happens."

The experience of middle-voicedness is perhaps most palpable when improvising with another person. Many of us have enjoyed the experience of neither leading nor following, but instead moving with, and being moved by another body. One body's weight and momentum flow into and with another body's shaping and trajectory making a double bodied co-motion. Or both bodies, seized by the same impulse, move in tandem, never touching physically but touched by a shared sensibility about the composition's needs. Or each body, knowing so intimately the other's whims and inclinations, simply incarnates as partner. Again, throughout this experience, there are many moments when one leads or is led, thus bifurcating action into initiation and response. But there are also spectacularly lucid moments when both bodies' actions coordinate and synchronize in spontaneous ensemble.

The concept of an operation that is neither active nor passive such as the middle voice profoundly challenges hegemonic cultural values that persistently force a choice between the two. Most theories about the significance of human action depend upon the conception of an individuated and isolated self located within a body that it controls and manipulates in order to achieve self-expression and fulfill individual needs. The self within the body tells the body what to do, and the body executes those orders, sometimes reluctantly or inadequately or deviantly, but never autonomously.[3] Other theories invest the state and capital with the power to transform the body/self into a desiring machine whose every impulse only enhances the growth of capital and the all-consuming power of the state. In these models, all individual choices merely maintain the appearance of independence. On closer scrutiny, however, the structuring of individual initiatives reveals their prior co-optation by governmental or capitalist channels through which power exercises its control.[4]

In either of these models of human agency, where the self tells the body what to do, or where both self and body are subsumed by larger political and economic forces, the body is relegated to the status of instrumental object. Robbed of all vitality, much less the capacity for agency, it endures as a mute, dumb thing. The experience of improvising, however, establishes the possibility of an alternative theory of bodily agency, one that refutes the body's mere instrumentality and suggests alternative formulations of individual and collective agency.

Improvisation provides an experience of body in which it initiates, creates, and probes playfully its own physical and semantic potential. The thinking and creating body engages in action. The presence of this body, cultivated during dance classes that enhance prowess at improvisational skills, is what recalibrates ego and superego, critic and comic, attentivist and activist, and individualistic and communal impulses to build a middle voice among them. This body, instigatory as well as responsive, grounds the development of consciousness as a hyperawareness of relationalities. Each next moment of improvising, full of possible positionings, develops its choreographic significance as all participants' actions work to bring the performance into proper proportion or relation. During this playful labor, consciousness shifts from self in relation to group, to body in relation to body, to movement in relation to space and time, to past in relation to present, and to fragment in relation to developing whole. Shared by all improvisers in a given performance, this embodied consciousness enables the making of the dance and the dance's making of itself.

Power circulates through the collective actions of such improvisation. It never has the opportunity to dwell in a specific joint of the body, or alight at the site of a particular individual, or hunker down among a portion of the group. Power is repeatedly "taken by surprise" so that it can never embed itself within a static structural element that would allow it to flex into hierarchies of domination and control. In improvisation, power can only keep on the move, running as fast as it can to partner, to empower performers, never overcoming them.

Improvisation empowers those who witness it as well as those who perform it. Watching improvisation, consciousness expands out of passive reception of an event and toward active engagement in the actual making of the event. Viewers participate along with the performers in the open field of possible choices and the performers' construction and selection of those choices through which meaning is determined. The middle-voiced play of desire and power envelopes the audience and invites participation in eventing.

The recasting of power and desire that takes place during improvisation, the new conception of human agency articulated during improvisation, and the special identity of body discovered through improvisation—these are insights of crucial importance. They impact on our understanding of history and political agency, and they provide us with an enormously rich source of tactics for navigating the next millennium.

MANIFESTO (*EPISTEMOLOGICALLY*)

In the original presentation of this essay, I read aloud, spoke extemporaneously, and improvised choreography, speaking and dancing simultaneously.[5] I had been asked to write a speech about improvisation, to fix on paper certain thoughts about the unpredictable and deliver these verbal ideas about dance to an audience. Two contradictions held me in their clutches: (1) that a written discourse about improvisation might never incorporate its essential spontaneity; and (2) that the translation from dancing to writing might erode the power and significance of the moving body improvising. In order to extricate myself from the first contradiction, I not only added extemporized comments; I also organized the writing into trajectories of inquiry, manifestos, whose open-endedness might invite further improvised dialogues. In order to escape from the second, I improvised a dance that sometimes illustrated and other times commented upon the talking. At still other times the dancing resolutely pursued its own interests oblivious to the speaking that was taking place. In this way I hoped to create a co-motion between two discourses, speaking and dancing, as they were being composed, more and less spontaneously, together.

This essay gestures in the direction of that co-motion, its body straining between conventional prose and other writing that might depict more accurately the interaction between words and dance (*rolling up her sleeve for the fourteenth time, the dancer grins*). The essay is intended to clear a space where choreographers and scholars, together as well as separately, might begin to consider the workings of improvisation in dance and in history (*wiggling, winding down, then almost winking*). Once begun, such a talking-dancing inquiry might well last for a very long time (*she walks to the podium and rights it before exiting the stage*).

NOTES

1. M***. *Mercure de France,* April 1734, pp. 770–72. For more information on Sallé, see her biography by Emile Dacier, *Une danseuse de l'Opéra sous Louis XV: Mlle. Sallé (1707–1756)* (Paris: Plon-Nourrit et Cie, 1909). For a fuller discussion of her *Pygmalion,* see my *Choreography and Narrative: Ballet's Staging of Story and Desire* (Bloomington: Indiana University Press, 1996).

2. Elizabeth Zimmer, "Richard Bull Dance Theatre," *Dance Magazine* (April 1985): 37.

3. This model of individual agency lies at the base of social-contract theories descending from those of Jean-Jacques Rousseau.

4. Michel Foucault was one of the first political theorists to advance this kind of perspective on body and agency.

5. The presentation was delivered as the keynote address of the conference "Taken by Surprise: Improvisation in Dance and Mind," organized by David Gere and Ellen Webb of the Talking Dance Project in Berkeley, California, June 10–11, 1994.

EXPOSED TO GRAVITY

Bruce Curtis

Often when I contemplated dancing while sitting in my wheelchair, and looked at all the wonderful bodies swiftly spinning and flashing across the floor, it would seem to me that I was another species of Human. It felt much the same way to me upon traveling to Guatemala, going to the end of the road in the rain forest and then wandering among the village people that live there. The people stopped what they were doing and stared at me while I was staring at them, everyone filled with curiosity.

Because my body looks different and moves differently, I've often wondered, how I can participate in this dancing when it doesn't seem that we share a commonality of movement. I would wonder how they ever learned to move like that. What was their secret? Lots of classes? Born with rhythm? Survival of the fittest? It seemed pretty clear, whatever the reason, that for me to dance the technique would have to come from my personal experience of how my body moves, not from copying how nondisabled people move.

When I first began to explore moving my body in rhythm (before I knew of Contact Improvisation), I wanted to dance like everyone else with grand gestures, lots of wiggles in the right places, relaxed and cool. But a body in a wheelchair doesn't seem capable of moving like that and it was pretty scary to experiment in front of people. So I would move my shoulders while shifting my weight to the rhythm of the music, dancing inside my body with grand gestures and lots of wiggles. At some point it occurred to me that this micromovement was just as much dancing as what everyone else did with their whole body. It may not have looked the same but the rhythms flowing through my body, unlocking the grip of my mind and fears, came from the same primal experience. With this realization, I began to lift up my hands, lengthen the movement of my arms, and deepen my reliance on the validity of the movements that were emerging from my body. I found my body starting to move in patterns that did not exist in my mind or in my previous experience. When I would dance in this manner, and look into the eyes of someone dancing next to me, a smile would spread across both of our faces from the joy in our hearts. The dance was within us.

I would like to explain very generally how Spinal Cord Injury (SCI) affects most bodies. To injure the spinal cord in the back or waist can result in paraplegia, with no muscle control in the waist or legs but normal use of the arms and hands. An injury to the neck can result in quadriplegia. Most quadriplegics are unable to move any muscles below a midchest level. Their shoulder, biceps, and wrist muscles are often good, with triceps weak and finger muscles nonfunctional. In those muscles that are affected by SCI, sometimes a movement will create a spasm that can start a leg or the whole body shaking or cause it momentarily to go rigid. Breathing is done through the diaphragm with each breath being shallow. There is usually no surface skin feeling below the midchest level so it is possible to cut or bruise this area without being aware that it has happened. (A good visualization of how a body like this moves is to look at a newborn baby. Its mind does not control how the head, each limb, or the body as a whole responds to gravity or positioning. If the head is not supported against gravity, it will immediately fall.) Each person's degree of function varies, depending on the severity of the original injury, their body tone before and after the injury, and the person's willingness to experiment with his body and environment. What is most important to remember is that each body, disabled or not, is unique and presents another opportunity to explore what movement is possible.

I am a quadriplegic but my lower body is able to feel pressure when touched; therefore I can usually guess where my legs or feet are positioned. Because my feeling is minimal, I often use my eyes to tell me exactly where my body is. My body is long (6 ft., 2 in.), lean, limber, and I love it. I have used a wheelchair for twenty years now, living, working, and playing around the world. My chair has become a part of my body. It has movements, sounds, and rhythms that describe the texture of the ground that I am moving across, defining the space that I am passing through.

Gravity is very noticeable to me as my muscles cannot stand in opposition to it. When sitting, my chair supports me above the ground. If I lean in any direction too far away from the center of my support, gravity will bring me down. (I really don't mind falling down as it's never that far.) My body will sense a lack of support against gravity immediately and, because my muscles can only delay the fall, I usually don't think about how to keep from falling, but rather, how to use the momentum of falling or a quick push off a nearby surface to help me arrive on the ground in a safe manner. Most of the time, I just prepare to meet the ground.

Gravity is very constant and dependable and I use it often to move my body when my muscles cannot. When sitting in my chair the ground is rarely level under me and I will feel gravity moving me in some direction. Because my arms are not awesome, I am always looking for ways to ride the flow of gravity, by analyzing the angle of the plane of the surface in front of me and then moving to a point that optimizes the motion in the direction that I want to go. For example, climbing up a hill against gravity is made easier by tacking diagonally across it. Often I will stop to rest by finding that place of balance where movement is briefly suspended between possibilities; then, with a slight push, I join with the flow once again. This is how I play while moving through the world, riding gravity and looking for cheap thrills.

I was first introduced to Contact Improvisation while on the March for Peace in Central America, some 250 people from thirty countries traveling overland from Panama to Mexico City. We had stopped for a rest at a coffee plantation high in the northern mountains of Nicaragua. Another marcher, Holly Hamilton, and I went for a walk and discovered an abandoned coffee-drying courtyard made of concrete with a view of the countryside for thirty miles. I had a cassette player with a tape of Andreas Vollenveider in my backpack and I offered to demonstrate how I could dance with my chair. To my amazement, Holly began moving with me in a noncontrolling manner without my having to explain much at all. After we danced, she told me about Contact Improvisation and I decided that this was an important discovery for disabled people. A dance form that uses movement, gravity, and their relationship to each other as revealed through changing points of balance seemed ideal for people like myself whose daily interaction with their environment is grounded in the same experiences.

My first experiments with Contact Improvisers Holly Hamilton and Arthur Hull involved moving with my chair in spirals, using the momentum of my partner as the force that moved me. Through the point of contact, I would feel the potential for movement waiting to be released, the intention to move shifting between me and my partner. For the first time I felt truly equal in the creating of the dance. At this stage, I was primarily looking at my dancing like a ballet: grand sweeping movements of my chair without my having to push it. For me the dance was to move across the floor in a graceful, fluid manner, while making interesting patterns and smooth transitions. This early work was videotaped and, after showing it to Alan Ptashek, a great teacher of movement, I began to learn with him how to have a physical conversation through the movement form Contact Improvisation.

I went through what must be familiar issues to anyone beginning to learn the language of Contact Improvisation. Keep your eyes open, don't get lost inside your head. Look for opportunities to support your partner, move in underneath them. Don't give or take weight without listening for the agreement of your partner's body. Let each move evolve from mutual agreement, rather than having an image in your own mind dictate what happens next. Mutual trust is based on uncompromised attention, so stay in the present moment.

In the beginning, my interest in Contact Improvisation was always oriented toward performing a choreographed dance by stringing together all the fascinating moves and deleting the "dull" spaces in between. When we began practicing for our first performance, I would always be asking Alan what movement we would start or finish with. It wasn't until the last rehearsal, while feeling totally nervous, that I realized that without a choreographed plan of action, our practices were always full of exciting moments of improvisation. Because Alan and I were creatively and unhesitatingly exploring our possibilities, what emerged was a fascinating conversation of movement. I also learned how important it was to remember to have fun while dancing. So I started playing with Alan the same way that I would play off the walls in a hallway or moving through cars while crossing the street: being spontaneous and playing together with gravity.

When I first started practicing Contact Improvisation, it was necessary for me to have music playing in the background. It was a strong habit: if you want to dance, put on some music. Initially, Alan discouraged this because the body tends to move to the rhythm of the music instead of to the internal rhythm of shifting weight, sensation, and the communication that goes back and forth between the dancers. As I listened more intently to Alan's body through the point of contact, minutely increasing or decreasing pressure against my body, I would notice afterward that I couldn't remember hearing the music while we danced. The attention of my mind was so focused that music, audience, monitoring my self-image, everything external to the next movement vanished. Now when we practice, we sometimes turn off the music to listen to the sounds of our breathing or the squeaks and grunts. At performances we would use taped or live music to help fill in the environment for the audience as well as set up an emotional mood.

The first time Alan lifted me out of my chair, I had no idea what was happening until I was looking down from his shoulders. For a person in a wheelchair, control over your own body's safety is never easily relinquished to someone else's judgment. My life is full of people who want to help me by grabbing my body or my chair and dragging me somewhere in an unsafe manner. On top of Alan's shoulders I could feel the ground *through* his body solidly supporting me against gravity. Whether sitting in a chair or wrapped around someone's body, when I feel supported against the flow of gravity, I am not afraid to let go of holding on; I am freed to explore new possibilities. Once after a performance Alan said, "When we dance together, I always feel that when I offer you two different options, your response is Yes-Yes. I rarely feel that you resist what I offer you." One reason: because I explore my movement by playing off of Alan's movement, any movement, they all have possibilities. Another: you don't have to say no to someone who is listening to your body.

In the beginning, I was concerned about how I looked while I was dancing. Was I sitting up straight or slumped down? If my leg began to spasm, jumped out straight, and started shaking, what would people think? In our discussions about these concerns, we agreed that these were not problems but opportunities. They were not to be ignored, feared, or repressed. The point was not to clamp down and control my body but to listen to it, accepting whatever movement was inherent. If a spasm did occur, we would just keep on dancing and let it happen, allowing the movement of the spasm to become part of the dance. Sometimes we would play off of the spasm, with Alan taking a rigid leg and using it as a pivot point to move my chair in a spiral. When we don't make fences around our bodies, all movements become acceptable.

Some time ago, I began practicing Contact Improvisation with Patty Overland, a disabled woman who uses a wheelchair. She had very little prior experience with Contact and I had never tried to teach it to anyone. So while we were trying to figure out how two people in wheelchairs do Contact, she was learning how to improvise her own ways of playing and shaping our duet. Even though music helped her to be more comfortable (Patty was used to moving her body in rhythm to rock and roll), we had to turn off the music so that she could easily listen to my body through hers. It is difficult to stay in close contact with each other because the chairs are rigid and don't wrap around each other like bodies do. Both of us have limited use of our waist muscles (and her right shoulder is weak), so we have been forced to experiment a lot. We have to lean out away from our chairs to remain in contact while allowing enough space for our chairs to move off the momentum from the shifting balance between us. We have also started working off each other's chairs as if they were bodies. Because we feel that our chairs are part of ourselves, it feels natural to grab hold of or push off of a chair if it is in front of us at the moment. At one point, I discovered that she could get out of her chair, down to the floor, and then back into her chair fairly easily, so we started incorporating this into our dancing.

We feel it is important that the dance comes from the realities of our bodies and our chairs, rather than trying to move like nondisabled dancers. We have a relationship with our disability that has three parts: how our bodies move, how our chairs move, and how they both move together. There is a great joy that comes from coaxing a subtle, minute movement from a part of our bodies that we do not control and then using the momentum of the changing point of balance between us, to slowly begin turning a wheel in a sweeping arc. Patty and I did not know each other personally before we started dancing, or the specifics of each other's body. It has thus been emotionally scary to explore how to combine all of these variables, while trying to be relaxed and comfortable enough to encourage our creativity. Our willingness to expose our awkwardness could become stifled because on the way to practice, someone on the street has once again violated our personal space or negatively affected our self-image so that when we arrive, our bodies aren't really open to being vulnerable. If our fears don't get in the way, the mechanics of moving can make it difficult for us to keep our communication tightly focused without interruption. For example, when our bodies are not centered in our chairs, there is a strong habit to stop dancing for a moment, straighten ourselves, and then continue. Yet, working within the physical limitations that we have sometimes requires us to break physical communication long enough to make the next move possible.

When you are in the present moment and listening to your partner's body, the point of contact can bridge the empty space between your bodies until the dance brings you both home again.

So what do I have in common with all those wonderful dancing bodies gracefully spinning and flashing all over the floor? Another wonderful body filled with the movements of the glorious life that is within every part of me, just trying to let those movements come out in all their joyful wiggles and spontaneous jumps. Another dancing body that is laughing and playing with the rhythms that join my body with someone else's body, communicating in the most intimate way our willingness to open our hearts and be vulnerable to each other. We are all dancing bodies, playing together to ignite the light that shines from our eyes and our smiles to touch the souls of all who can see us dancing.

I am a disabled person who has spent my life trying to open more possibilities in society for myself and other disabled people through legislation, civil rights demonstrations, community organizing, and the Independent Living Movement. Yet all of these accomplishments have not caused the able-bodied strangers that I would encounter in my work to open their hearts and let their eyes show how happy they were to see me. It is just as important to talk about what we as human beings share as it is to show it: through the joy that we have in each and every one of our physical movements; through the fearlessness of our hearts, forged by the daily journeys into the dark of our souls; and through the beauty of ourselves that we are willing to reveal to the able-bodied and the disabled strangers that we meet. As disabled people, we have shown that we can survive in this world. Now it is time to show that we can dance too. The world needs our joy, our dancing.

NOTE

This is a slightly edited version of an essay originally published in *Contact Quarterly* 13, no. 3 (Fall 1988): 18–21.

DANCE

A Body with a Mind of Its Own

Ruth Zaporah

I am a physical performer of improvisation theater. As both actor and dancer I weave images through movement, language, and vocalization. I enter the performing arena with no prearranged concepts. I begin with a spontaneous action and then, step by step, build a scenario until the content is realized and the piece feels complete. Within it, I introduce characters, events, and situations that reflect the mingling of imagination, memories, and sensory input. The pieces are often dreamlike landscapes, grounded in humor and pathos. I am endlessly surprised by what happens.

Fig. C1. Ruth Zaporah, 2001. (Photo: Michelle Baker. Courtesy Ruth Zaporah.)

The year was 1976. I was performing in Ann Arbor. I had asked the presenters to create a set within which I would improvise. That evening, the set included a Raggedy Ann–like doll, which was lying on the floor downstage center. Early on, the doll drew my attention. I named her Alice. Within the first fifteen minutes of the improvisation, Alice died. The remainder of the show focused on how others in her life responded to her death.

As I was bowing at the end of the show I noticed three women sitting on the floor near where Alice had been lying. While everyone else clapped, they were completely still. Later, they came to see me backstage. Through their crying, they told me that a year ago, that very night, their mutual and dear friend, Alice, had died. Before my performance, they had gone out to dinner together to honor her passing. A shock went through my body and left me trembling. The territory of embodied improvisation that I had just visited had implications beyond my comprehension. If I were to continue, for my own safety, I must observe very closely.

When I refer to the body, I am also referring to the mind, for the two are known through one another and are inseparable. The body knows itself through the mind as the mind knows itself through the body. Sometimes it is convenient to talk about the body and the mind as separate entities. We can talk about taming or disciplining the body, quieting the mind, relaxing the body, focusing attention. But can you imagine doing any of these without both body and mind?

I have been practicing physical improvisation for thirty years. My mind and body, their oneness, is the instrument of my art. Sometimes my body seems to have a mind of its own. It fidgets, slumps, and jerks while my mental attention is elsewhere. And conversely, my mind (as we all experience in meditation practice) fidgets, slumps, and jerks while my body appears to be calm and still. We talk about the mind and body as if they were separate but, in fact, it's our attention that is split. Through improvisational practice, awareness expands to hold our entire self.

"Ruthy, dance for us." I'm four years old. At every family event, this invitation is spoken by someone. I never decline. I am shy, but when I dance I have a voice, I am seen. In the family, I am a Dancer.

Simultaneously, another and quite different realization was brewing. At age six in 1942, I began formal dance studies. Three afternoons and most of Saturday mornings of each and every week, I attended ballet class. This regimen continued through high school. Ballet classes in those days were exceedingly impersonal. The student was seen only as a body. A student arrived, silently changed clothes in a grey and metal locker room, careful not to let her gaze turn toward another naked body, entered the glistening white and mirrored ballet room, and, within the vacuum of her isolation, inched along toward mastery. At the end of the session, students clapped their hands, left the room as silently as they had entered, and stuffed their stimulated young bodies into plaid skirts and penny loafers.

As I write this, it is clear that those hours in ballet class were often a place of pure bodily experience. Yes, there were times charged with judgment, moments filled with confusion, self-hatred, or pride. But there were also stretches of nonthought that drew me back and back again. That state of nonthought was restful, calm. I relaxed into the action itself, losing all sense of self, of Ruth, of me.

Dance is silent. The lips are shut tight. The motion can be either serene or violent. Either way, there is no guarantee that because the body is filling every moment with action, the mind can't also be filling every equivalent moment with disembodied thought. For me, the thoughts were often about the action: judging, evaluating, or directing.

Can we stop thoughts so that our body and mind are aligned into a singular happening? I'm not sure we have to stop anything. What I remember is that I came upon a secret place of silence and I was repeatedly drawn to it. Neither my family, friends, nor teachers guided or prepared me. At the time, I couldn't have talked about it either. It just seemed right. I was continually drawn to this place, more like space, and that space became home.

Dance itself is thoughtless. It is its own event. It doesn't follow anything and it doesn't lead anywhere. It is not about gain or absolution. Dance dances itself and is not at all tied to the conceptual world or even the concept of dance.

Until my thirties, I danced, danced, and danced. I took classes, created dances, and taught both technique and improvisation. Only when dancing did I feel truly peaceful. I knew my body and its capabilities and danced within my limitations. I remained focused on the actions themselves, and they always offered cues for further explorations. I remained relaxed and imagination thrived. I knew that if I was fascinated, so too would be the audience. All of this knowledge integrated into my awareness. Awareness danced.

Then, in the early 1970s, I became restless with the confinement of silence. I felt handicapped. I wanted to talk, to be heard, to explore "real" life, grapple with its issues. I began to experiment with speech, character, and vocalization of feeling. Wrestling with these forms for a very long time, I tripped over myself continually, forcing, analyzing, and constructing. I was determined to create meaningful content. All this led to more separation, myself from myself. Eventually, however, I got a clue. I felt my mouth moving. My mind had relaxed its hold on content. I experienced speech and feeling as their own dance—movements arising and falling away, mouth moving, mind moving, thoughts, feelings, all moving.

I sense the body as no different than the space it is moving in and the sound it is moving to. If I am improvising with a partner, each of our bodies becomes an extension of the other. I perceive her body as no other than my own; her voice, my voice; her story, mine. If I am dancing in a public dance hall or a private party, I merge into the larger body of sounds, colors, heat, sweat, motion. I am not alone in this. Dance has served through time and cultures as a collecting force, a softening of the hard edges that separate one person from another, an activity of communion.

> Bob and I are improvising together on stage. The performance begins with both of us standing, playing conga drums. We chant. My voice is inside of his and his is inside of mine. We wail. I begin a narrative on top of the clamorous beat. My voice and the sound of the drum rise, swell, and recede together. I tell of a woman, sitting before the fire in her living room. She feels the familiar cold wind slipping in from under her front door. She's tried to seal the space under the door many times, to no avail. The wind continues to torment her as it slams against her fragile body.

> As these words escape from my lips, I sense that I'm following a script that is writing itself. Each word comes on its own. I discover it as I hear and feel it forming itself. The beats of Bob's drum and the timing of my words are riding on the same energy. Even though we're not doing the same thing, our bodies have merged.

> Abruptly, as if we were being directed, we stop. Bob crosses the floor. He sees a river between us and is intent on crossing its hazardous waters. I too see the river and share his distress. I reach out to him and throw him a line of a song which he repeats. I sing, he sings, again and again, until we are both on the same side of the river.

In the altered state and extraordinary space of performance, Bob is me and I am him. No boundaries exist between us. His river is THE river, real and tangible; his distress, mine; his safety, also mine.

For many years, I struggled with the awkward moments that follow a performance. Audience members would come backstage to offer their appreciation, to tell me how much they loved the piece or me. If the performance had been a struggle for me, if I had been plagued by judgments, I would feel ashamed, as if

I'd put one over on them. Or, I would feel exposed, the soft belly of my psyche hung out on the line of spectacle.

If I had sailed through the show without a disembodied thought, I would still be unable to receive their praise. Here they were talking to Ruth and yet, ever so vaguely, I suspected that it wasn't Ruth they had witnessed. Ruth wasn't there. Instead the dance had danced itself.

After years of practice in performance, I have learned to no longer identify with content as it arises. I don't know where it comes from—certainly not always from my personal experience. The episode of the Raggedy Ann doll, Alice, begins to make sense. If the performer is truly riding the energy of the moment, without any ego interference, the audience recognizes this dynamic and relaxes into it. The performance becomes a collective experience, the audience and the performer meeting in a clear space.

> I am leading a training in Freiburg, Germany, July 1995. It is the fourth of what is to be ten days of work. The students are grappling with an improvisation score that focuses on relationship. Whether their partner is projecting an image through movement, vocalization, or speech, they are to respond with a contrasting form. For example, if one speaks, the other must move or make sounds. After several rounds of sluggish practice, I suggest that the students shift their perception and accept their partner's action as their own—to view their partner's body and all its actions as extensions of their own body with no sense of separation. They are to consider that one body, not two, is expressing itself. They are to experience the improvisation as an ongoing stream of action.
>
> I feel the room lighten and the energy become fluid. Students relax. They are quicker to respond.
>
> Afterward, they say this idea of no ownership has helped them to view all action as having equal value.

"Ruthy, dance for us." The dancing that began with a child's need to be seen became, over the years, a release from the separate self.

Movement, speech, action. It is all dance—emanating from the inside out, one moment nourishing the next, uncoiling itself.

You reach your hand out.

> Hand reaches.
>
> > No hand.

NOTE

This essay was first published in *Being Bodies,* ed. Lenore Freedman and Susan Moon (Boston: Shambhala Publications, 1997). Reprinted by arrangement with Shambhala Publications.

THE CUTTING EDGE OF AWARENESS

Reports from the Inside of Improvisation

Kent De Spain

Improvisation is a form of research, a way of peering into the complex natural system that is a human being. It is, in a sense, another way of "thinking," but one that produces ideas impossible to conceive in stillness.[1]

Fig. D1. Kent De Spain. (Courtesy Kent De Spain.)

There are so many reasons to improvise: warming up; creating specific movement for choreography, bonding groups of people together, exploring new movement qualities, achieving a particular somatic state, creating a performance, having fun. In such cases, improvisation can be seen as a kind of tool for accomplishing some purpose. Tools, as an extension of our intentions, have a way of becoming invisible at times. You don't tend to think about the iron, or even the experience of ironing; you think about eliminating the wrinkles. Once the wrinkles are gone, you unplug the iron and leave.

One of the things I find fascinating about movement improvisation, however, is that most of the longtime practitioners I know treat it less as a tool and more as an end in itself. For such people, the primary purpose of improvisation is simply to experience themselves improvising. Even the movement that results is secondary. The purposes listed above do not govern "why" they improvise so much as "how" they improvise, forming part of the structure of the perpetual "now" that both determines, and is determined by, their actions. Put into words: improvisation is a way of being present in the moment, and your awareness of yourself within that moment both challenges and refines your presence in each subsequent moment. In an interview, Steve Paxton explained to me that there was no longer a clear dividing line between his everyday life and his improvising. I know exactly what he means: once you have developed and honed your awareness, you can attend to the improvisational quality of any moment of your life.[2] But how does this "improvisational awareness" work? And what can it tell us about what an improviser experiences while moving? To put it another way: where do we go, and what do we know about ourselves and our world, through improvisation?[3]

WHERE TO LOOK

As an improviser/researcher, I am constantly searching for ways to delve into the specifics of improvisation.[4] My approach has been based on the assumption that if you want to understand how something as subjective as improvisation really works, you need to ask improvisers; they are the "authorities" in this field. In theory, this might seem simplistic. In practice, it is not.

If you are only seeking a general understanding, then reflective thoughts gathered through spoken or written interviews are useful. But if what you want to investigate relies on "improvisational awareness" while moving, you need to find some way to access improvisational experiences right as they are happening, and then translate them into language that can be understood and analyzed by others. In other words, you need to find a way to transform an individual's experiential understanding into theory. The problem is how to access "real-time" experiences without disturbing or destroying the improvisational state in which they are occurring.

After reading up on other experiential research, I became inspired by a project on the "flow" experience (as defined in the work of Mihaly Csikszentmihalyi and others) that used telephone pagers and written questionnaires to gather information on the state of mind of the participants at random times during their day.[5] Realizing I could not reasonably ask improvisers to stop moving long enough to fill out a form, I developed a method for recording experiences while moving that used two audio tape recorders: the first played a mostly silent tape during which, at random times, my prerecorded voice broke in to say, "report now"; the second, connected to a microphone, recorded anything the improviser said. Using this method, I set up a series of solo improvisation sessions, each forty-five continuous minutes, and recorded the verbal reports of seven experienced improvisers: David Appel, Asimina Chremos, Ed Groff, Roko Kawai, Eric Schoefer, Leah Stein, and myself.[6]

As quantum physicist Werner Heisenberg taught us in the last century, the very act of observing a system alters that system, so there is no question that my method of recording our experiences during these sessions affected the nature of the improvisations in progress.[7] The presence of the tape recorder, my voice breaking in, and the need to translate somatic experience into linguistic reports invariably changed aspects of each improviser's process. At the same time, this structure allowed them to keep moving, placed the burden of translation on the person best suited to know what was being experienced, and retrieved the experiential reports at the very moment they were occurring. While no method can ever be ideal, the results of our sessions were eye-opening testaments to the usefulness of this approach.[8]

WHAT I FOUND: STRUCTURE

Because improvisation exists for the improviser as a movement-based somatic state, the challenge to each participant, and therefore the core of significance for this kind of research, resides in the real-time translation of experience into language, and the acknowledgment that such a translation can only approximate what is felt. In other words, what we can know or surmise about improvisational experiences must be based on a kind of echo that survives the constant disappearance of the improvisational "now": the language of the individual reports. And because both language and experience are complex phenomena, there are any number of ways to extract meaning from their interaction.

Before beginning to analyze the reports of others—each improviser did one session for me—I needed to understand the reporting process thoroughly. So I performed five solo sessions, giving as many reports as the other participants combined. To analyze such a large number of reports effectively, I concentrated as much on what my patterns of language use could reveal about my experiences as on the content of the individual reports. The first thing that struck me as I read through my reports was that I seemed to be speaking about my experiences in two ways: as an "I" interacting with the elements of improvisation, and as an unidentified observer of an improvisation in progress. "I'm drawn to the black curtains at the back of the space," clearly identifies me as the protagonist of an experience, acted upon or attracted by outside forces, but still acknowledging and owning my desires. But "that rhythmic pattern has transformed, transitioned into something else about walking . . . and arms," indicates a detachment from the action quite different from the quote above. My consciousness while improvising seemed to be bifurcating between "I"-ness and the activities performed by the "I," which appear to have an implied force or will of their own. My identification or detachment has little to do with how the improvisation might be understood by an outside observer, because in all cases I was the person moving. Instead, the differences seemed to arise from the internal experience of intention: did I feel that I was directing the action, being acted upon, reacting, observing, or some combination or interaction of those choices and others?

Another important element defining and clarifying aspects of my experiences arose from my choice of verbs; I found three categories of verbs to be particularly revealing. A narrow understanding of movement improvisation might predict that most of the verbs used would be *movement descriptors,* and those were certainly present. Words such as "swaying," "shifting," "walking," "running," "crawling," and "reaching," could be found throughout all of my sessions, clear indications of movement action. There were other kinds of verbs present, though, words such as "listening," "feeling," "tracking," "sensing," "noticing," "thinking," and "scanning." These words were nearly as common as the movement descriptors, but referred to *actions of information gathering and acknowledgment* with respect to both the state of my environment and my own somatic state. Such actions would be more difficult for an outside observer to identify than the movement actions; nonetheless, they were just as important to my experience of the improvisation. A third category of verb was present almost as often as the first two and it merits special attention. These verbs, words such as "playing," "responding," "exaggerating," "letting," "forcing," "manipulating," and "following," seemed to indicate *the nature of the relationship between myself and the improvisational material* (movement or otherwise).

So, from the construction and choice of verbs alone, the following is clear: that I was moving, that I experienced a variety of states regarding my intentions within that moving, that I experienced a variety of relationships between myself and the improvisational material, and that I was seeking and acknowledging information about the state of my self and my environment. This seems like a good skeleton for a description of improvisational process, one that could be fleshed out by adding the voices of the other improvisers to my own.

WHAT WE FOUND: CONTENT

As indicated in the previous section, one of the first things that becomes apparent from the content of the individual reports is that there is a clear and sometimes radical difference between an improvisation as it is experienced from the inside and that same improvisation as it might be understood if viewed from the outside. The internal awareness of the improviser can encompass a rich stew of sensations, images, memories, intentions, aesthetic considerations, and much, much more; the only aspects of this internal life that can be directly seen by an outside observer are those that bubble to the surface as muscular tensions affecting movement, shape, or expression. So, to substantiate the range and depth of this internal life—in essence, to track where an improviser has traveled during a session—I tried to categorize and analyze the specific words and phrases used to describe each experience. By mapping out and comparing/contrasting each improviser's "sphere of experience," I hoped to identify overlaps, revealing areas of uniqueness or common ground that would lead to a more complete understanding of improvisational process. Using a selection of quotes from the reports (indicated by the improviser's initials), here is a brief synopsis of our inner travels.

The World Inside

To sink beneath the apparency of movement is to come into contact with the intricacies of somatic experience. A good place to begin is to track the dancers' consciousness of their own proprioception. These internal sensations can influence, and be influenced by, externally visible movements, but are, in themselves, invisible from the outside. There was "residual tension in my hand after its release" and "feeling too narrow" (KD), "my skin is real hot and I notice that my head's still achy from the other day" (AC), "feeling sits-bones shifting" and "internal pressure . . . imploding, high-intensity, squeezing in me" (EG), and "something in my hands is really heavy . . . heavier than my head" (LS). But it is not just what improvisers sense inside that is important, but how they interact with those sensations through moving: "sitting, rocking, feeling somewhat autistic, very passive, hands swollen, heavy, limp" (EG), "feeling my heartbeat and matching it with the rhythm of a small hand gesture," and "my wrist is feeling the movement and that feeling is finding its way to other parts of my body"

(KD). In this last example, I was moving, then became aware of the internal sensations of that moving, then used those sensations as material for more moving, in a continual cycle created by the relationship of sensing to moving.

The next category of reports—mental images—reveals even more of the richness of the internal life: "[I] put my markings down in different places, to lay out skeins, threads of movement . . . in the space" (DA), "foot exploring space . . . have eyeballs in my toes" (EG), "an image like a monk . . . I'm looking out into the space from my protected monk cocoon" (KD), "it's almost like a Cinderella or an immigrant maid who scrubs floors" (RK), and "I feel like a grasshopper . . . it's like my feet have wings and my hands are anchors" (LS). The poetry of these words evokes images of shape and movement even in a sedentary reader, so the power of images to inspire and reflect movements and somatic states in an improviser should be clear. What is interesting to consider, though, is how movements inspired by such imagery would affect an outside observer, and whether, through the conduit of improvisation, there are moments where improviser and observer discover and experience powerful images simultaneously.

Although it was not mentioned often in these sessions, improvisers can also become aware of their own emotional states, and even use them as an element for interaction: "eyes closed, I've found a quirky little character that stands and shifts and gestures. . . . the character's emotions seem to shift and shift and shift depending on how he stands" (KD).

One last significant category of internal experiences concerns the improvisers' aesthetic reactions to their own moving. Such assessments can clearly have a considerable effect on subsequent movements and choices, but only the improviser knows how and to what extent. "My feelings at the moment are those of dissatisfaction and are growing as I continue, as I realize I have to take into account being in a larger space" (DA), "thinking about whether this whole dance has become too shifty, too movement-y" (KD), "now I'm working on a leg dance 'cause I noticed that I've been using my arms a lot today" (AC), "that wasn't a bad turn . . . grounded into the floor like that class I took" (RK), and "I'm getting a little frustrated with this work, my voice is a little strained. . . . I feel . . . sometimes I feel stupid as I explore these different characters" (ES).

The World Outside

While cataloguing poignant images, emotions, and other elements of what I might call the internal landscape, it is easy to forget that improvisers are constantly interacting with an equally engaging world beyond the boundary of their skins. From the outside, this external sensing—using the classic "five senses"—can also manifest as visible movement because of the necessity to direct and focus the action of sensing organs such as the eyes or skin. It can be difficult, though (and perhaps unnecessary), for an outside observer to discern the expressive from the pragmatic. "For a while there I was exploring the space with my eyes closed, which really tuned me in to tactile sense and sounds" (AC), "feeling the floor against the skin of my feet" (KD), and "I just opened my eyes and I saw the light shining on the floor" (ES). Although there were no examples of taste or olfactory sensing mentioned during these sessions, I have certainly experienced them in the past as a part of improvisational work.

But, as with the world inside, it is the connections between sensing the environment and moving that engender the richest improvising: "a fly just landed on my finger . . . and left . . . it's dancing a small duet with me in this area of the space . . . and I join it" (KD), "right now I am experiencing visual stimulus . . . I'm looking at the chairs and the black thing and I'm turning" (AC), "I was seeing that light and then my movement was doing a weird thing with the reflection of the light . . . it's like a balance, and then I play with the reflection, and then (*snaps her fingers*) change" (LS). Scanning and responding to the environment, conflicting or not conflicting with it, pursuing mental or emotional images associated with it—all reflect the improvisational possibilities inherent in the relationship between movers and the world in which they move.

Memory

Although the next two categories—memory and intentionality—are really a part of an improviser's "world inside," I prefer to focus on them separately. It seems ironic that memory matters at all in a process that revolves around being present in the moment. Nonetheless, two types of memory that seem to be crucial to improvising: associational and kinesthetic.[9] *Associational memory,* as I am defining it here, concerns images, facts, and movements or movement qualities that are stored in memory until triggered by existing conditions during an improvisation. Those conditions might be other movements or images, or perhaps other situations or aspects of the environment that encourage associative connections. The triggering mechanism appears to work in any combination (that is, movement triggers memory, memory triggers associated movement, situation triggers memory and movement). By *kinesthetic memory* I refer to the seemingly unconscious ability of the body/mind to remember and reproduce specific movements and/or qualities, complex coordinations, or habitual movement responses. Kinesthetic memory is thus similar to associative, but I do not know whether or not it is the result of actual associations or some other process.

There were several cases of associational memory during these sessions: "developing that gesture becomes a stroking of my face which makes me think of '29 Effeminate Gestures' by Joe Goode" (KD), "I was remembering Simone (Forti) on her side this way, kind of what she was doing at The Kitchen . . . thinking of her as I was doing this funny sideways thing" (LS), "I was thinking about Jennifer Monson a little earlier" (AC), "Walt Disney . . . I'm thinking of those cardboard picture books of Walt Disney cartoon stories . . . but all the text was in Japanese" (RK).

Examples of kinesthetic memory are more difficult to identify and understand. One illustration of this phenomenon can be pieced together from a series of my own reports. The beginning of one of my sessions involved the exploration of a movement theme built around a small rocking motion: "I'm sitting cross-legged with an autistic sort of rocking motion while I make tiny finger gestures with each hand," "the tiny rocking has grown much larger," and "continuing to explore aspects of rocking." After a few minutes, the improvisation moved on in other directions; however, fully half an hour of improvising later, I reported that "the dropped released quality has sort of melded together with the early rocking quality." For whatever reason, that rocking motion had reappeared without any conscious intention on my part. Was this movement theme triggered by some association? Was that just how my "body" (as separated from my conscious "mind") wanted to move that day? Was there some underlying and unconscious meaning structure connected with these movements? How do we categorize and understand aspects of improvising that come to us unbidden? The answer is probably beyond our grasp because most of the clues are subliminal; nevertheless, it is important to acknowledge ways of exploring, knowing, and remembering that lie beyond "consciousness"—which brings up the issue of intentionality.

Intentionality

Intentionality, and the reports that relate to it, proved to be the most fascinating and complex area of concern arising from my research. Part of the complexity flows from the ontological confusion inherent in the fact that all of our actions and intentions and reactions and movements are centered in the same somatic entity, but occur across a spectrum from the conscious to the subliminal. We are not, probably cannot be, aware of more than a small percentage of what we intend; even if we know what we want, we do not know how our intentions will be carried out. Efficiency in action and clarity in consciousness demand that much of what we do relies on training and templates, on unnoticed needs and autonomic functions. In the improvisations of our everyday lives—walking down a crowded street, or choosing the words of a sentence before we are completely clear about what we want to say—we use real-time creativity as a tool to manifest our desires. But the "space" of improvisation (and by that I do not mean Euclidean space, but rather a separate and specialized place/time/context), and the power and clarity of a honed improvisational awareness, can be a dynamic instrument of inquiry into the intricacies of human behavior and experience. In other words, if we want to know more about the relationship between what we want and how we act in the world, being aware of ourselves while improvising may just be the best way to find out. To help make some sense out of all of this, I have divided the discussion of intentionality into three areas of prime interest within the sessions: the relationship between intentions and movement, between intentions and the physical body, and between intentions and elements of artistic form.

The reports dealing with the relationship between intentions and movement indicated a wide range of interactions. Basic reports about movement—"spinning" or "walking" or "pushing"—would seem to represent a straightforward approach (what I would call "direct intention": you want to move a certain way and then you do so). But the following report, "by releasing some muscles, gravity is slowly rolling me across the shoulder . . . to I don't know where" (KD), shows an example in which direct intention accounts for only a part of what transpired. In this instance of "indirect intention," what initiated the movement (in this case "releasing some muscles") resulted in a further action not specifically directed ("gravity is rolling me"), toward an unspecified goal ("I don't know where"). And in this last report, "I stopped dancing and something else was making me dance" (LS), the improviser indicates even less ownership of her intentions. We can suspect that no one was actually making her dance against her will (she was alone in the space), but rather that this was an example of "intending the unintended" or "allowing," that is, choosing (read: intending) to allow conscious intentions to step aside for a moment while something else (we can only make intelligent guesses as to what) directs the action.

The movement/intention relationship further reveals a side of an improviser's internal life that outside observers could not see (although, perhaps they could sense it), in other words, intentions can be consciously acknowledged but not acted upon: "there's an editing process going on, you're in the middle of something and you think, 'boy, all of a sudden I'm just going to go there and take a big jump,' but, in fact, then you edit, at that moment, say 'no' and then continue" (DA).[10]

Moving on to the relationship between intentions and the "physical body," again, the realities during improvisation were wide-ranging, from simple to quite complex. For the exigencies of discussion, by using the term "physical body," I am isolating the body from its function in movement and from its more holistic context as the "body/mind" or "soma."[11] I do, however, also believe that the body is and has its own intentionality, and that the need to separate it linguistically arises from the incredibly complex interactions among multiple aspects of body, mind, spirit, intentions, and actions. "I'm standing, making a gesture with my right hand that's very tense, but that tension isn't really affecting the rest of my body. It's separate . . . almost not a part of me" (KD). With this gesture I was attempting to split my body into separate intentions; the first to be as tense as possible, the second to not allow the tension in one part to have an effect on the rest of me. At first this was successful, but then the persistent tension in my hand began to spread, overcoming my intention for it not to: "the tension has affected my face" (KD). Later, I made a change: "I'm letting the tense hand go, but it doesn't release because it's been tensed for so long" (KD). My intention to release the tension in my hand was, by itself, insufficient to accomplish my goal, leading to another discrepancy between body and intention, so in the report: "Increment by increment, I'm forcing it [my hand and fingers] back to straight" (KD), it becomes clear that, in order to fulfill my desire to release the tension in my hand, I was compelled by my body to amend my intention and force my hand back to normal. I believe that this subtle interplay between body and intention occurs consistently, and mostly unconsciously, throughout improvisational process.

The relationship between intention and the body can also be found in the improviser's interaction with communications (for lack of a better word) from the body itself. Instead of a conscious-mind–over–body hierarchy, there seems to be a much more fluid feedback loop of intentionality. "Responding to a kind of need to stretch, to feel into the length of my legs and my back, I've draped over and developed an odd kind of leaned-over walking" (KD), finds movement in response to the sensed "needs" of the improviser's body—instigating what, from a third-person perspective, might be viewed as an "aesthetic" choice. A similar idea can be found in an improviser's occasional inability to execute clearly intended movement ideas: "I slightly lost my balance on one of my steps that made me cross over, so I've picked that up as a pattern" (KD), is a case where, instead of just acknowledging and accepting the unintended loss of control, it becomes the intended basis of new material.

That brings us to the relationship between intention and the elements of artistic form. Because these sessions had no predetermined improvisational structure beyond the place, the time, and the reporting procedure, some questions emerge: How were these sessions formed artistically? From where did the shape and flow and progression of each session arise? In "I feel like my opening gambit is to get the lay of the land . . . let myself traverse back and forth as many times as possible, trying out different things . . . to allow things to remain open, in the sense that they don't move into any of the material that I previously have been working on" (DA), we see the acknowledgment of a strategy appear—what I would call an "agenda" for improvising. As conditions and context shift, however, so can strategies, in the very midst of moving. Later in the same session, "I find myself now drawn toward toying with the material I've been working on for the last two months" (DA), shows a complete reversal in the acknowledged agenda.

It is easy to assume that we are clear and single-minded about our intentions in moving, but improvisation mirrors those facets of our lives in which it is not always easy to know what we want. Eric Schoefer clearly demonstrated this version of the "intentional fallacy" when, in two distinct voices (Characters A and B), he had the following conversation with himself:

A: Okay, so what do you want to do now?

B: You know.

A: Do you want to move?

B: Sort of, but my body is hurting and I don't feel like movinnnnggggg.

A: Well, okay. Then what do you want to do? What's the problem with this character work? Why not keep exploring different characters?

B: But I don't want to explore characters. I don't want to.

A: Why don't you want to? Huh? Okay. Okay, if you just want to move, then just move. You are moving.

B: Yes, but I'm tired of moving without having the other parts of my brain be a part of it.

A: Well, then, let's see. What do you want to do then? Do you want to go back to voice, or do you think you should start, start, start with the story?

Some of this intentional schism may result from the real-time interaction of two clear points of view: the internal and the external (or, to put it differently, the improviser and the audience). Although there was no audience present during these sessions, improvisers (particularly those experienced in performance situations) can be very aware of how their process might be experienced by someone watching. This bifurcation of attention was reinforced in these sessions by the presence of the tape recorders and the odd necessity to translate experiences into reports for public consumption. This prompted both a questioning of intentions: "Am I doing vocals here because that's what I do? . . . Or is it because I'm very aware that there's a tape here? . . . I don't know, it's probably both" (RK); as well as a recognition that intention and action have taken you to a place beyond linguistic translation: "Slow, (there is a very long pause here) elbow . . . I can't . . . I don't know how to say it" (LS).

When improvising, our intentions can act simply as a filter for our movement choices—or, with more complexity as an evolving feedback loop concerning the relationship between what we want and what we do. But, as with any of the elements of improvisation, intentionality itself can become the primary focus as we enter a space where movement choices become less important than sensing and exploring the very nature of desire.

BEYOND WHAT WE KNOW

If improvisation is a form of research, improvisational awareness is the scientific method. Through it we become aware of our own theories and biases, our histories and desires, our delimitations and our methods, and even our results and conclusions. It is the weapon with which we cleave the good from the bad, the desired from the unacceptable—at least in a given moment on a given day. But that awareness, like the moments it is attached to, is fleeting. We can feel it ourselves through the process of improvising. To explore it in others, however, and thereby better understand the cultural and/or personal sources of our commonalities and differences, requires literacy and translation.

My own experience tells me that where we go, what we know, and how we know it is intimately connected to the linguistic stories we tell ourselves in our minds (that might be one definition of the word "consciousness"). The verbal reports under scrutiny here, by their very linguistic nature, urge those aspects of our awareness to the fore. But verbal language has limits. By looking at those limits, at the places where our ability to articulate our experiences begins to break down, we see how improvisation can take us into realms of awareness that extend beyond literacy, a place of synapses and chaos and unvoiced intention. While the linguistic content of these reports is consistently, even gratifyingly, compelling, as students of human experience we must find the discipline to feel past these words and into the negative spaces around and beyond.

But in those spaces beyond are some experiences in improvisation that are not easily categorized—not inside, nor outside; in fact, somehow dissolving that existential border. In these moments, we seem to sense and respond to ("dance" with) something ineffable; something, although we tend to avoid the word in this culture, that might be described as "spiritual." David Appel reported such an experience:

> I just finished a sequence of events where I became acutely aware of the edge, of the border, of the line of play between movement that's erupting, billowing forth, and a sense of experience, craft, body knowing, that [is] there from previous times; how these two mesh, and meld, and interact, and encounter each other, and converse. . . . There's a feeling in dancing that something is singing itself as I'm moving. I don't know whether it's me that's doing the singing, or whether, in fact, what I probably think it is, is that something is singing through me. There's a question of allowing myself to be a conduit for that. And at the same time, I'm noticing that I can be responsive to that song in some way.

Our consciousness is like a body interacting with the exterior world. Because our nerves cannot extend beyond our skin, we only really sense ourselves in contact with a larger world, but separate from it. In the same way, we only "know" what is present within our consciousness, yet by touching it, by dancing with it, we can sense the contours and textures of an infinite world that exists beyond the boundaries of knowledge.

But the "cutting edge of awareness" cleaves deeper than that. Improvisation, as I understand it, is an attentional practice: the more you attend to movement and memory and sensing and intention, the more you play (improvise) with all of the elements of what we call living—and the more you come to understand that reality itself is based on the relationship between our attention and the world. You sense that your attention is both selecting and forming your experience in real time, but that what is being selected and formed is not completely of your choosing, because the world is improvising too; and that dance, your interaction with the world, forms you just as you form the world.

NOTES

1. This is a quote from my "Dance Improvisation: Creating Chaos," *Contact Quarterly* 18, no. 1 (1993): 21–27.

2. Steve Paxton, personal interview, August 4, 1991.

3. The "improvisation" I have focused on has been (quoting from my dissertation): "non-choreographed, spontaneous dancing as developed and practiced within the modern and post-modern dance traditions of the United States and Europe . . . with their attendant historical and cultural connections to European paradigms and their subtle appropriation of aesthetics and forms derived from African-American and other cultural influences."

4. The most complete example of my research in this area can be found in my Solo Movement Improvisation: Constructing Understanding Through Lived Somatic Experience (Ph.D. diss., Temple University, 1997).

5. A good general guide to research on the "flow" experience can be found in Mihaly Csikszentmihalyi, *Flow: The Psychology of Optimal Experience* (New York: Harper Perennial, 1991). The methodology, called the "Experience Sampling Method," is de-

scribed in F. Massimini and M. Carli, "The Systematic Assessment of Flow in Daily Experience," in *Optimal Experience: Psychological Studies of Flow in Consciousness,* ed. Mihaly Csikszentmihalyi and Isabella Selega Csikszentmihalyi, 266–77 (Cambridge: Cambridge University Press, 1988).

6. Each of these wonderful dancers easily met my criteria, which was that participants should have a minimum of ten years of improvisational experience and have performed improvisationally in professional settings, a standard intended to identify improvisers who would have the experience to minimize the impact of the reporting process on their dancing.

7. Although this altering is never stated directly by Heisenberg, it can be clearly inferred from his writings on the Uncertainty Principle and other aspects of the observation and measurement of quantum phenomena. For an introduction to some of these ideas, see Werner Heisenberg, *Physics and Philosophy: The Revolution in Modern Science* (New York: Harper, 1958).

8. The value placed on "usefulness" is an important indicator of the underlying research aesthetic of my work, which follows a "constructivist" model (also known as "naturalistic inquiry"). More information can be found in Yvonna S. Lincoln and Egon G. Guba, *Naturalistic Inquiry* (Beverly Hills, Calif.: Sage Publications, 1985).

9. I am not using these terms in any academic sense, and my descriptions of them may or may not correspond to similarly named concepts in the literature of memory. I am only using these terms as descriptors for specific categories of phenomena that commonly appear during improvisation.

10. One mechanism of sensing such "undanced" movements could emerge from what I term "predictive understanding": the ability as a viewer to sense yourself in the moment of the improvisation and therefore "feel" what will (or could) happen next. The difficulty is in distinguishing between your own choices and those of the improviser. In other words, can you sense that the dancer onstage considered a possibility without actually dancing it, or are you only sensing the difference between your own choice-making and his/hers?

11. This isolation is not arbitrary on my part. Because improvisation, in my view, is an "attentional" practice (that is, a practice primarily focused on the "what" and "how" of our attention to ourselves in relation to our environment), I separate interdependent categories such as body and movement because we can "attend" to them as separate entities (e.g., I can attend to my arm regardless of how it is moving, or to its movement qualities apart from the fact that it is an arm).

A DUET WITH POSTMODERN DANCE

ANNA HALPRIN AND IMPROVISATION AS CHILD'S PLAY
A Search for Informed Innocence
Janice Ross

The end of all our exploring will be to arrive where we started and know the place for the first time.
> *T. S. Eliot*

We start at innocence, go through experience and in doing so, are able to return to a higher, informed innocence.
> *William Blake*

In the mid-1960s, Anna Halprin forged a reputation as a choreographer of provocative, socially current dances. These works were noteworthy for their celebration of the natural and for shaving ever finer the line between life and art. Much of the emotional immediacy of these dance works, however, came from large parts of them having been arrived at through improvisation. They were improvisations not just of movement designs, but also of fictitious and real social relationships. These works, such as *Parades and Changes, Ceremony of Us,* and *Apartment Six,* were theatrical spectacles with specifically scripted situations in which open-ended movement choices were made by the individual, often at the moment of performance. This information throws into new relief Halprin's fluency in dealing with difficult social and personal issues through dance. Viewed with this knowledge, her theater becomes not so much the result of a deliberately designed message as the shaping of what bubbles to the surface.

Halprin became associated with improvisation because of her interest in blurring the line between the figure on stage and the private person behind that stage presence. Although never labeled as such, improvised movement had also been a part of Halprin's training as a dance student under Margaret H'Doubler at the University of Wisconsin.[1] In her own work with children, and later with her San Francisco Dancers Workshop, Halprin was rediscovering the utility of improvisation. She, like H'Doubler, avoided using the term improvisation.[2] Yet improvisation it was and it became a very contemporary way of generating performance material for Halprin in the 1960s.

Halprin's early work with children, then, informs us about where she ended up because it represented a vital period of transformation for her. Stylistically it was a departure, but conceptually it was a return. The decades of the late 1940s to the late 1960s encompassed the period in Halprin's life when she was forging her own voice in dance and moving away from the formal, grandly narrative works of her immediate mentor, Doris Humphrey. Her goal was a more personal vocabulary with more intimately scaled dramatic content. Experiments with children in loosely structured dance formats showed her that new possibilities of invention were feasible and could, in fact, yield richly personal work.

Halprin's working with children in dance had begun many years earlier when, as an undergraduate at the University of Wisconsin at Madison, she had a decidedly inauthentic experience. In 1938, in a class on dance pedagogy taught by Blanche Trilling, then chair of the dance department at the university, Halprin and the other students were instructed to "act like children" while another student practiced "teaching" them.[3] Halprin later recounted that she found this exercise so stupid she stormed out of the class and never returned.[4] The memory of this improvisation of falseness, its bitter aftertaste, has stayed with Halprin throughout her life.

Halprin was on a quest for a natural balance between structure and freedom. She wanted to discover through dance the preconditions for spontaneous behavior within disciplined order. Halprin had actually taught her first class for children in 1941 as an undergraduate dance major at the University of Wisconsin in H'Doubler's program. Because as part of her course of study, Halprin was also required to teach in the community, she spent a year in the public schools of Madison teaching dance once a week to elementary school children. "I thought that the children were fresh and that working with them would eventually enable me to work spontaneously," Halprin said of that time. "I thought they were closer to natural sources of movement and creativity. But I was concerned with giving the class a shape and providing safe boundaries."[5]

Halprin continued her work with children in Boston after graduation. Newly married, she commuted to work daily on her bicycle, splitting her time between teaching in Boston's elite Windsor School and teaching at an inner-city settlement house. Her husband, Lawrence Halprin, was completing his architecture and landscape architecture degrees at Harvard under Walter Gropius; thus, the Bauhaus aesthetic also began to shape Anna Halprin's ideas about movement invention and space.

Once she left the university and began teaching her own classes for children, Halprin took each child's individuality as a starting point in dance class. At first tentatively, in Boston (1942–44), and later more boldly in her Marin Children's Dance Cooperative classes (1946–68), Halprin pushed for spontaneity in children's dance actions, for movements that felt comfortable regardless of how they looked.

The genesis of what grew into her thriving Marin County Dance Cooperative was a 1946 lecture demonstration on children's dance that Halprin gave for a parents education workshop. Within the first decade this network of children's dance classes around the Bay Area had grown to more than eight hundred boys and girls between the ages of three and sixteen who were studying modern dance at six sites from Marin to Palo Alto.

"I was captivated by the unpredictability of what the kids would do," Halprin said of the open-structured movement exercises she gave. "I was interested in getting the children to be present," she recalled. "I might say something like 'Skip' and then I would close that direction by saying 'backwards,' 'faster,' 'smaller.' I was most interested in just generating an idea."[6]

As with her own work Halprin preferred that movement have its own meaning rather than stand as a symbol for something else. And the way one arrived at this meaning was through guided improvisatory work. "I cannot approach art symbolically or literally with any enthusiasm," Halprin wrote in a letter to the parents of her young students in 1960, "and therefore I cannot teach this way. The most rewarding part of teaching children is that the child's art is one of complete immediacy. It is impossible to bottle it up into the art labels of adulthood."[7]

Halprin says she started teaching dance to children because she had children of her own and she wanted them to dance. Yet the actual founding date of the Marin Children's Cooperative in 1946 predates her oldest child's birth by two years. Also, children's dance classes were a core part of the curriculum at the studio she shared with Welland Lathrop in San Francisco beginning soon after her arrival in the Bay Area in 1945. Teaching children served Halprin as both an educator and as an artist, because she learned best by helping others learn. Indeed, the creating of conditions in which learning could take place would prove to be her paramount gift as a dance maker. Her first choreographic goal was never the movements themselves, but rather imparting to the dancer the tools for unlocking movements within oneself.

In linking her children's dance classes with the beginning of her own family, Halprin was also probably acknowledging the conflicting tensions of the time, which saw satisfaction for women largely tied to the fulfillment of their duties as wives and mothers. Halprin had already opted for a personal life over a strictly professional one when she moved to the Bay Area. The Marin Children's Dance Cooperative, although it eventually proved profitable and artistically inspirational for Halprin, was, in its early years, a means of keeping the two halves of her life connected, mother-and-wife and woman-artist. Through improvisation Halprin was exemplifying a maternal approach to creativity. Her goal was to tap the instinctive and internal in children. From her perspective, feeling and instinct were valuable repositories of emotional reserves that improvisation could mine.

In the 1950s a typical class for four- and five-year-olds in Halprin's Marin Cooperative would begin with a focus on good posture. It would rapidly progress to what is listed in Halprin's notes as locomotor movements (walks, runs, the introduction of rhythmic distinctions, body gestures of the trunk); isolation of parts of the body, explorations of force, space, and time; and finally, the introduction of composition with the shaping of material into a beginning, middle,

Fig. E2. A view of the dance deck adjacent to the Halprin home in Mount Tamalpais, California, c. 1957–58, from a film by Lawrence Halprin. (Courtesy Anna and Lawrence Halprin.)

and end. While this list of specific movement skills is ambitious, it also rests comfortably within the boundaries of creative movement skills that were being emphasized by American specialists in children's pedagogy during the 1930s and 1940s. There was a great deal of latitude for individual styling and inflection within the improvisatory guidelines Halprin gave.

During the 1950s and 1960s Halprin's dance cooperatives served as a prime laboratory for exploring the possibilities improvisation offered the dancer. Here Halprin and her staff of dance teachers taught hundreds of Bay Area children, from preschoolers to high school teenagers. The method Halprin used, which was almost entirely structured improvisation, would form the basis for her subsequent movement explorations with her own adult company, the Dancers Workshop.

"My whole concept in working with children was to have them appreciate their aliveness," Halprin said in a recent interview.[8] "I wanted to give them a sense of believing in themselves so they weren't worried about being right or wrong. It takes a lot of self-confidence to be a dancer because you are totally exposed all the time. It takes the most courage [of any performing art]. Kids have to grow up believing they are just fine the way they are. I did this through improvisation because with improvisation you aren't right or wrong, you just are."

The idea of "just being," a supremely natural and at the same time elusive state, propelled Halprin's search for the innate and authentic in her own work throughout the 1960s and indeed into the subsequent three decades. "Natural-ness" and "authenticity" in this regard implied innate, unmediated responses and behaviors, an indifference to conventions. For Halprin the notion of improvisation involved the discovery not of a single correct path but of multiple possibilities; one chose the one among the many that would be the one for that moment. "One of the biggest things motivating me," Halprin said recently of her use of improvisation, "was that I was trying to get away from cause and effect relationships in performance. I wanted to free myself from preconceptions. The real goal was to perceive reality in a fresh way. And what was reality?"[9]

This notion of improvisation as a tool for modeling reality was readily apparent in Halprin's work with children for the more than two decades she directed the Marin Children's Dance Cooperative. "Improvisation was a tool, the most important tool, I used with the children's dance collective," Halprin said. Indeed, her teaching was strongly centered on helping kids chart their own paths to their interiors. Halprin departs significantly from the norm for children's dance classes of the time, however, with what she called her "methods," a list of six objectives imbued with a rich improvisatory sensibility. She lists the following ambitiously curricular objectives for her four- and five-year-old pupils:

The overall aim of a creative approach to dance is to give the child a rhythmic dance training that is a natural and joyful art expression. The method of achieving this aim is to deal with the child as a whole human being—physically, mentally, and emotionally—establishing an integration and balance of personality. Thus, the dance experience becomes part of the child's well-being and growth. Specific Aims for 4 & 5 year olds:

1. A conscious awareness of the simplest, most natural movements.
2. Having fun.
3. Explore [sic] and Self-discovering.
4. Repetition of general class pattern with fresh material each week *so that a routine as such is never established.* (Emphasis added.)
5. Encouragement . . . make the child confident, help him find himself.[10]

What is interesting about the tone of this document is its respect for the child as an individual.[11] Examined against this backdrop, Halprin's use of improvisation takes on a new tenor. It is not the refuge of a dance teacher short on activities for active children; rather it is a means for seeking out the private person in each child and fostering the tastes, inclinations, and movement distinctions of that unique individual.

A link might be made between this faith in the inventive powers of the unencumbered child and a trusting of adult improvisation to yield more genuine movement than the conscious mind could design. An early draft of what appears to be the mission statement for the dance cooperative reveals her lauding of these abilities buried in the child, abilities that she will shortly try to wrest free from adults through improvisation:

Young children are endowed with the gift of seeing the world around them intuitively, with an innocent freshness as yet unaffected by the rational dictates of experience.

This natural ability is akin to the awareness of the artist, although it may be less conscious. One of the chief concerns in the use of the creative process is to retain as much as possible the natural awareness in the child and yet provide a method of training that will truly let the child grow, develop and mature.[12]

As other women artists in America in the 1940s were discovering, improvisation could also be a steady state of mind in a society not yet conversant with two-career families and "juggling" as a long-term condition. The lines between Halprin's private life and her performing life would continually cross as the obligations she felt as a parent and wife steadily informed the subsequent choices she made as an artist. The author Diane Middlebrook, in writing about the poet Anne Sexton (who came of age as a mother and artist during this same period as Halprin), has observed that the key issue for women artists of this period was just how they negotiated the conflicting demands of motherhood and art.[13]

Curiously, Halprin's creation of the dance cooperative as a forum for her own balancing of these roles may also have made it attractive to other mothers who were striving to do something for their children *and* for themselves. It was parental involvement that really got the cooperative going and that kept it salient for the next twenty years. From among the parent volunteers who shouldered the administrative chores, Halprin would draw some of her most important collaborators, including the designer Jo Landor, whose children took class at the original Halprin-Lathrop Studio on Union Street in San Francisco. Landor became a director as well as prop and set designer for Halprin for the next decade. Halprin also recruited children who had moved through her classes, in addition to her own two daughters, Daria and Rana. Kim Hahn, Yani Novack, Melissa Davis, and Norma Leistiko all began as free-spirited children dancing with Halprin before they evolved into Dancers Workshop artists.

So there were notions of family, of community, wrapped into Halprin's children's classes and, by extension, her use of improvisation. Photographs and film footage of the first decades of the Marin Children's Dance Cooperative reveal a strong sense of the individual reflecting her immediate environment. Preschool boys and girls, for example, are shown at the start of class lounging on the floor and leaning against their mothers, the moms languidly moving the children's arms as if testing for a state of complete relaxation. Improvisation for Halprin was about becoming attuned and sensitive to the external as well as the internal, to using insight to broaden outlook.

The task of finding a movement solution to a communal problem then took on the attributes of a social response. Improvisation was becoming a means to connect as a group. "Many of the children devoted the whole Saturday to being at the dance co-op," Halprin said recently. "So I tried to create a family feeling with older children working with the younger ones." Halprin was tapping into a generational story in using improvisation with children in this way. As we grow up, our discovery of our self always needs to be mediated in relation to how it affects our relationships with our families and others. So too for the improvising child: respect for and cooperation with those around becomes crucial.

For adults too these would prove to be some of the thorniest problems improvisation prompted. Just how free can a dancer be in a studio filled with others all cutting loose and looking within? Indeed by the late 1960s Halprin had pushed to the limits of how personal adult improvisations could be and still be viewed as art.

A single fragment of black-and-white film footage dating from 1957 or 1958 attests to the strong ensemble quality of these early children's classes in improvisation. Shot by Halprin's husband with a hand-held camera, this film unfolds as a slice of spontaneous play. It begins with a chain of little girls, led by Halprin's daughter Daria, dashing downhill to Halprin's outdoor dance deck. Like nymphs from the woods come to frolic in a forest glade, they skip wildly around the gnarled madrone trees that poke through the dance deck, each child a study in the naturalistic beauty of simple skips, jumps, and running turns.

Next, faces serene and bodies blissfully limp, the children lie on the deck and take turns relaxing and letting each other gently lift and rotate their arms and legs in a sequence Halprin called "floppy flop." One little girl in a black leotard looks as if she were dreamily floating while another child softly tugs her limp arms and legs until her whole body flops over in a sleepy roll. One of the most touching passages depicts Halprin's oldest daughter, Daria, who appears to be about nine years old, and a younger child whom she tenderly pulls to standing. Daria conveys intense focus and investment in the immediate task as she leans back to get more leverage on the soft body that she is tugging. Her concentration suggests a maturity well beyond her years.

One can imagine the attraction this kind of meditative focus would have held for adult performers in the 1960s when "being present" was such an important social as well as aesthetic goal. In this quest for the natural person, children's dance and improvisation were keys to this suppressed state of the modern person. In the December 1957 *Dance Magazine,* Halprin is quoted as saying:

> All co-op teachers share [my] underlying conviction about the importance of imbuing and maintaining in the children a genuine pleasure for discovering dance ideas in all their experiences. The primary motivation is to encourage each child to realize and understand the basic values of creative movement. He is instructed in percussion and singing, so that dance becomes an integrated art experience. Classes draw upon the multiple stimuli of poetry, drama, painting and sculpture.[14]

Halprin's belief in improvisation as a serious tool of dance invention is ironically most apparent in her framing it as something for which the body must be physically and emotionally prepared. She developed clear warm-ups that were later codified into her *Movement Rituals One, Two, and Three.* These warm-ups were designed to prepare the body for improvisation. "The movement rituals are about coming back to feeling the body and feeling the integration of yourself," Halprin said. "It's a basic identification of how you are as a dancer."[15]

As improvisation, particularly the kind of improvisation that seeks a response that is as unmediated as possible, "floppy flop" was to become a staple of Halprin's teaching and a means for listening to the first murmurings of the conversation with one's body that improvisation initiates.

The final few minutes of the film footage show three girls in a pose that echoes the twisted lines of the large madrone branch next to them on the dance deck. One by one they propel themselves around the branch, echoing the form of its smaller branches with reaching arms and stretched legs. What is most captivating about this final section of the film is not so much its fascination as dance as a performance product (which even Halprin would probably agree is negligible) but what it reveals about the dancer's attention to her environment. It seems that the first step in finding out what is inside is acknowledging and responding to the forces of the surrounding world that impinge on our sheltered interior.

This acknowledgment of the environment was one of Halprin's most salient discoveries. It was territory she would pursue aggressively in her seminal work of the mid-1960s. Not a quest to go wild but rather an effort to become real propelled her. "In the 1960s we [Halprin's company, the San Francisco Dancers Workshop] were using improvisation all the time," Halprin said. "We used a lot of open scores for work later as well," she continued, referring to her process of scoring or scripting a dance so that the general parameters of action might be sketched out while the actual details (for example, how a dancer might interpret the directive "lock eyes with a member of the audience and slowly remove your clothes") were left up to individual interpretation.[16]

Later, Halprin would use improvisation in company rehearsals as a way to generate material and move through a tight spot. "We might take a chair or branch that was a fixed element in the dance and we would improvise with it, so through that we would develop a more fixed relationship [between the dancers and the prop]."[17] She continued: "But it was never the same twice because it was part of the here and now philosophy of being present in the moment."[18]

In the late 1950s, in an address she gave before the annual recital of one of her Marin Children's Dance Cooperatives, Halprin noted: "We are children once in a lifetime of art. The way we experience it [art] in our youth may open its world of seeing, enjoying, creating for the rest of our lives." So here is a second attraction improvisation held for Halprin: a process of discovery, of engagement with the world that, once revealed, could become a path and a process to be visited again and again. Improvisation and its discoveries were for Halprin a way of being in the world.

Halprin felt she was on a mission to foster creative vision. For this reason, after the 1960s, she chose terms other than improvisation (for example "open scoring") to describe what she was doing. For her, improvisation was a word saturated with casualness, a casualness antithetical to what she saw as the purpose of her children's dance classes. For her this purpose was the very serious task of enhancing a child's natural awareness while, in her own words, "providing a method of training that would let the child grow, develop, and mature."[19]

A second film of her Marin children's classes, dating from the early 1960s, documents an indoor end-of-the-year festival. The children dancing here range from toddlers with their mothers to teenagers; for each age group the reality of their moment in life in the world is also the text of their dance. This text is played out in a very curious exchange between a dark-haired sixteen-year-old boy and a long-haired blonde teenage girl. Facing each other they stare for a long moment into one another's eyes—then the boy dodges the girl as she lunges for him, their play fraught with the awkwardness of budding sexual attraction. The film then jumps to another teenage girl who sits, covered in layers of lace petticoats, atop a Victorian settee, a prop from Halprin's improvisatory adult dance of sexual encounter, *Apartment Six*.

Today Halprin continues to be cautious about using the word improvisation with regard to her work. The reasons are complex. In this reticence one senses Halprin's objection to the notion of improvisation as work that was generally careless, unconsidered, tossed-off, "winged." Not to call what she was doing improvisation was a way to get a serious hearing for behaviors that otherwise might be readily dismissed as frivolous.

Particularly for the kinds of work that Halprin was investigating beginning in the early 1950s and extending into the 1970s, improvisation might well have stood for an escape from the demands of artmaking. For her, loosening the bonds of movement invention implied a flight into what she saw as riskier, more gutsy realms of discovery and expression. "The key factor is that our experimentation then was taking many forms," Halprin said. "We were looking for a way so that the audience wouldn't be passive."[20]

For Halprin, improvisatory methods were choices prompted by practicality and pragmatism as well as art. She had begun openly embracing less structured ways of working soon after she arrived on the West Coast in 1945, but these didn't blossom into her signature dance-theater works until after she returned from performances in New York in 1955 as part of the ANTA (American National Theatre and Academy) Festival.

Struggling to find her own voice as a choreographer, Halprin turned to what might be called "structured improvisation" to find out who she was as an artist and an individual. She felt the leading modern dance techniques of the time interfered with her ability to create something authentic for herself. Interestingly, however, her belief that dance should address social problems clearly connected her conceptually to the dance modernists of the preceding generation.

By the time the Halprins had moved to the West Coast, children's classes were a firm part of Halprin's dance identity. Once she was in California however, these classes, like Halprin's own work, began to change. To begin with, there was the dance deck, a wooden outdoor studio designed by Arch Lauterer and Lawrence

Halprin, that sat perched below the Halprins' home on a California hillside next to Mount Tamalpais. This natural setting, which significantly influenced Anna Halprin's own work, also began to shape her ideas in the rented classrooms in Marin where she taught burgeoning numbers of children's classes. "I had begun to realize that a class didn't have to be orderly, that it wasn't so bad if a class was unstructured," Halprin remarked recently. "If a certain amount of chaos didn't bother the children why should it bother me?"[21]

In retrospect Halprin also began to find that H'Doubler's model of using improvisation in dance was becoming more influential. In class H'Doubler had spent hours having students explore the motion of various joints of the body as the wellspring of movement invention. For Halprin alone on the West Coast, this notion of discovery within the body's own set parameters was a model to which she would return again and again. It was one that allowed her to find herself without relinquishing total control. In fact, Halprin would come to see these methods as a means for putting more areas of the creative individual in the service of making art. "I would look for structures I could use that told each child what but not how," Halprin said. "As a guide I had to be open and flexible."[22] For Halprin, teaching children's dance and using an open structured form of teaching movement evolved together. With the added influence of the California environment and the dance deck, she was finding a way to let the individual speak through movement choices.

In pursuit of unleashing this same unpredictability in adults, Halprin began to explore similar methods in the series of seminal workshops she gave on her dance deck in 1962, 1963, and 1964. The same improvisatory techniques Halprin had begun using as a tool of progressive education with children suddenly had a new currency as tools for adult personal growth in the 1960s. Movement improvisation had shifted from being looked upon as a throwback to Isadora Duncan to being regarded as a very contemporary way to get in touch with oneself.

Ironically, Halprin used improvisation during this period in a way that her most influential students would later refute. For her it was a means for physicalizing intuition, for giving feeling a physical form. Trisha Brown, Simone Forti, and Yvonne Rainer, alumnae of her summer workshops, would later channel the use of improvisation Halprin exposed them to into the new territory of postmodernism. They would use it to create movement that was more instead of less objective.[23]

By the late 1970s, the techniques stemming from H'Doubler's teachings, the children's dance classes, and the California landscape, would inform Halprin's dance work with her new pool of student-performers, individuals challenging cancer and AIDS (she had only recently returned to dance after a seven-year period dealing with her own cancer). Halprin's initial investigations into a balance between control and freedom—the very investigations that had led her to children's dance classes—were now leading her to the adult and the infirm. In the process she had found that it isn't necessary to loosen all the restraints for one to be in the grip of the imagination. The crucial elements are the setting of the conditions for movement discovery in the studio and then a willful submission to a larger force. This relinquishing of personal control can produce the stimulating frisson in which abandonment to the moment leads to discovery of the innocent self. Rather than being a starting point, Halprin's use of improvisation with children was an important transitional phase in her development as an artist. In the process Halprin helped transform improvisation into a prime tool of the performance avant-garde.

NOTES

1. Hermine Davidson, telephone conversation with Janice Ross, Madison, Wisconsin, June 25, 1996.
2. Hermine Davidson, interview with Janice Ross, Madison, Wisconsin, March 23, 1996.
3. Interview with Janice Ross, Kentfield, California, January 25, 1996.
4. Interview with Janice Ross, Madison, Wisconsin, May 14, 1994.
5. Interview with Janice Ross, Kentfield, California, December, 21, 1995.
6. Ibid.
7. Interview with Janice Ross, Kentfield, California, January 25, 1996.
8. Ibid.
9. From an archival curriculum sheet on the Marin Children's Dance Cooperative, Anna Halprin Archives, San Francisco: Performing Arts Library and Museum, undated.
10. Philosophically it echoes the sentiments of the educational progressives of the time, and Halprin herself was a product of the premiere progressive educational system, Carleton Washburn's curriculum for the Winnetka, Illinois, public school system.
11. Diane Middlebrook, conversation with Janice Ross, Stanford, California, April 24, 1996.
12. Halprin, Anna, "Introduction to New Members," Anna Halprin Archives, San Francisco: Performing Arts Library and Museum, undated.
13. Interview with Janice Ross, Kentfield, California, December 21,1995.
14. Halprin, Anna, "Introduction To New Members," Anna Halprin Archives, San Francisco: Performing Arts Library and Museum, undated.
15. Interview with Janice Ross, Kentfield, California, December 21, 1995.
16. Ibid.
17. Ibid.
18. Ibid.
19. From an archival curriculum sheet on the Marin Children's Dance Cooperative, Anna Halprin Archives, San Francisco: Performing Arts Library and Museum, undated.
20. Interview with Janice Ross, Madison, Wisconsin, May 14, 1994.
21. Interview with Janice Ross, Kentfield, California, January 25, 1996.
22. Interview with Janice Ross, Kentfield, California, December 21, 1995.
23. Copeland, Roger, "Dance, Feminism, and the Critique of the Visual," in *Dance, Gender and Culture,* ed. Helen Thomas (London: MacMillian, 1993) pp. 139–150.

ANIMATE DANCING

A Practice in Dance Improvisation

Simone Forti

The stage. Walking out. "They see me now. Let them see me, get used to the sight of me. Quiet down. Open." I choose a place. I stand there. I glance at the audience. To see them, for them to see my face, my whole stance, just a look of recognition that I consider a hello. I begin. With what presents itself. A memory, a shape in the performance hall. I trust this first thing and I begin. I hope that the audience, having met me, follows my interest, my involvement. I return in my mind's eye to the northern slope of Bald Mountain on which I live. I look around and—pronto! Something happens. I see snow. I jump and curl in air. Hands and feet in air. Heavy rattle winter wind smashes dry sunflower stalks. Again. Again, smash, jump! Snow thud falls from laden roof. Feet slide out, thud. Whole body, thud, flat to floor.

I met Anna Halprin in 1955. My main focus at that moment was painting. I was twenty-one and went on to study and dance with her for the next four years. I had been taking one or two classes per week, just for fun, at the Halprin-Lathrop Studio in San Francisco. The work at the school of Anna Halprin and Welland Lathrop was based on Martha Graham's technique. One evening, instead of the usual technique class, one of Anna's senior students, A. A. Leath, taught a dance improvisation class. I clearly remember that he had us work with the idea of upwardness. I remember a moment of deep and joyful involvement, lying on the floor, every cell in my body reaching upward. And from the edge of the room I saw A. A. make a gesture as if to cast a fishing line and reel me in.

Anna was just in the process of breaking away from the school and starting her Dancers Workshop. Her new studio was an outdoor deck in the woods at the foot of Mount Tamalpais. In her book *Moving Toward Life,* Anna writes: "I left the city and began to dance in this invigorating outdoor environment. I cut my ties with modern dance and began to search for new directions."[1] It was a tremendous gift to be a participant as Anna developed a system for teaching dance improvisation. Her approach was similar to the way the visual arts had been taught since the groundbreaking work of the Bauhaus School of Design in

Fig. F1. Simone Forti, 1994. (© Isabelle Meister. Printed with permission.)

prewar Germany (which in fact Anna acknowledges as an inspiration). She often invited guest teachers from other disciplines, such as musicians Terry Riley and La Monte Young, her landscape-architect husband Lawrence Halprin, visual artist Jo Lander, and people from theater and psychology. The visual artist Robert Morris often participated in our classes.

I felt right at home with Anna's way of teaching, which I recognized from my experiences in art school. It was a process in which the teacher gave the student a point of departure for an exploration. In art school it might have been an exploration of the qualities of line. Thick, wet brush stroke; fine, hesitant pencil line; sharp, boldly ruled line. Each with its own feeling in the making and in the seeing. The teacher's instructions would not give the outer shape of what was to be achieved; they would provide a focus (sometimes called a "problem") for which each student would find his or her solution.

A major part of our movement training with Anna was based on anatomical explorations: for example, understanding the bone structure of the shoulder area and then spending a half hour exploring its range of movement, engaging muscles or releasing them to the forces of gravity and momentum, pushing, taking weight, noticing the resulting dance as the whole body supported this exploration (fig. F2). And then we would show each other what we'd found, teaching each other actual movements or presenting short improvisational studies. Anna had been introduced to this experiential approach to anatomy by Margaret H'Doubler at the University of Wisconsin. We found that with the exploring of so much movement, our movement vocabularies gradually expanded along with our strength and facility, and a great variety of movement qualities became accessible to us.

One of the instructions Anna sometimes gave was to spend an hour in the environment, in the woods or in the city, observing whatever caught our attention. Then we would return to the workspace and move with these impressions fresh in our senses, mixing aspects of what we had observed, with our responses and feeling states. The crinkly bark of a tree might be quite still. But one's eyes would scan its texture with a rhythm that might show up in the crinkling and flickering of the surface of one's back. Then as the surface of the back came into focus in the mind's eye, the whole body would become alive with more tree trunk information. Perhaps a certain woodiness in the neck, a certain flickering tonality in the solar plexus. With a tilt of the head, eyes focus at the edge of the canopy of leaves. This process brings particularity. The tree comes back to mind as a set of very particular sensory impressions. A white burst of sunlight as the eye-shading leaves suddenly part.

An important part of maturing as an improviser, indeed as an artist, is the process of choosing for oneself what to work with and how to work. Within what parameters, with what focus. Isadora Duncan, one of the founders of dance improvisation in America, reached across time and space to find a precedent for the

Fig. F2. Simone Forti, 1976. (© Peter Moore.)

dancing she felt she needed to do. She found inspiration and confirmation in the figures dancing with abandon, which were brushed onto the vases of ancient Greece. They seemed to be dancing with abandon.

I once spent some long summer days traveling in the Outer Hebrides, the northwestern islands of Scotland, so far north that dusk and dawn mix for an hour or two without the coming of night. There, a local woman asked me what I do. She listened, and told me that once, in school, her teacher had brought all the little girls up to a mountain meadow where they had danced naked, somersaulting and frolicking to their heart's content. "Yes, that's what it's all about, isn't it." she said. "I got to do it once."

For those little Scottish girls in the high fields overlooking the North Atlantic, the sudden freedom, the wind, the incline of the land could easily precipitate gleeful and energetic outbursts. But this is not the usual context. And there always has to be a context. Even Isadora Duncan, who stood silently still in the center of her studio waiting for a movement impulse, was working with this very particular problem she had given herself, of clearing the environment and listening for an inner impulse.

Perhaps choreography is like oil painting. And improvisation more like watercolor where the immediacy of the mark, or gesture, is an important part of the poetics. And yet an improvisation doesn't just spring forth from the void. Each new one is in context with others that came before. And it can be followed by another and another in a series. Ideas can be worked out. Elements can be tried out in various ways. Each new improvisation with its own particular essence. The whole experience leading to new ideas, building the ground for the next series.

I like to think of rehearsal or preparing for performance as a wave that will crest into the lap of the audience. A great deal of dancing goes on in the studio, getting an idea going, getting into the swing of it. The performance should be full of discovery. Yet even as it requires an unobstructed carrying through on impulse, it also requires keeping an outside eye. A complex of judgments regarding what it is that is evolving, an awareness that there is something that you are making. Is it fresh? Is it going somewhere? Is it accessible to the audience?

There was a time when my improvising was anchored in observations of animals. Mainly in zoos. And what finally stopped me was the sadness of captivity. But I used to spend time in the Bronx Zoo making sketches and taking notes (fig. F3). I guess there were two main things that interested me, besides just sharing a visit with those captive spirits. One was their very movements, their gaits, the functioning in movement of their various body structures. Brown bear walk: front limb steps and whole side contracts to pull back limb into place. Boom boo-boom. Boom boo-boom. Boom boo-boom. Giraffe: back limb steps, crowds fore limb which steps ahead. Boom-boom. Boom-boom. I liked to see myself as one variation. Watching them move helped me understand my own movement in a very basic way, clear of historical or stylistic values. "This is my body, this is how I move." Also, to my surprise, I found that there were dancers among the captives in the zoo. Individuals who found ways to enrich their lives with movement games and practices of their own invention. I saw a chimp that stuck his finger in a hole in the ground and ran in circles, leaning out from that tiny point of support. Three brown bears running back and forth up a ramp and turning by rising up onto their hind limbs, reaching and spiraling their noses skyward to drop again facing a new direction. I saw what I took to be a functional ritual, the biggest male of the Pere David's deer doing a terrifying leap straight at but just short of the newborn fawn. I saw many examples of what I took to be the roots of dance behavior. Cubs sparring. Even the big cats' compulsive pacing at the fence, which seemed to provide a modicum of relief. And this gave me a new view of what it was that I was doing when I was dancing. I abstracted some of the gaits, some of the movement games, and took them on into my own body. I walked through the halls of the Museum of Natural History, watching the evolu-

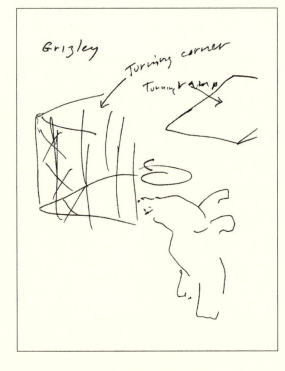

Fig. F3. Drawing by Simone Forti, 1980. (Courtesy Simone Forti.)

Grizley

Turning corner

Turning ramp

tion of the reptilian thigh bone. The foot. I wondered how a tadpole's movement developed from a lateral undulation for swimming into the symmetrical hop of a frog. I tried it. I was delighted to read that young frogs often fall over; it made sense in my body. My dances were studies, explorations wherein I ran the various possibilities through my body.

When I took this material into performance, it was in collaboration with musician Peter Van Riper. I have often worked with music. Always in collaboration with a musician who was also improvising. It seems important that each of us bring to our work sessions something that we have already been working with, some tangible point of reference or vocabulary in movement or in sound. Then, working together, we can find how these elements can coexist, influence each other and commingle. I love the tension of staying focused on the heart of what my dance is, while being pulled and finding myself responding in unusual ways, intuitively taking into consideration the quality of concentration, the energy and timing, the music of my partner.

In the mid-1980s I started developing a dance/narrative form. I started speaking while moving, with words and movement springing spontaneously from a common source. This practice has been a way for me to know what's on my mind. What's on my mind before I think it through, while it is still a wild feeling in my bones. My subject matter tends toward landscape, ruminations on the news, my family, garden, vegetables, weeds, roots, the way in spring a worm will dash for cover as I pull out the winter rye. The thoughts and images seem to flash through my motor centers and my verbal centers simultaneously, mixing and animating both speech and physical embodiment. Spatial, structural, emotional. I call this *moving the telling* or *Logomotion*. I see it as a performance form, and as a practice.

I have often experienced a change from one way of working to another. Such a transition always evolves out of a feeling of need, either coming from within the work itself or as an adjustment to changes in my personal life. In 1985 I was looking for a support group of people finding themselves at a turning point in their work but not yet clearly seeing what direction to take. So I offered a workshop called Work in Progress, and gathered a small group of dancers and others. We read our journals to each other, offered feedback, and gave each person a chance to try things out with the group. One woman was looking for ways to access her feelings about the information that was coming to her through the news media. She had joined, thinking that working with movement might help her. The ways she had us work with the news opened some doors for me. My father, the family's official knower of the news, had recently died and I had started following the news myself. It wasn't coming easily to me but I started to experience, at least during the act of reading, a sense of familiarity with the stories, with the major players. Most of all I started to accumulate kinesthetic impressions of pressures, wedges and currents, balance shifts and impending collapses. So much of the language of the news media is in terms of physical dynamics: the dollar in *free fall,* Lebanon as a *slippery slope,* and Iran sending *human waves* into the in-

vading Iraqi army. So I started dancing the news. Talking and dancing, becoming the ships, the lands, the peoples, the strategies, the connections. It was a practice that helped me remember the bits and broad strokes of information. And as I ran it all through my body, I could see how it all fell together in my mind, in my imagination, in my feeling.

When I did this in performance, I called it *News Animations* (fig. F4). And I always began by carrying in a pile of newspapers and using them to make a path to walk on. Often I would begin in darkness except for a flashlight dangling from my waist, illuminating feet, newspapers, and busy hands. Somewhere along the way I would get the idea for what topic I was going to start with. I would turn the flashlight off, and as the lights came on I would be shaping the papers around on the floor, making them into maps. And I would start talking and animating the human dramas above ground, interwoven with the seismic/tectonic dramas below.

> Up to balance on shoulders, oil pump. Whack down! Whack! Pump feet to ceiling, whack down! Human waves across Iran. Splat, roll beneath fly ways of bird migrations. Roll above jumble of continental plates, Arab peninsula drifting into Europe raising snow mountains jumbling and pressing pockets whole body high pressure twisting writhing pressing pockets of fossil ooze. Human waves soak red where Tigris and Euphrates fallopian tube rivers hug the cradle of civilization and flow into the Persian Gulf where ships take on oil and slide on back past Chinese silkworm missiles.

One of my teachers in art school, Howard Warshaw, once said that when working with subject matter there are always three points, or stations, that are dynamically interacting. That which you're looking at or referring to. The way you're perceiving or approaching it. And the actual thing you're making. You might choose to draw a grove of trees. You might further choose to work with the layering of branches seen through branches seen through branches. You look at your empty page, make some choice and touch down for the first mark. The page is changed. You look up and see the trees differently. The whites of the birch among the black maple branches jump out at you. When I am moving the telling of some material, I am as affected by my own movement as by the subject. There is a feedback and a responsiveness that is set up in my dancing body, in my dancing mind. I still have all the concerns of space, of timing, of movement interest. There are moments when I purely get lost in the movement. In the sound and rhythm of the words. I often feel that movement is like paint and words like pencil, or vice versa, together on a canvas. They can contrast or follow one another, with a time lag or contrast of perspective, a detail against a broad indication. The references turn back around one another building a whole quite spontaneously.

In 1992, after spending increasing amounts of time in Vermont, northern and rural, I finally settled there. I got my hands into the dirt for the first time, bathed in cold streams, and got lost in the woods. And this place became my focus and source of subject matter. I started collaging some wildlife stories into the middle of my *News Animations.* Then started doing a *Gardening Journal,* drawing on the intimate experience that gardening is. And the thoughts that might come through while weeding, or rolling heavy rocks and collapsing for a rest on the supergravity-charged earth. Gouging and pulling the invading burdock, its deep taproot giving way at dusk with a pungent artichoke smell. The more invasive herbs snaking runners into one another's territories, trying for a greater mint, a greater thyme, a greater chamomile. How to explain what I learn from the snow, from the compost bin, from the stars? When a fresh wind is blowing down the mountain, I absolutely gulp it down. Stand there in the field and gulp it down. Gulp it in. Or reaching into the dirt for the potatoes, my self dives into my fingers and I am the dry crumbly ground. I am the cool round things, of delicate russet skins, emerging miraculously clean.

Meanwhile, from 1986 to 1991, I worked with a group of dancers (K. J. Holmes, Lauri Nagel, David Zambrano, David Rosenmiller, Eric Schoefer). We went by the name Simone Forti & Troupe (fig. F5), and we mainly focused on land portraits. Going to different locations, spending time in the environment, reading about the social and natural history of the area, letting these kinds of information influence our dancing, our improvising. We worked in solos and groups of various configurations reflecting how different ones of us had shared particular experiences. One of us, David Rosenmiller, knew a great deal about geology. Our land portraits always included a choreographed reenactment of how the land in that spot had moved and formed, indeed, was still moving. At first our

Fig. F5. Simone Forti & Troupe, 1987. (© Peter Moore.)

pieces would always include a solo of mine in which I would be moving and speaking. I would usually work with some poignant image, some event in the history of the place. Eventually, we were all speaking. Sometimes in duet form, with one supporting the other. Sometimes with simultaneous independent stories which, coming from experiences in the shared location, had surprising points of overlap and resonance. And the place we were rendering seemed to emerge full of color and detail.

In my sixties I continue to perform, and of course teach. Still moving the telling, still working with landscape and garden. But now also opening up to whatever topics come to my mind, and simply calling my improvisations *Animations*. On the day of performance, by way of preparation, I look for a prop, whatever I can find, and I call this my arbitrary object. A big iron washtub or a little plastic honey bear container of honey. I never know how I am going to involve it in my improvisation, but miraculously, I always do. And I do a twenty-minute continuous timed writing. If I'm lucky, this gives me an outline that I can play off of.

Timed writing is a practice developed by writer and teacher Natalie Goldberg, clearly presented in her books *Writing Down the Bones* and *Wild Mind*.[2] I first came across this practice through Christie Svane, whose workshops integrate moving, writing, and voice. Essentially, you must commit yourself to writing for a prescribed length of time. It could be three minutes, ten, sixty minutes. And you must keep your hand moving for the duration. You may use a word or topic as a starting point or through line. I often start with "I remember" and see what comes. I love how at those moments when I would usually pause to reflect, I must keep going. So my mind grabs at those thoughts, images, and memories that are flitting through with their own wild connections, with jumps that are irrational but resonant, and shadow thoughts I might not usually express or even know I have.

Goldberg also practices Zen meditation. Her title *Wild Mind* reminds me of poet Gary Snyder's *The Practice of the Wild*. He too is a Zen practitioner. My sense of his meaning of "wild" is that most of our experience, most of what surrounds us, and indeed most of what goes on in us, is undomesticated. Out of range of human plan or control.

Following is a slightly edited twenty-minute writing I did a few hours before a performance in Venezuela. I began by opening my Spanish-English dictionary and randomly pointing to a word. *Vinicultura,* wine growing. I have found that even with a random word I will gravitate to my own experience, but with an unexpected slant.

> Sssss I know the name starts like the start of own name Sssss yes! Ssstrasbourg. And the valley of wine. Alsace. The wines of Alsace. And the glasses for drinking wine. Green edged. A stem, delicate, and I prefer white wine. Image of father and his friend Bertelli. Bertellone. Drunk at the gates of the city. Florence. And the news at five o'clock- (theme music)
>
>   dom
>
>   dom   dom
>
> dom
>
>   dom
>
>   dom
>
>   dom
>
>   dom
>
> I go for the bottle. Never before the news. And I hear the news. How can it be that it's such a moment of safety, hearing the news. Quebec. If Quebec separates, then the

Northeast Kingdom (northeastern Vermont) becomes a corridor between Canada and Canada. And the Indians with treaties with Canada? Wine. The vines. The valley of Alsace. The way the vines are, the way the towns are. Wine. White wines in delicate stemmed glasses. I remember in art school drawing a delicate stemmed glass the way it feels in the fingers, in the mouth. Light thin glass. We went to California to the wine, vinicultura, to the olive groves. Father never spoke English. We always drank red wine. Red his favorite color and yes mine too. Red. Red Mars. In Vermont so many guns. It comes from the image of the complete community. Firewood, earth to cultivate, guns for meat and in case . . . every 25 years we vote whether to remain in the union. It's a feeling. Like wine. Kisses sweeter than wine. And guns. Guns. I'm sure it's different in war. In pain and exhaustion. But meanwhile, I me wine 5 o'clock news. Why speak of the place where there's war, what is the attraction? And yes, there is attraction. Ask any . . . ask any . . . I don't know. Look at the bible. Look at . . . I ask the dictionary for a word, I get vinicultura and what do I talk about? War? Stop, Simone. Talk about olives. Wine. The culture of wine. Simone, the castles in Alsace. The one, the special small one in ruins. I could feel the people in it. The men and the women and the deaths in childbirth. The deaths in the mouth of the wolf. The battles between brother and brother. Between cousin and father. The women. The laughter, the rocking the babies, the stairways, the falls and yes, vinicultura in Alsace even then yes and olives and rabbits, deer, weapons, Mars and wine. Wine! Simone red red red.

WORKSHOP ANNOUNCEMENT
LOGOMOTION

Always, words and movement work together towards what we need, building our understanding and our expression. By speaking and moving at once, following our impulses and responding to the resulting dynamics and images, we integrate various aspects of our knowing and give expression to a fuller spectrum of our world. The workshop will include a warm-up practice to awaken our kinetic juices and mindfulness, and timed writings to put us in touch with our wild thoughts and observations. We will focus on improvisation, including exercises for perceptual and compositional awareness and for developing an intuitive flow between our movement and our speaking.

To me this work seems very natural. And yet it is subtle. It is not illustration. It is not mime. It is not even linear thinking. And in a way, that is the key. A shift of frame of mind. I have found that we think differently when we are in motion. And this is the thinking I am trying to access. In the workshop, we do an exercise I call *movement memory snapshots*. It is based on a communication behavior we often experience in our daily lives. Something we call body language. For instance, once, at a party in Vermont, a woman told me how at dawn she had looked out of her back window and seen a bear. "It was real young. Skin loose like a puppy." And she took three bounding steps without losing conversational distance from me, letting her flesh bounce on her bones. I saw the snow, the young bear lunging, bounding. We do the *movement memory snapshots* while sitting in a circle. We each tell about something that has stayed in our memory because of some aspect of movement. I ask people to go right for the image that comes up. The very moment of movement. The snapshot. And to forgo the lead-up or linear story. I don't say anything about moving, but it is hard not to get animated or even stand up when you are telling a movement story. So we do. I love how the images that the narrative calls up to the mind's eye are seen simultaneously with our actual movements right there in the studio space. And when the students are inspired, I love the feel and taste of each story, how I get to know each individual, especially when someone breaks through to a surprising moment of total body response to, and identification with some aspect of his "story," some detail or central quality. When we have gone around the circle and all have offered their snapshots, we try to play back some of the movements we saw each other do. A shrug, a lunge, a shape in space.

Written at brook, while thinking about starting this article:

A green leaf at bottom of quiet pool. Above, on surface, water striders. One scratching its hind right leg with its foreleg. Shadow of something across surface, a bird? A butterfly? No, a leaf. Sitting on rock, hardness getting uncomfortable even through folded towel. Later I'll bathe. Waiting for a thought for writing, a thought in the context of a particular writing. From the pool here, to a reader maybe at the breakfast table, morning light slanting in east window, maybe snow. Water striders always so easy to see, over the years always so easy to observe I don't take seriously. If a little brookie, a little trout, were to show itself, now that would be something. Something. At this pool I smell fish. Smelled it the minute I got here from the pool below, the pool below that the waterfall falls into, that pool which is something, which you can mention to someone and they'll say, "Yes, I go to the waterfall, I sometimes bathe there." Light through pools, light through falling water, roots and rocks, little island beach pebble mound. And dancing? There's a function that functions in our sleep. So that as we dream we're running, we lie still. Sometimes a cat will twitch its paws, its face in its sleep, but basically lie still. Seeing the fractured rock face shunting water one sheet here one there my eye follows sharp edges. My teeth try the stone I breathe the falling water and am the soft air smelling of me, the bright tree root curve of sun-soaked moss, pulsing circles of light bopping water. And only by the grace of that which holds me still do I hold still.

NOTES

This article was first published in French translation (trans. Agnès Benoit) in *Improviser dans la danse* (Alès, France: Editions du Cratère théâtre d'Alès, 1999), 14–28. It was subsequently reprinted, also in French translation, in the Belgian dance journal *Nouvelles de Danse* 44/45 (Fall–Winter 2000): 209–24. The original English text first appeared in *Contact Quarterly*, 26, no. 2 (Summer–Fall 2001): 32–39.

1. Anna Halprin, *Moving Toward Life: Five Decades of Transformational Dance,* ed. Rachel Kaplan (Hanover, N.H.: University Press of New England, 1995), xi.
2. Natalie Goldberg, *Writing Down the Bones: Freeing the Writer Within* (Boston: Shambhala, 1986), and *Wild Mind: Living the Writer's Life* (New York: Bantam Books, 1990).

LEARNING TO SPEAK

An Apprenticeship with Simone Forti in Logomotion

Carmela Hermann

I met Simone Forti in the winter of 1998 in Los Angeles when I was a graduate student at UCLA in the Department of World Arts and Cultures. She was teaching improvisation as a guest faculty member, and I was getting my master of fine arts degree in choreography and performance. I asked her to be my guide in a one-on-one independent study course in choreography. We would look at art and work on composition assignments. I would learn some tools to give my ideas form. I didn't think of our connection this way at the time, but in retrospect I realize that approaching Simone helped me uncover a hidden desire: I wanted to learn to speak. Not only did I want to speak as an artist but literally to say things with words and with movement. Simone seemed the perfect guide.

Our first outing was to a museum. We went up the huge freight elevator that carries art and Simone lay down on the elevator floor. When we got out she said, "Let's split up and we'll draw each other into a painting." In the midst of this extraordinary excursion, it seemed to me I had never seen art before. I spent time absorbing the details, colors, shapes, contrasts. I sat on the floor and stared at a painting of naked red women. After awhile I turned around and Simone was standing behind me.

That summer we continued with a series of weekly meetings. Simone gave me composition assignments, I would work over the course of the following week, and then show the results to her. For the first assignment I was to buy a couple of postcards from the museum bookstore and create movement studies with the postcards as my source. This was difficult. I was more connected to working from my kinesthetic sense than from visual impressions. For the second assignment I read the newspaper and created movement studies from two different articles. I chose one about laws for transporting goods in and out of China and another on the transformation of Princess Diana's family estate, Althorp, into a public museum. Both seemed to me to be about negotiations for space. I continued through the summer with a deeper exploration of Princess Diana, whose life and death had intrigued me. At Simone's suggestion I bought a book

Fig. G1. Carmela Hermann, 2000. (© Carol Petersen.)

full of pictures of Diana, studied them carefully, and re-created several of them in movement. I examined Diana's posture, emotional tone, and breath. A year later this study became my solo, *Diana*.

Simone and I had just completed our summer of working together and were wrapping up our last meeting. She had two evenings of improvisation scheduled at Highways Performance Space in Santa Monica. "What are you planning to do for your concert?" I asked her. After a pause, she said, "Actually, I was thinking about doing something with you." My heart skipped a beat; this was news to me. She explained, "Well, I have been working with you, and I thought we might do a duet." I had never performed an improvisation before. I had never talked onstage before. I had no idea what we would do, but I was excited. I said, "I'd love to, but I don't think I could do any talking." "We could do a movement piece. We don't have to talk," she said. Yes, I definitely wanted to do it.

We started by dancing in the studio on Thanksgiving Day, moving together spontaneously, becoming familiar with our dancing relationship. Making the shift from teacher/student to partners in a dance. I was a little intimidated at first. It was funny. We danced well together, getting into a groove. We started by doing solos for each other. Then duets. Just following our impulses, no structure. Getting to know each other, finding what was there.

Simone had chosen the UCLA Botanical Gardens in Westwood as inspiration for our piece. I had never used the environment as a source for movement before. We took several trips there, observing, feeling, seeing, and eventually translating our impressions into our bodies. Before we began, Simone gave me the manuscript of an article she had written (now published in this book). In "Animate Dancing," Simone writes: "One of my teachers in art school, Howard Warshaw, once said that when working with subject matter there are always three points or stations that are dynamically interacting. That which you are looking at, or referring to. The way you are perceiving or approaching it. And the actual thing you are making." These three points of reference guided my approach to improvising with the environment as my source. I did not have to look like the bamboo tree. What came through my body would be my physical impressions of what struck me about that tree, a physical embodiment of what I saw and the energies I felt. I could become the tree itself, without trying to copy what the tree looked like from the outside.

I had never looked at nature with such attention and awareness. We hung out at the Botanical Gardens for a few hours at a time, seeing, feeling, noticing, talking. As the hours passed, the small details of the place emerged and we sank deeper into the experience. Shadows, colors, and shapes of the plants and trees became art. We spent thirty minutes knocking on bamboo trees, hearing the different pitches emanating from each hollow trunk. We wondered about things: Do plants have a spirit? Do the trees consciously decide to grow around each other when one is in the way? What will happen to that baby bamboo tree that looks like it is blocked by all the other big trees surrounding it? Will it grow? One day I found myself drawn to some moist earth under a tree. I wanted to dig my hands in it, cover myself with it. I felt a hunger in my bones to connect to that soil. But we felt a little self-conscious there and held back. Later, we went into the studio and I danced that I was rolling in the earth, rubbing it all over my face and my body, probably as I would have done when I was a young child.

After our outings, we went into the studio, wrote for twenty minutes about our impressions, and read them to each other. Timed writings are a tool borrowed from writer Natalie Goldberg, author of *Writing Down the Bones* and *Wild Mind*.[1] In this practice, you write for a predetermined length of time on a topic. You keep your hand moving. You let your first thoughts come out on paper, no matter what they are.

We wrote without editing for the entire time, letting our thoughts flow. Sometimes our writings overlapped, illuminating our shared experience. Sometimes they revealed personal feelings about our lives, unrelated to our trip to the garden. The reading felt personal, scary, intimate. We found out about each other. Again, we improvised alone and together, our movements now based on images from our writings. The bamboo trying to grow around the other bamboos, the cactus that looked like a penis, the orange vine that looked like a claw about to grab you. It all came out in our dance.

During our second rehearsal we had difficulty connecting. It occurred to me that doing some Contact Improvisation might help us reach a new level of connection. The next day, Simone said, "I thought we'd do some Contact." We started with the basics, following a point of physical connection, exchanging weight, rolling. It helped. The physical touch helped us relate energetically. We started to relax. In the next rehearsal, we did Contact while simultaneously describing with our bodies, without words, the things we saw in the space. While exchanging weight and staying in constant physical touch, I became the light bulb, the shadow on the wall, the sweatshirt on the floor. She became the crack in the ceiling, the doorknob, a dangling wire. We stayed in relationship, each with our individual impressions. It was fun. Spontaneously, we then began to verbalize our descriptions as we moved: "I'm the red sweatshirt, I'm the white light, I'm the ladder rungs."

Simone seemed happy for us to do a movement improvisation at Highways, but I kept feeling that talking would be more interesting. She was so fascinating when she performed her talking work, and I wondered what would happen in a duet format. We tried a little of it but it felt awkward to me. The night of our first show we decided we would talk, but sparsely. During the piece, when Simone began to speak, a friend later told me she saw this look on my face that said, "Oh no, I'm going to have to *say* something now." I was not ready. Simone and I discussed this after the first performance and it became clear that, for the second night, we needed to do a movement piece without speaking. That night our warm-up was silent. We connected with our energy and movement. Then Simone looked at me and said, "Good." We were ready.

Our performance turned out to be strong, focused, funny, connected. We became the garden. My fingers transformed into the red spider crawling up her leg, she became the tiny bamboo stump trying to grow as I became the other trees pushing her down. We embodied the environment, and it was good.

I continued to be intrigued with Simone's movement-and-talking work, so I signed up for her Logomotion class at UCLA. Many of the students had taken her class the previous year and I watched them with admiration. Some of them seemed so at ease, the words flowing effortlessly as they moved their experience. I wanted to find that place in myself where moving and speaking became effortless.

Underlying my motivation to learn this form was the knowledge that I would have to face some hidden fears, a confrontation that would be frightening but ultimately rewarding. My fear was in facing the block between my moving and my speaking. When I spoke, I felt cut off from my body, from myself. Dance has always taken me to a deeply physical world. Once in, I never wanted to emerge. There was either talking or there was dancing. Feeling or thought. The two didn't connect. Deep down I think I was afraid to be seen, exposed; that what was really inside of me would be horribly ugly in some way I could not reveal even to myself. In a paper I wrote for Simone's class, I talked about my struggle:

> I have been contemplating my discomfort with this moving and speaking process. I feel disconnected because I *report* my experience as opposed to speaking while being in the experience. I experience the thing and remove myself from it in order to explain it. So I decided to try another approach, to take myself back to the experience in my imagination and to try to speak as I re-experience it, to remember and let things come to me in the moment, to be surprised. It felt scary to let myself do that. Like I went into another world in front of everyone. I guess I do that when I dance, but I don't talk about it. And to try to talk from my experience feels so raw, like my voice is coming from a place I have not experienced before.

I met with my teacher, Mariane Karou, founder of the Dance Alive Method, whose work takes people deeply into their physical experience, heightening awareness of unconscious sensations and feelings. I told her about my struggle with Simone's work. "I can't speak and move at the same time. I feel disconnected." After a moment she said, "I sense that you are not used to talking and feeling at the same time." As I lay on the floor with her hand on my chest, she asked me to bring my attention into my body and when I was ready, to speak from the place of feeling within me. I was silent for a long time. There was no sound. Just as when I would dance, there was no sound. I did not want to speak. Eventually I started to make a sound. The sound turned into a soft *nooooooo.* Like a whine. Like a small child. Emotion built into more sounds and then words, words out of the sounds. Images entered my mind, images of a long-ago loss, images that had been said but not felt, felt but not said. And then tears, cries from deep inside my body, my heart. All tumbling out. Voice, words, feeling.

At the end of the session, Mariane said to me, "You couldn't just start performing Logomotion. You had to get through this layer of connecting your voice to your feeling."

After we wrapped up the session, Mariane suggested that I start letting myself talk nonstop, for five or ten minutes at a time, to familiarize myself with my voice, my thoughts. The idea was to speak without editing. I started talking stream-of-consciousness, in the car, at home, on walks. For me this was the beginning of being able to know my thoughts, to appreciate the nonlinear direction, the random changes of subject, the childlike feelings. I no longer felt bound by pre–thought-out ideas. I was learning to follow what came to me in the moment, to give up control. This was the beginning of my ability to do Logomotion.

Later, I led one of Simone's Logomotion classes in Santa Monica and I presented nonstop, or stream-of-consciousness, talking as an exercise for the students. We were used to doing timed writings, but not timed talkings. I had a particular student in mind when I taught that exercise. She reminded me of myself. She would often say that when she spoke in an improvisation, her voice felt stuck. As she described this she would bring her hands to her throat. The exercise I gave was to walk in partners around the room. One partner would speak nonstop for five minutes on a topic. The other would keep a hand on the speaker's shoulder or back, following the speaker wherever she went. They did not have to dance, only to walk. We would incorporate more movement later. The girl I originally had in mind said that she got a lot out of the exercise, that it allowed her to loosen up. Later I thought to myself that it was probably less a matter of loosening up than of reestablishing pathways of communication between the moving and speaking bodies. While this process is complex, it occurs to me that the real complexity lies in our ability to separate these two aspects of ourselves as young children or adults. It takes effort to conform to conventional modes of verbal communication: we learn to reference our intellect in disconnection from our physical senses.

Based upon my experience, there are several stages in learning to perform Logomotion. One of the first steps is allowing imagination to become communicated through spoken language in a deeply physical way. This stage in itself is a major accomplishment and is difficult for many people—perhaps because, as Simone says, we are used to organizing and communicating our thoughts based on socially accepted ways of communicating. When you tell a friend about a place you saw once, you probably try to speak in full sentences: "It's got huge, red rock canyons. The rocks are enormous." If you were doing a Logomotion improvisation, speaking from your most immediate impressions of this place as you relive it in your imagination, you might say, "Red . . . red . . . and black . . . sharp, enormous. The rock so steep you could slide right off of it." You are still communicating about the place, but your words are inspired by your experience of the place; you become the place, feel it as you talk about it, and the way you speak changes.

Then comes the next step. Once you have gotten comfortable embodying thoughts, ideas, and images from memory or imagination, you can begin to focus on making a cohesive improvisational piece. Simone sometimes says that when we put an idea, a movement, onstage, we are like painters adding something to the space that was not there before. When we leave the stage, we rinse our brush before reentering with a new idea. Later, in Simone's class, I wrote, "I have been struggling in my mind to create an approach to making something with this work. The paintbrush image has given me a different perspective on how to approach the space. In my mind, the stage has become a canvas and every presence, every movement, every shape makes the painting. My decisions are based on how I can add to or create the total picture. Still working with being in the experience as I talk, but now also working with an awareness of what it is I am creating as I talk and move." This phase of work never seems to end. As you improvise you continually find new ways to create onstage, while sharing ideas, experiences, feelings.

Ultimately, I learn from my teachers, not by what they say, but how they embody what they are teaching. A lot of what I learned about Logomotion came from watching Simone in action, seeing her use this or that approach. When it came time for me to do an improvisation and I had an impulse, I would remember, "Simone did something like this. I can try this, too."

Simone's approach to moving and speaking offers limitless possibilities. Sometimes she connects deeply to becoming a tree or a bush with her body; at other times she discusses her thoughts on some random topic, her movement not specifically describing anything she is talking about, yet related because it springs from her physical impulses in connection to her thoughts. What makes all her approaches engaging is her total interest and involvement in whatever she is doing. While there are certain exercises that help to connect moving and speaking, ultimately this form is wide open to include any way that inspires you. There is no wrong way. What is important is that you are connected to your moving when you are moving and your speaking when you are speaking and to both when they are happening together. Your impulses will not always make sense to you. You might think, "Why am I moving like *this* while I'm talking about *this?*" You don't really need to know why or to try to change what you are doing so that it makes sense. You need to listen to yourself and follow your impulses.

In August 1999 Simone and I performed together at the Seattle Festival of Alternative Dance and Improvisation. It was my first Logomotion duet with Simone. We took Seattle as our subject. I was terrified. We had a dress rehearsal and it went well. Later, in performance:

> We walk onstage. I suddenly remember looking down on the freeway from the bridge. My arms become the cars rushing by. I begin to speak. Simone begins to speak. Simultaneously. About different things. Listening for the pauses between each other's words, for the musicality in our speaking. I remember the berry bushes that we dug through, picking, eating sweet blackberries by the freeway. I talk about reaching for the blackberries and how good the stretch felt. What a great stretch. I reach. Simone talks about the guy we saw jogging at the park. Did she think he was cute or not? She runs

around the stage like he did. Full of himself. I talk about the dizzy feeling I always get looking down at the cars from the bridge. How I am always secretly afraid I'll jump off. Also secretly afraid I will push Simone off. "You were thinking that?" she asks me. She talks about her secret fantasy of being in a bar and throwing a mug of beer at the mirror, dancing the dance of the mug flying, the beer miraculously staying in the mug and crashing. Our themes start to overlap. She talks about a berry that was at the crotch of the tree. I say, "A tree doesn't have a crotch, Simone." She makes a "v" with her fingers and explains how a tree has a crotch. We come together on an image. We go on, the images flowing. I crawl between her legs, speaking about the little hole we saw, just big enough to fit a homeless person. Safe.

The performance was a success. People said it was strong. We each carried our own weight. We each retained our individuality, and the feedback was that our differences complemented each other. And I was speaking.

"You must have a method. Carmela must have learned how to do this through your method!" Nina Martin, the San Diego–based choreographer and improviser, was impressed and wanted to know what Simone had done to get me to perform at this level. Nina had seen some of my work at UCLA during the year I had been studying Contact Improvisation with her, and had never seen me do anything like this before. Simone looked perplexed. She didn't think of her work as following a method, didn't have an answer. She said, "Carmela wanted to learn it. She just went for it and pulled the information out of me. She asked lots of questions." It was true. During our rehearsals I had pumped her for information, asking her about her state of mind as she dance and spoke, what she was thinking, how her process worked.

We went on to perform Logomotion duets at Highways Performance Space and at Judson Church in New York City. After our performance in New York, we were sitting in a restaurant. Simone said, "It's time for you to do a solo." She was reading my mind. I had wanted to do a solo. I was terrified and excited but knew that I was ready. That same night I got a message from the performing arts manager at the J. Paul Getty Center in Los Angeles. She wanted to know if I would perform my choreography as part of their Friday night dance series. They were also interested in my improvised work. Here was my opportunity.

Simone and I began to meet weekly to rehearse solo structures. I was working with Simone's practice of picking three random words from the dictionary and using the words as source material for my improvisation. The intention was to let my impressions, inspired by the words, weave together to create a seamless stream of related ideas. The ideas didn't have to connect in a linear or expected way. The challenge was to stay open to my thoughts and allow my unconscious mind to make the connections as I worked. It was almost impossible to foresee how I could make a cohesive piece out of words like *reading, superstitious,* and *unholy.* I had seen Simone use this structure before and had been astonished at the connections she could make. The first time I tried it, I was surprised to find that I was able to make those same kinds of connections too. It was as though the mind itself holds the creative key to connect anything it is given.

When I performed my solo, *Thoughts on Three Random Words,* at the Getty Center, I didn't just want to do something interesting or spontaneous. I wanted to make a piece that developed a theme in a cohesive, yet unexpected way. I was interested in finding out if I could arrive at the same level of content and structure in an improvisation that I had seen achieved in good choreography. I found that in the three-word structure the mind would unconsciously make significant connections between the three words. I would be talking about one thing and suddenly my mind would make a leap to a seemingly unrelated image. I learned to follow these thoughts because eventually they led to something that tied into a previous idea, building on it in a new way. The words unleashed images, metaphors that eventually communicated some larger thing that was there to be said. The work was completely improvised, yet I experienced that within the unconscious lies an intelligent order. When I allowed this order to unfold, it revealed, in the best of times, perfectly structured choreography.

I decided to bring a dictionary into the audience and ask for volunteers to pick three words for me. I got *decompose, decorate,* and *courage.* There was a cross-fade and the piece began:

DECOMPOSE. I think of death. I talk about coffins that have holes at the top. If the corpse wasn't really dead he could ring a little bell tied to his finger by a string running through the hole. I lie down in the coffin and reach up through the hole. I say, "My greatest fear was to be buried alive." DECOMPOSE. I think of Princess Diana. Yes. DECORATE. I explain how they had to borrow a black dress from the prime minister's wife to carry her body from France to England. I run my hands down the sides of my body. "It was black and just her size." COURAGE. I think of Diana's two boys. I describe the card on top of her coffin that said "Mummy" on it. And the news coverage of the funeral. "Barbara Walters said that it was heartbreaking." I think of JFK's children. Small. I get on my knees. "To be a small boy and see your father wheeled out in a coffin and to hold your mother's hand, and not totally understand, but to feel like somebody's not . . . . Not courage, but you just do it cause that's what you have to do."

What's next? I wait. Yes! Nails and hair. I talk about how when I was a child, someone once told me that nails and hair keep growing when you die. How the nails curl like the guy's in the *Guinness Book of World Records.* My hands curl. "They might even come through the hole at the top of the coffin so that instead of the bell ringing, you'd see this little nail . . . ." I move across the front of the stage, feet pivoting underneath me, arms out, nails extending out into the universe. "That guy must have had to do everything with his feet! His job was to get in that book! How would you unbutton your pants with your feet?" I lie down on the floor and try it, unsuccessfully.

In my mind I see the picture, that famous picture of Jackie and her two children at the funeral. I back up on the diagonal. COURAGE. DECORATE. "The little boy and the little girl, and the mother with that hair and those glasses, standing so still and so calm, while the whole nation . . . they felt it for them . . . with them." I see Diana. Her legs pinned under the seat. I become the seat with my body. "Maybe if she'd used her feet more she wouldn't have . . . maybe she would have . . . one leg was under the seat, and, and her arm, and . . . it was bad." I talk about the famous photo of Prince

Charles kissing Diana as she turns her head away. Her head, a blur from turning it so fast. I dance that kiss. My head whips around and back, over and over, replay. "It was a blur! He was . . . and she was . . . and . . . it just said it all!" COURAGE.   "It took courage to leave." I lie down again in the coffin. In the same place I began the piece. "When you're cremated you don't have to worry." I reach up. My arm goes limp.
   . . . I end.

It has been a year since this article was originally published and two weeks since terrorism devastated the World Trade Center in New York City. In the past year my focus has drifted from Logomotion, turning toward other sources of inspiration to create my dances. However in light of recent events I find myself again reflecting on the importance of language, having a voice, knowing what that voice must say. This is a time when communication and the attitudes that motivate our communication play a critical role in how we will recover and how we chose to act.

Today I heard the poet Maya Angelou say on television, "I am speechless. But that doesn't mean I have nothing to say." In the days and weeks following the unimaginable, Logomotion has offered many of us who are speechless a place to find our voices. And we find our voices in connection to our moving bodies—bodies that we find ourselves suddenly grateful for as never before. We voice our reactions, our fears, our sense of loss, our anger, our thoughts, and our hopes.

During the past two weeks in Simone's class, we have been doing large-group Logomotion scores. One of the topics was "Hard Times: Personal or Ancestral." We did some timed writings, read them out loud in a circle, and then we danced for forty minutes, using a familiar format that included solos, duets, and groups. Sometimes we supported someone else's image, sometimes we initiated our own. Sometimes one of us would simply move, noticing what was happening in the room, or dance with momentum and energy, releasing some of the intensity in the atmosphere. We felt speechless, and yet we all had something to say. Sometimes we spoke through movement, throwing ourselves against the wall or walking slowly as one who is lost, old, grief-stricken. Sometimes we found words, discussing past memories of violence, re-creating present images of the towers collapsing, still so fresh in our minds. We improvised, a room of speechless voices resounding together, without judgment. Afterward we reflected on the clarity of every voice, each one so different, so equally valuable.

Timed writing, Simone's class 9–21–01:

Hard times. Now. The towers collapsing, the moments of terror before. All trapped in that building and just today I found the photos of Simone and me at the top of the World Trade Center (we visited in preparation for our New York performance). What if they had chosen that day? Now. Everyone in Shock. Flags. And now is the hardest time there is. And before that, *then*. Then was the hardest time. The day my mother went into the hospital and didn't come out. That was the hardest time. Family gathering in shock, little girl, adults. We didn't expect that, never expected those kind of hard times. My family came to America from Russia. Granny the only Jewish girl in Southampton High School. Boys didn't notice her. Jew girl. Myself fifty years later, atheist family in Christian neighborhood. Why don't you believe in God? Prejudice, hatred. Hard times, now. All those hard times collected to make now. Keep going, keep going, keep going, we just keep going because what else is there? You have hard times and you live in shock and grief and terror and you try to get into action and you keep going, speaking in silence, out loud, to no one, to the world.

NOTES

This essay is adapted from "Hearing/Miraculously/Structure," originally published in *Contact Quarterly* 26, no. 1 (Winter–Spring 2001): 15–25.

1. Natalie Goldberg, *Writing Down the Bones: Freeing the Writer Within* (Boston: Shambhala, 1986), and *Wild Mind: Living the Writer's Life* (New York: Bantam Books, 1990).

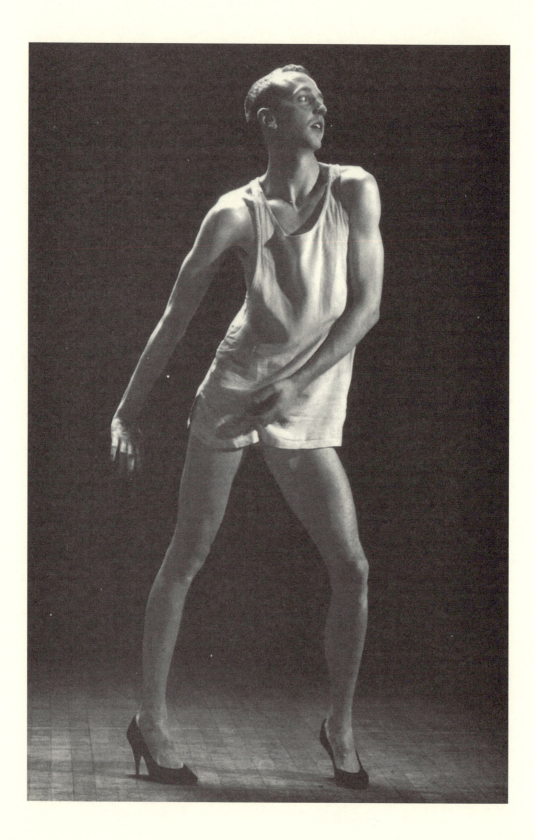

SPONTANEOUS COMBUSTION

Notes on Dance Improvisation from the Sixties to the Nineties

Sally Banes

Historically, improvisation in postmodern dance has served a variety of functions and signaled different meanings since the 1960s:

spontaneity
self-expression
spiritual expression
freedom
accessibility
choice
community
authenticity
the natural
presence
resourcefulness
risk
political subversion
a sense of the connectedness of playfulness, child's play, leisure, and sports

Although improvisation can mean all of these things, different aspects/values/goals have emerged at disparate historical moments. And even when some of the same issues arise, they do so in a different key, given new historical circumstances. Dance improvisation in a culture of abundance in the 1960s had a different significance—both for doers and watchers—than dance improvisation did in a culture of scarcity in the early and mid-nineties.

THE SIXTIES AND SEVENTIES

The sixties and seventies saw an emphasis in postmodern dance on freedom, abundance, and community; improvisation often served to embody these values, not only in dance, but in the other arts as well. These were political issues, although not always stated explicitly. In the 1960s, artists like Anna Halprin on the

West Coast and Simone Forti on the East Coast were committed to improvisatory methods, what one might call either "indeterminate choreography" or "open choreography" (as opposed to determinate, "closed" choreography), "situation-response composition," or "in situ composition." Unlike chance procedures, which took the choice-making element out of the self, improvisation seemed to many during this period a way of engaging the deep, untapped creative resources of each person. Various improvisatory events were held, such as Concert #14 of the Judson Dance Theater in April 1964, which included seven dances created by individuals and one twenty-five-minute group piece. (Although critic Jill Johnston complained the evening "couldn't get . . . off the ground," Yvonne Rainer's contribution to the event, *Some Thoughts on Improvisation,* included as a "soundtrack" a recording of Rainer reading an important theoretical essay she had recently written on the workings of the situation-response method.)[1] Also, groups devoted to open choreography emerged. An all-women's group, the Natural History of the American Dancer, organized in the early seventies by Barbara Dilley, has long since been forgotten. But there were two visible and memorable stimuli to dance improvisation during this period: the Contact Improvisation movement and the group Grand Union.

Contact Improvisation, a form that evolved out of explorations by Steve Paxton in the early seventies, began as a series of experiments for men in duets dancing together in ways that might avoid aggression and embrace tenderness.[2] But it soon became a gender-integrated form that allowed both men and women to investigate various means of moving in one-on-one or small group encounters: giving and taking weight, lifting, carrying, leading, following, wrestling, and partnering in myriad ways; finding movement templates in social dancing, sports, and martial arts, such as Aikido.[3] Since the 1970s, Contact Improvisation has become a worldwide practice. One finds communities of Contacters in the United States, Canada, Europe, Japan, Australia, and New Zealand. Probably the bulk of Contact Improvisation happens in nontheatrical settings, in "jams" where dancers and nondancers get together to work out. Contact Improvisation is thus not primarily a theatrical form but an ongoing practice. Occasionally, Contact Improvisers will show the work in a theatrical setting, but in a casual way in which the audience feels it is more or less observing the jamming behavior that would occur even without spectators. Besides its worldwide networks of practitioners meeting regularly to jam together, the movement spawned a journal, *Contact Quarterly,* that publishes articles on Contact experiences and related body therapies, as well as names and addresses of groups around the globe.

For Steve Paxton, Contact Improvisation both signified and helped create a set of interconnected values important to the artistic avant-garde in the sixties and seventies: playfulness, freedom, spontaneity, authenticity, and community. "I like it when bodies are free and when the emotional state is open and accepting and sensitive," Paxton has remarked. "When the psychology isn't hassled or political or tied in knots. I like it when people can do things that surprise themselves." Paxton continues, "Where it comes from is just human play, human exchange—and animal play. It's like horseplay or kitten play or child's play, as well." Comparing the mental state of the Contact Improviser with that of an alert, confident basketball player, he concludes, "I enjoy the sharings that have come out of it, with other dancers and with the people who have seen it. . . . It seems a way of learning that I like a lot."[4]

As Contact Improvisation spread in the late seventies, it became associated with other countercultural or alternative culture trends, including gender issues of equality, of women's strength, and of men's sensitivity. In Contact Improvisation, men could lift men, women could lift women, and women could lift men. All-men's Contact groups in the United States and Britain, such as Mangrove and Men Working, created situations in which men could partner one another in gentle, nonmacho ways, harking back to the origins of the form. Women could find strength, and men could find support.[5]

Ramsay Burt stresses the surprising, spectacular elements of the form.[6] Yet for many improvisers of the eighties and nineties (some of whom were born in the sixties and had no firsthand knowledge of the origins of postmodern improvisation) Contact Improvisation gained a reputation as a perhaps too gentle, passive, even boring way of dancing. Instead of focusing on the occasional unexpected lift or handstand, younger artists saw only dancers tangled together, endlessly rolling around on the floor. Moreover, they felt that Contact did not function primarily for the viewer, but for the participant, and therefore it could not always deliver a satisfying theatrical product. For the younger generation, Contact became a negative foil against which to invent a new approach to situation-response composition.

Grand Union, an improvisatory group to which Paxton also belonged, was entirely a theatrical phenomenon. Lasting only from 1970 to 1976, the Grand Union grew out of experiments Rainer had initiated in her dance *Continuous Project—Altered Daily,* in which she gave the performers permission, as she put it, to improvise blocks of material. If Contact Improvisers saw situation-response composition as an ongoing process done outside the theater more often than inside, and only occasionally witnessed by spectators, Grand Union improvised solely for audiences. The group was so committed to open, in situ choreography as theatrical performance that once it was formed, its members (Paxton, Yvonne Rainer, David Gordon, Trisha Brown, Douglas Dunn, Barbara Dilley, Lincoln Scott, and Nancy Lewis) prided themselves on never meeting offstage to have rehearsals or practice sessions, but instead, coming into each performance "cold." Though there were occasional crashes, more often the Grand Union took off from that cold base like a collective rocket.

Still, the Grand Union was committed to process, in a way that was consonant both with other contemporary movements in the arts and with collectivist political movements of the early and mid-seventies. Part of its risk-taking was to lay both the process of improvisation and the process of group dynamics open at all times to public scrutiny in performance. The group explored movement interaction and social intercourse in various "keys" of reality: fictional, dramatic, metatheatrical, and everyday. Material might be learned, rehearsed, or performed in a finished state. Structures were invented, repeated, dropped, and remembered. And everything was commented upon, analyzed, mock-ritualized, and transformed in an ironic mode that made the group's antics resemble a surrealistic vaudeville. They danced, sang, played records, quoted movies, took care of one another, took star turns, argued, found partners, did solos, created images with objects and flamboyant costumes, and altogether created the feeling that the stage was a place where anything could be imagined and tried out.[7]

Trisha Brown's description of her earliest experience performing with the Grand Union conveys the group's style. Brown had never been part of Rainer's company, and she explains that as a Grand Union member she did not want to learn any material from *Continuous Project—Altered Daily,* because she believed in an "unpremeditated . . . blank slate approach" to improvisation. Brown remembers:

> At Rutgers on November 6, 1970, my first performance with the Grand Union, I worked alone, unable and unwilling to participate in "known material." This self-imposed isolation caused extreme discomfort, there were so many of them throwing pillows in unison and so few of me looking awkward. Luckily, Steve stepped into my dilemma and asked, "Would you like to dance?" as he extended his arms in the traditional ballroom position of the male lead and we were off . . . for about five years.[8]

She describes other key moments:

> Steve Paxton arriving with a burning candle installed on his hat symbolizes [the beginning stage of Grand Union] for me. That and the night we verbally reduced a foam-rubber mattress to a kitchen sponge. . . . If you said "Drop a hat," everyone threw them in the air. Subversion was the norm. Everything was fair game except fair game. . . . There were time lapses, empty moments, collusion with the audience, massive behavior displays, pop music, outlandish get-ups, eloquence, bone-bare confrontations, lack of concern, the women's dance, taking over, paying deference, exhilaration, poignancy, shooting one's wad, wadding up one's wad, making something out of nothing, melodramarooney, cheap shots, being oneself against all odds and dancing. Dancing and dancing and dancing.[9]

If Contact Improvisation, with its (not always exclusive) focus on the duo, stripped away everything but the bare bones of partnering, Grand Union maximized all sorts of group situations and dynamics, as well as metatheatrical commentary, to proliferate both texts and imagery in an open choreography of constant surprise.

Oddly enough, Contact Improvisation and the Grand Union—both in their different ways embodying an ethos of leisurely movement exploration, bodily richness, and collective or cooperative politics—flourished in the seventies, a time of economic recession and political quiescence (in terms of mass political movements). Perhaps this disjunction is not so strange as first appears, however. The initiators of these groups came to artistic maturity in the sixties, a time of political and artistic upheaval and economic abundance. While these forms of indeterminate choreography fiscally suited the seventies (in that they were inexpensive to produce), they remained rooted artistically and sociopolitically in the sixties. They carried forward into the seventies an oppositional sixties attitude toward bodily, imaginative, and political liberation.

THE EIGHTIES AND NINETIES

The eighties and nineties saw various changes in the postmodern dance world. For one thing, a new form of inter-art avant-garde collaboration flourished in the eighties, a unified *Gesamtkunstwerk* that—marketed now to attract larger audiences combining art, music, theater, and dance spectators and involving several artistic contributors from different artistic fields—could not always risk the uncertainties (both financial and artistic) that open choreography implies. Also, generational succession in an avant-garde always questing for the new meant that a fresh crop of choreographers and dancers emerged, a generation trained and inspired by the generation of the sixties and seventies, but in search of distinctive, dissimilar paths. By the nineties, a key area of difference between the two generations developed: the content of the dance tended toward an explicitly stated politics of identity, in terms of gender, sexual preference, race, and ethnicity.

The late eighties and nineties saw a reemergence of interest in improvisation, but diverging in both motivations and meanings from those of the earlier generation. If many dancers in the sixties saw situation-response composition as a way of accessing the "authentic" self, postmodern culture in the eighties and nineties declared that there is no singular, authentic self, but only a fragmented multiplicity of shifting identities. This stance was nicely exemplified in John Jasperse's improvisation (from a Hothouse event at P.S. 122 in New York, December 1993) in which his body was marked not as blurring boundaries between male and female, in the androgynous mode of the seventies, but rather, as simultaneously extremely masculine and extremely feminine. By the nineties, the debate about self and identity had become complicated. There is a contradiction between postmodernism/poststructuralism and identity politics in regard to the notion of subjectivity. While identity politics does not necessarily require essentialist notions of a group (either racial, ethnic, gendered, or sexual) still, it often reverts to essentialist rhetoric. And even the position that some have called "strategic essentialism" asserts that there is—if only contingently—a genuine "I" (whether gay, black, female, Latino, and so on), whereas postmodernism in the cultural/theoretical sphere denies it. So this debate about self, subjectivity, and affiliation has affected danced representations of identity, or questions thereof.

If dancers in the sixties saw open choreography as a way of expressing freedom and creating community, cultural critics in the eighties and nineties questioned the meaning of freedom and community—even the community that identity politics might promise. Several decades ago, improvisation was a leisurely means for exploration, participating in a culture of abundance. But the recession of the seventies seemed at the time only temporary; by the early nineties, the prospects of worldwide financial crises made abundance and leisure seem antique, nostalgic notions from the past.

Finally, while avant-garde dance improvisers in the sixties and seventies were predominantly white but influenced by an African American aesthetic (especially as practiced in the progressive jazz music of the period), in the eighties and nineties, many more people of color appeared in avant-garde venues. Groups such as Urban Bush Women brought African American improvisatory traditions directly into postmodern dance practice, sometimes using improvisation to create material and sometimes leaving room for open choreography in performance. Those traditions include an interweaving of music and dance and a view of the relationship of the individual to the collectivity as not only a political, but also a spiritual value. Jawole Willa Jo Zollar, artistic director of Urban Bush Women, declares that "improvisation is a spiritual philosophy as well as a movement tool. It includes the Marxist concept of collectivity, the African notion of cooperative tribal action, the Native American council."[10]

This is not to say that African American dance groups (for instance, that of Dianne McIntyre) were not using improvisation all along. But in the sixties and seventies, the African American vanguard in dance took an entirely different direction from the predominantly white avant-garde, so that both venues and audiences for the two worlds separated. Postmodern dance was seen by many African American dancers as dry formalism, while African American dance was considered by some white postmodernists as too emotional and overexplicit politically. In the eighties, a wave of African American postmodern dancers emerged, while at the same time a heightened political sensibility—often focusing on identity politics—and a renewed taste for direct action led white postmoderns to prefer explicit content. For some, situation-response composition served as a metaphor for Realpolitik, in that it requires tactical thinking and acting in public, in response to issues of power and choice in the group. In contrast, closed or determinate choreography molds the world to a vision. Practical politicians have no such luxury.

Improvisation, of course, continues to be used in dance in a variety of ways, not only to generate material for performance that will later be become permanent (this, of course, has been a compositional method used for untold ages), or as a shifting component of a set piece of choreography, but also as offstage daily practice or preparation. But in the early nineties, there was an efflorescence of improvisation as direct performance: not as preparation for the event, but as the material of the event itself. Festivals and series abounded, including Hothouse at P.S. 122, Bread to the Bone at the Knitting Factory (both in New York), the New York Improvisation Festival, and Engaging the Imagination in San Francisco.

If the improvisations of the sixties and seventies created the feeling that "we've got all the time in the world to play and explore," those of the nineties had a sense of urgency, a feeling of grabbing you by the lapels. Young dancers may turn to indeterminate choreography in each generation, but the nineties generation was one that felt frenetic—responding, as Jennifer Monson put it, to the violence and risky energy all around it, as well as to shorter attention spans. "Improvisation now is different from the seventies," she pointed out. "Contact Improvisation was slow and gentle; I needed to explode. There is a fierce physicality that may be an impact of the New York City environment [as opposed to Vermont, Steve Paxton's home for the past thirty years]. For me, improvisation has political overtones. What I do is related to the work of the Lesbian Avengers, a direct action group."[11]

The nineties generation inhabited a very different historical moment than did its predecessors. Freedom took on new meaning in a post–cold war world. And erotics have altered implications in a world with AIDS. Spontaneity, resourcefulness, attitudes toward time and bodies—all had added layers of significance in a world of urban homelessness and violence in the eighties and nineties.

Yet even in the nineties group, there were echoes of certain values of the previous generation. For Jasperse, seeing people think, make decisions, and act—all in real time—is part of the method's excitement, recalling Paxton's excitement about witnessing surprises. And Jasperse's sense of satisfaction that making improvisatory work increases the ephemeral nature of dance, leaving no product to purchase or to hang on a wall, harks back to the conceptual artists of the seventies. Still, his interest in finding "extreme physical states and unachievable scores," his use of heavy-metal music that assaults the ears, his cross-gendered images—all are pure nineties.[12]

I also see differences in approaches to improvisation on different coasts. In New York I see a search for extremes, for physical risks. This is a view of community that is different from the preceding generation: one not so much of harmony and health, but rather one that recognizes splits, differences, and pains, as well as pleasures. At the same time, the politics of New York improvisers seem less explicit, more a metaphoric function of onstage actions. In California, where Anna Halprin still teaches, there seems to be more of a holistic approach in several senses. Not only is open choreography connected to mind/body therapeutic modes, but dance improvisation also shares personnel and venues with theatrical improvisation and performance art. Generational relations, as well, are continuous, not oppositional. At the same time, however, perhaps because of the connection to theater and performance art, dancers such as Rachel Kaplan present more explicit, even confrontational political agendas in their work.

On another front, the enterprise growing out of Contact Improvisation known as DanceAbility, which joins able-bodied and disabled dancers in movement explorations based on a broad range of human movement, extends to its logical and radical implications the sixties' promise of democratic accessibility for *all* bodies in postmodern dance. It implies not just accessibility, but empowerment, because disabled dancers lead and teach able-bodied dancers, as well as vice versa. DanceAbility expands the egalitarian idea of the sixties in its attempt to create equality of *condition,* not just of opportunity. That is, it reconfigures the dance so everyone can be a dancer. The ordinary movements valorized by postmodern choreographers in the sixties were still the ordinary movements of able-bodied dancers. In the sixties, even in the avant-garde and even in the counterculture, to be all-inclusive was still (albeit unwittingly for many) to exclude those whose marginal status—whether due to color, race, ethnicity, or physical ability—made them invisible to the majority. Disability is the final frontier for dance, where DanceAbility has extended the egalitarian franchise. In this sense, DanceAbility becomes an important expression of identity politics.[13]

CONCLUSION

Although the younger generation of improvisers often positions itself as contesting the practices of an older generation, some familiar aspects of improvisation reemerged in the early nineties: a yearning to take chances, a delight in surprise, a desire to collectivize creation. Yet history never repeats itself exactly. What came in between the effervescence of the sixties and the riskiness of the nineties was the Reaganite eighties, a decade of bodily and political *control.* In dance, this fascination with control often took the form of physical virtuosity that flaunted a highly regimented body. In the nineties, although a fitness craze still obsessed our culture, there was a reaction formation in the avant-garde to fetishizing discipline. While younger improvisers looked for physical extremes (which can still be a virtuoso gesture), they also wanted—and needed—to let go, to let the body and the imagination overflow all boundaries.

This desire to let go was sharpened by a feeling of carpe diem, an urge to seize the moment and to live to one's utmost in the present. Especially in the age of AIDS, to overflow one's bodily boundaries can symbolize danger. But it can also stand for a refusal to cut off human contact, even in the face of danger. It can serve to criticize the sexual and other forms of bodily repression that have trailed the AIDS pandemic. And, in a larger sense, it attacks an increasingly puritanical view of the body by mainstream culture. Thus the nineties strain of improvisation combined two seemingly contradictory facets: open-endedness and urgency. Perhaps what fueled the nineties taste for improvisation (not only in dance, but also in comedy and theater) was a millennial sensibility that various ends were close at hand.

NOTES

1. Jill Johnston, "Judson 1964: End of an Era: I," *Village Voice,* January 21, 1965, p. 12; reprinted in *Ballet Review* 1, no. 6 (1967): 8; Rainer's essay was published in her *Work, 1961–73* (Halifax, Nova Scotia: The Press of the Nova Scotia College of Art and Design; New York: New York University Press, 1974), 298–301.
2. See Sally Banes, *Terpsichore in Sneakers: Post-Modern Dance* (Middletown, Conn.: Wesleyan University Press, 1987; 1st ed. Boston: Houghton Mifflin, 1980), 64–65.
3. See Cynthia Novack, *Sharing the Dance: Contact Improvisation and American Culture* (Madison: University of Wisconsin Press, 1990) for an in-depth study of Contact Improvisation and its cultural meanings.

4. "Beyond the Mainstream," directed by Merrill Brockway, *Dance in America*, PBS, WNET, New York, 1980.

5. Issues of gender in Contact Improvisation have been discussed by both Novack and Ramsay Burt, *The Male Dancer: Bodies, Spectacle, Sexualities* (London: Routledge, 1995).

6. Ramsay Burt, *The Male Dancer: Bodies, Spectacle, Sexualities* (London: Routledge, 1995), 154–55.

7. For an in-depth study of the Grand Union, see Margaret Hupp Ramsay, *The Grand Union (1970–1976): An Improvisational Performance Group* (New York: Peter Lang, 1991).

8. "The Grand Union, Q & A," in Banes, *Terpsichore*, 225.

9. Ibid.

10. Quoted in Sally Banes, "Dancing in Leaner Times," *Dance Ink* 2, no. 3 (Winter 1991–92), repr. in Sally Banes, *Writing Dancing in the Age of Postmodernism* (Hanover, N.H.: Wesleyan University Press, 1994), 343.

11. Telephone interview with Jennifer Monson, June 5, 1994.

12. Interview with John Jasperse, New York City, May 28, 1994.

13. On DanceAbility and the identity politics of the disabled dancing body, see Ann Cooper Albright, *Choreographing Difference: The Body and Identity in Contemporary Dance* (Hanover, N.H.: Wesleyan University Press and the University Press of New England, 1997).

EXPANDING
THE CANON

STEPPING, STEALING, SHARING, AND DARING
Improvisation and the Tap Dance Challenge
Constance Valis Hill

On the night of November 21, 1964, at the Village Gate in New York City, jazz tapsters Groundhog and Chuck Green faced off in the fiercest tap challenge of their lives. Groundhog was back in town. Rumor had it that a group of dancers locked him in a Harlem cellar, making him show his steps, feeding him liquor while stealing his stuff. Groundhog, strictly a hoofer, a dancer's dancer and the best that most had seen, was challenging Chuck Green, protégé of the great John Bubbles. "I've been waiting to battle Chuck Green for twenty years," Groundhog rasped before the event. "Dancing is like a gang war and tonight, I'm up against one of the best. Every dancer is my enemy." Drummer Max Roach, singer Abbey Lincoln, comedian Nipsey Russell, and artists from the jazz world took their seats in the audience as the Jo Jones Trio took their places on the bandstand. The battle began.

Green went on first, without an introduction. Tall, lean, and totally cool, he shifted back and forth between medium and fast tempos. Twirling and gliding to Jones's slithery brushstrokes, he earned cheers for an effortless cascade of taps. Then Groundhog, a short and mischievous-faced man with a gap-toothed smile, burst onto the stage in his new black patent-leather shoes and exploded a wild assortment of eccentric and acrobatic steps. "Let's do it à la Charlie Parker," he ordered the drummer, as he bopped through a rat-a-tat of machine-gun taps, all the while boasting, "Now watch this one." Scuffing and pigeon-toeing, digging and scraping the varnish off the floor, he called Green back onstage and signaled him to dance, and keep on dancing. "I'm gonna put something on you," Groundhog growled, as the audience whistled and shouted, and he flung his arms wide open and skittered across the floor. Green's return was all the more quiet. Trusting the even timing of his taps, the milliseconds of silence between each tap, he sprawled into a leggy, languid tap Charleston. "I know you can do better than that," Groundhog charged, as Green floated into a graceful tapping turn. "Oh, you want to play show biz?" Groundhog roared, returning with a staccato of flamenco-heels that made his patent-leathers skate across the stage.

Fig. l1. Savion Glover and Colin Dunn in a video still of their challenge dance from the 39th Annual Grammy Awards. (39th Annual Grammy Awards telecast, February 26, 1997. Courtesy the Recording Academy®.)

The audience went wild. Max Roach jumped from his seat to the stage and ousted Jo Jones from the drums, as Groundhog and Green copied and cracked on each other, charging the musicians to keep up or shut up. Then, tired of words, the hoofers went with the hands. Throwing their arms around each other, they rocked back and forth in rhythm until, suddenly, Groundhog pushed Green away, flew into the air, and plummeted into a split-second down-and-up knee drop that left the audience gasping. Sweating, laughing, crying out over and over again, "I've never lost a case, I've never lost," the show ended when Groundhog decided he won—but everyone knew, that night, that Groundhog was the undisputed King of the Gate.[1]

This performance, reconstructed from reviews and interviews with tap dancers, some of them my teachers, is a sublime example of the tap dance challenge. Motivated by a dare, focused by the strict attention to one's opponent, and developed through the stealing, trading, and riffing of steps, "tap challenge" is my term for any competition, contest, breakdown, or showdown in which dancers compete before an audience of spectators or judges. As such, the challenge is the dynamic and rhythmically expressive "engine" that drives American tap dance performance. Fiercely competitive, the challenge dance sets the stage for a "performed" battle, and engages dancers in a dialog of rhythm, motion and witty repartee; and forces the audience to respond to the moment with a whisper of kudos or roar of stomps.

Improvisation is integrally related to the concept of the tap dance challenge as a performative practice that forces the dynamic exchange of rhythmic ideas. Like improvisation in jazz, improvisation in the challenge can take form as the spontaneous creation or composition of a percussive statement in performance. More often and most generally, however, improvisation in the challenge is the act of responding spontaneously (to an opponent, musician, or member of the audience), in the moment of performance. If the challenge is the *call* to action, the putting forth of a rhythmic statement by the challenger, then improvisation (or more aptly, the improvisatory imperative) is the *response* (and not only an "Amen")—the answer to the call that is spontaneous, creative, and reactive, compelling the challengee (who in turn becomes a challenger) to look, to listen, and to respond in the moment, with any and all means necessary. Even when the challenge dance is built on previously rehearsed materials that are not freshly composed, what is essential in the dynamism and fierce excitement of the challenge is that it at the very least be *perceived* as an extemporaneous, or improvised, battle: an in-the-moment happening that may never again be repeated the same way. The temporal notion of spontaneity and spontaneous invention in the challenge, as it relates to improvisation, must always and at the very least be implied.

The oral and written histories of tap dance are replete with challenge dances, from jigging competitions on the plantation (staged by white masters for their slaves) and challenge dances in the "walk-around" finale of the minstrel show, to showdowns in the street, displays of one-upmanship in the social club, and juried buck-and-wing dance contests on the vaudeville stage. There are contemporary forms of the tap challenge as well that I shall identify in this discussion of the tap dance challenge, its relationship to improvisation, and its ethos of spontaneity and invention.

Tap dance is an indigenous American dance form that evolved over a period of some three hundred years in America, initially as a fusion of Irish and West African musical and step dancing traditions. As early as the 1650s, thousands of Irish and Scottish men, women and children, who were deported during the Cromwellian wars to the Caribbean as indentured servants, came in contact with the first wave of enslaved West Africans. Both these groups of people often labored, side by side, on the English sugar plantations. Through time, the Irish jig (a musical and dance form) and African *gioube* (the general term for sacred and secular stepping dances) juxtaposed and fused into early forms of tap dance. Musically, the flowing $\frac{6}{8}$ meter of the Irish jig can be distinguished from the polyrhythms of West African drumming, with its propulsive, or swinging quality. The fusion of these musical opposites in America yielded a form of dancing that by the late 1700s was identified as "jigging." Most often considered a "Negro" form of step dancing, jigging was accompanied by tunes that were "ragged" or syncopated on the fiddle. No one knows the extent to which improvisation functioned as a catalyst for the fusion of the jig and *gioube* forms that produced American jigging. But surely, if there was a West African component in the meld, improvisation must have been involved: improvisation with traditionally designated materials was then and continues to be integral to all forms of West African music and dance. Gunther Schuller, in *Early Jazz,* writes that in West African drumming, the drummer's skill as an improviser is judged by his ability to vary the material with maximum of variety, with variational principles including a number of expositional techniques in which the "seed pattern," or rhythmic theme, is varied, manipulated, augmented, diminished, fragmented, or regrouped into new variants.[2] Marshall Stearns, in *Jazz Dance,* states that one of the major characteristics of African dance that helped identify the African influence on jazz dance in the United States was the importance of improvisation, satirical or otherwise, which allowed for a freedom of individual expression.[3] And Kathy Ogren, in *The Jazz Revolution,* theorizes that it was from the African participatory heritage of call-and-response and a strong tradition of improvisation that jazz in America developed as a distinct language and a unique form of oral performance that encouraged spontaneity, invention, and interaction between performer and audience.[4] Thus, African retentions of improvisation as an expositional technique that allowed for freedom of expression and spontaneous interaction between performer and spectator were rooted strongly in American vernacular dance forms, especially in tap dance.

The congruence of belief systems and the shared competitive traditions of the transplanted Irish and West Africans in the Caribbean also perpetuated the key features of the challenge dance, which was sparked by spontaneous retort. Both the African myths of Oriki-Esu and the Gaelic legend of Airthirne are described by an oral tradition of folk tales and songs of slander, which shaped an "insult tradition" of verbal abuse and satire. Esu-Elegara, the divine trickster figure of Yoruban mythology, was a "divine" linguist who spoke all languages, and was known for his powers of magic, parody, and satire; while Airthirne, whose exploits are recounted in ancient Gaelic manuscripts, was a divine poet who was feared for his "word magic," and so powerful in his poems of slander that he could demand the single eye of a king. The "Song of Marvels," or Lying Songs of the Irish,[5] for instance, which were sung in competition, used fantastic inventions of lying, boasting, and verbal trickery to amaze, dumfound, and entertain its listeners. Rapparree, the legendary Irish rogue from eighth-century Bruidhean tales, was a prankster with a fondness for music and poetry who indulged in outrageous trickery, which certainly would have included elements of playful improvisation. Similarly, it was believed that the West African songs of derision were so powerful that an intended victim paid griots *not* to sing them. And in the *Sundiata,* an epic of old Mali told by generations of griots dating back to the thirteenth century, the hurling insults and boasts of two warring kings of Mali is recounted in a verbal exchange that, even when read today, exudes spontaneity: "Know then, that I am the wild yam of the rocks, nothing will make me leave Mali," says one king; "Know then, that I have seven mastersmiths who will shatter the rocks. Then, I will eat you," threatens the other:

> I am the poisonous mushroom that makes the fearless vomit;
> I am the ravenous cock, the poison does not matter to me.
> Behave yourself little boy, or you will burn your foot, for I am the red hot cinder;
> Then I am the rain that extinguishes the cinder.
> I am the silk cotton tree that looks from on high;
> I am the strangely creeper.
> Enough of the argument—You shall not have Mali. Know that there is not room for two kings . . . you will let me have your place;
> Very well, since you want war, I will wage war against you.[6]

Musical forms and expressive narrative traditions such as these were retained and recited in the Caribbean, circum-Caribbean,[7] and southern United States by slaves and servants. Sung in fields, danced in slave quarters, recited to fiddle tunes, they cast satirical aspersions on masters and became the basis for blues songs, "cutting" contests, and jigging competitions, in which insults were added ammunition to the trap-hammering of the feet. In Yoruban ceremonies practiced in America today, drummers incite the gods to manifest themselves by calling out insults, or the names of other gods; when the gods are activated, worshipers fall to their knees in immediate praise. Like the Dahomean drummers who shout disparaging remarks to the dancers to make them dance harder (and like Groundhog, who shouts, "I know you can do better than that," to Chuck Green), the insult motivates an opponent to action—as does the copying and stealing of steps. Unlike European ballet, with its codification of formal technique, tap dance is learned by listening to, and by watching, people dance.

"Technique" is transmitted visually, aurally, and corporeally, in a rhythmic exchange between dancers and musicians. Mimicry is necessary for the mastery of the form.

From cornshucking festivals in the 1840s, where slaves danced mocked versions of the minuet learned from watching their white masters dance it, to the Hoofers Club in Harlem in the thirties and forties, where tap dancers gathered to practice and compete, there was one unwritten rule: "Thou Shalt Not Copy Anyone's Steps—Exactly!" Veteran hoofers, like my teachers Charles "Cooky" Cook and James "Buster" Brown, have confessed to sitting in the first two rows of the Lafayette Theatre to hawk the opening tap act, then rushing back to the club during intermission to copy and "modify" what they saw. Such creative modifications, in which previously "rehearsed" steps were recombined, rearticulated, and reaccented in every iteration, became the very stuff of tap improvisation.

In the challenge dance, you must copy an opponent's steps, only to reinvent them on your own terms. What you copy and how you copy it shape your reputation as a dancer—the how becoming the particularities of tap improvisation. You steal, but you alter and then allow inspiration to carry your performance in new directions in the moment. Williams Henry Lane was hailed "King of All Dancers" after beating the reigning white minstrel, John Diamond, in a series of challenge dances in the 1840s. Lane, a freeborn Negro, was a jig and reel dancer of exceptional skill who is credited for grafting an African American style of stepping and shuffling onto the more exacting techniques of Irish and English jig and clog. Lane was crowned "Master Juba," not only for his technical mastery of steps but because he could skillfully imitate the specialty steps of all the reigning white minstrel dancers of the day—after which he would execute his own specialty steps, which no one could copy. "He will give the correct 'Imitation Dances' of all the principal Ethiopian Dancers in the United States," states a handbill in the 1840s, and continues to name all those reigning white minstrels of the day, "after which he will give an imitation of himself."[8]

The challenge sharpens the ability to copy, fuse, and reinvent dance movement. It is a creative act that requires a mastery of the form and the ability to "deform" the mastery—to creatively extend or embellish the form in order to reflect the individual expression of the creator.[9] In Lane's case, his mastery of the exacting technique of Irish jig and clog, and subsequent grafting of an African American style of step dancing, wrought a highly individual style of tap dancing. One important aspect of Lane's challenge was his signifying: an aggressive style of joking in which you put down, berate, sound, diss, or pull rank on someone by referring to an aspect of his or her behavior.[10] Lane's practice of signifying on Diamond's best steps demonstrated his technical mastery over Irish jig, and at the same time elevated his own superlative style of stepping.

While signifying in the tap challenge can be traced to a number of African tribal groups, and identified as a predominantly African American form of black troping,[11] the obsession with technical perfection falls on the Irish side of tap dance's family. In New York City in 1868, for example, the *New York Clipper* reported that "Charles M. Clarke, a professional jig dancer . . . had a contest on the evening of the 3rd at Metropolitan Hall . . . for a silver cup valued at twelve dollars. Clarke did a straight jig with eighty-two steps and won the cup. Edwards broke down after doing sixty-five."[12] One-on-one competitions such as this one between Clarke and Edwards developed by the turn of the century into juried buck-and-wing contests on the vaudeville stage, where there were three judges: one in the front evaluating the movement and performance style of the dancer, one to the side judging the variety of steps, and one beneath the stage listening for the speed and clarity of steps. Improvisation, in the form of spontaneous invention of new material, does not appear to be present in contests that required a well-rehearsed, technical knockout of a routine, unless we look closely at the improvisatory imperative operating in the performance.

Willie Covan was sixteen years old when he entered *In Old Kentucky*'s Friday night buck-dancing contest; the touring musical show on the black vaudeville circuit was famous for sponsoring contests between members of the company and local buck-and-wing celebrities. Covan, who was born in Savannah, Georgia, and raised in Chicago where he learned to tap dance by mimicking street dancers, had been working up ideas all year for the event. Assigned a late number in the competition, he noticed that all his predecessors that evening began with traditional time steps in their routines. Each contestant was allowed no more than six minutes onstage. Covan decided to cut the time steps in his routine and instead jumped out with the wings, grab-offs, and rolls that would have ended his routine, squeezing in new variations on these steps before time ran out. He won first prize for the virtuosity of his variations, which undoubtedly had to be improvised.

Around 1895, when black musical comedy burst onto the American stage with the vigorous, double-metered, syncopated music of ragtime, tap dancing underwent its most significant transformation, developing as a musical form parallel to jazz. By the twenties, tap dance began to share with jazz its rhythmic motifs, polyrhythms, multiple meters, elements of swing (offbeat phrasing and suspension of the beat), and structured improvisation. By the thirties, "jazz tap" dance was "refined" into a concert form by the so-called two-man class-act tap dance teams. Dressed in tuxedos, top hats and tails, these elegant-dancing men tamed the challenge for the stage by taking the edge off fierce competition (though what was gained, in this heyday for tap dance, was the development of complex rhythmical ideas in the challenge). The most traditional elements of the tap challenge—verbal insult, mimicking and mocking steps, and the drive for physical endurance and technical perfection—may not have been immediately visible when watching Buck and Bubbles, Cook and Brown, Stump and Stumpy, Chuck and Chuckles, and the dozens of class and comedy tap-dance teams of the thirties and forties. But the challenge was still the churning engine in these swing-era performances. Instead of being pitted against each other, they were partners (often billed as "brothers") who, instead of one-upping each other, combined their specialties in building to a climax a routine in which structured improvisation was reserved for sections of dance, most often solos. Instead of mimicking each other's steps, the two moved as one, each a mirror image of the other. Instead of copying each other for the purposes of mocking, the practice of signifying evolved into the repetition of rhythmic phrases that progressed into whole paragraphs of sound and movement. When traded back and forth, these phrases became a lively and witty dialogue between dancers: technical perfection personified. Even when the solos were set, the very structure and form of the class act challenge dance, in which patterns were repeated, varied, traded, and one-upped, allowed for a dynamic exchange of rhythm and movement that gave the performance the look of being improvised.

A sublime example of the way in which the tap challenge was extended from its traditional form into a most sophisticated rhythmic expression is evident in a scene, featuring the Nicholas Brothers, from the Twentieth Century–Fox musical *Down Argentine Way* (1940). Although the scene must have been preset and exceedingly well rehearsed in order to facilitate the operation of a multiple-camera film shoot, certain elements of improvisation are key to the performance. The scene opens with Fayard and Harold, handsomely dressed in tailcoats, handing their top hats and canes to a pair of doormen as they enter the Club Rendezvous and move on to dance floor. The Latin orchestra is playing the eight-bar introduction to "Argentina," a tightly structured written arrangement that alternates between the $\frac{2}{4}$ rhythmic feel of a samba and the steady $\frac{4}{4}$ of swing time. Harold opens by singing the title song in Spanish, Fayard accompanying him by shaking a pair of maracas; they come together on the last four beats of the bar to dance.

The second chorus sets the "theme" of the tap dance, with the brothers performing smooth slipping and sliding steps. Harold solos with cramp rolls, back-slipping chugs, and variations on the slide, in which he rubs the whole of the foot along the floor. Fayard adds skidding steps and a break in double time, passes the dance to Harold, and then tries to take it back by waving his hands toward Harold, who mimes being stretched and released like a rubber band. When Harold snaps free, he dives into six rounds of his own signature trenches, which he repeats with a surprise ending: a split propelled by a front flip.

When Harold struts away, waving the dance back to Fayard, it is clear he has challenged his brother to come up with a better split than the one he just did: the challenge has begun. Fayard jumps into the air with legs splayed and drops right down to the floor into a full split. From that position, he makes eight half-turns on the ground, pulling himself up to a stand. Harold answers by diving into a forward flip into a full split; on the recovery, he does a one-arm flip and split, and then repeats the entire flip–split-rhythm phrase, walking away by sending Fayard a cocky "Top that!" salute. And Fayard does: holding the ends of a white handkerchief he has gallantly unfurled from his breast pocket, Fayard jumps over the handkerchief to land in a split; he then pulls himself back up to jump back over the handkerchief again to land in a split. Standing proud with legs outspread, Fayard replaces the handkerchief in his pocket as Harold, who has been standing behind him, takes a running slide through Fayard's legs. He pulls himself up just in time so that the brothers can finish with a slip and a slide, a fast rhythm break, bow and exit.

Given the constraints of having to perform this staged challenge before the camera and within a tightly written musical arrangement for orchestra, there was little room for spontaneous composition in the Nicholas Brothers' performance of the challenge. During the rehearsal process, however, they were able to improvise variations on the slides, which they extended into slip-sliding glides, which in turn were pushed to their farthest extension with splits, and in turn translated into a dazzling variety of acrobatic maneuvers. They were certainly aided by the fact that the choreography was structured as a series of solos, in which patterns were repeated, varied, traded, and one-upped. This dynamic exchange of rhythm and movement in their performance before the cameras gave it the look of being improvised.

Down Argentine Way, the Nicholas Brothers' first film for Twentieth Century–Fox, incorporated a routine from the film taken from the brothers' act at the downtown Cotton Club in New York. Even after recording the routine on film (which was such a smash, Twentieth Century–Fox offered them a five-year contract), the brothers continued to perform it in clubs and theaters throughout the United States and Europe. On the surface, and to the eye of someone who may have seen it performed at the Cotton Club, the routine fundamentally looked and sounded the same. But shifts in mood caused adjustments to be made to the music each time they performed with a live orchestra, whether Duke Ellington's, Jimmie Lunceford's, or Cab Calloway's. In the sequence of solos in the challenge section of the dance, there was always the opportunity to improvise. While the dances were arrangements of popular jazz standards that specified the number of choruses, the tempos, and the musical segues, there were always differences, however slight, in the manner the music was played, in the manner the brothers responded to the music being played, and most of all, in how the audience was responding to the musicians and performers. Given the narrow range of "basic" tap steps that compose the tap dance lexicon (shuffles, slaps, hops, riffs, pickups, slides, digs—which are in themselves variations of drumming the floor) the repetition of steps and rhythmic patterns implies variation, relying on the principle of improvisation. The challenge in fact provided the brothers with one of the few opportunities they had to improvise before an audience. Says Fayard: "The only time we'd improvise was after we did our act, and we could have some fun. We'd go back onstage and I'd go to the mike and say, 'Thank you very much, ladies and gentlemen, and now we're going to do a little challenge for you.' And my brother and I would improvise."[13] What he implied was that they were able to play, freestyle, with the very steps that they had discovered and varied in rehearsal, drawn freely from their technical storehouse of rhythm steps and jazz-dance vocabulary.

The swing era was at its peak when *Down Argentine Way* was released; its spirit had completely enraptured the American public. There were other venues where the challenge dance thrived in the swing-era forties. At the Savoy Ballroom in Harlem, New York, big swing bands battled each other nightly from their bandstands, and lindy-hoppers challenged each other nightly on the dance floor. On Sundays at the Savoy, "Opportunity Contests" were staged with prizes of ten dollars awarded to the best dancers. "We started getting ready for Sunday on Saturday," Savoy dancer Shorty Snowden recalls. "The deal was to get our one sharp suit to the tailor to be pressed Saturday afternoon. Then we'd meet at the poolroom and brag about what we were going to do on the dance floor the next night."[14] It was off of the basic step of the lindy (a syncopated two-step, or box step, that accented the offbeat) that Snowden claims to have created the breakaway step on the dance floor at the Savoy. "I got tired of the same old steps and cut loose with a breakaway," he said about the step in which dancers spin away from each other to improvise in freestyle a dance break. "Anything you could dream up was okay for the breakaway, you tried all kinds of things. Everybody did the same starting step, but after that, look out, everybody for himself." Snowden also claims to have invented the step called the Shorty George while improvising in the lindy breakaway: "I just made it up. I've put together new steps in the breakaway by slipping and almost falling. I was always looking for anyone dancing in the street or just walking or doing anything that suggests a step. If I could see it, I could do it."[15]

Snowden's remark that he "just made it up" points to his ability to improvise, to invent new moves and steps in the moment of performance. His skills as a dance improviser most resemble those of an improvising jazz musician. Jazz improvisation is the spontaneous creation of music as it is performed, without the benefit of written music: the act of composing on the spur of the moment to create an immediate composition of the entire work, or variations within the existing framework of the composition.[16] Improvisation in the challenge can also result in the spontaneous creation of music (be it rhythmic) as it is being performed. Jazz improvisation is not a chaotic, free-for-all response but a freshly composed statement. So it is with the challenge. Within the provisional framework of the choreography, the improviser draws on a storehouse of steps, rhythmic phrases, and body moves to create a richly resonant percussive statement that literally "re-sounds" the material at foot. In order to improvise in jazz, one has to know everything about the language that is being spoken. In the challenge dance, similarly, the soloist must have a mastery of "technique" in order to play with the possibilities within the framework of the conception.

Ironically, technique is what is forgotten when improvising; the ability to play is the thing, and in the challenge dance, there are a number of ways to play, or improvise, a response. The dancer can either embellish and enhance the "theme" of the previous statement with complementary steps, or play within the realm of the rhythmic statement; as the revolutionary alto saxophone improviser, Ornette Coleman said, "Forget about the changes in key and just play within the range of the idea."[17] The dancer can follow the direction of the music (as the jazz saxophonist Steve Lacy advised, "Each thing you hear determines the direction you go. You just follow the music, and if you follow the music you can go any-where")[18] or shift the direction while playing. The dancer can choose to trade on two, four, or eight bars of music in a structured exchange with another dancer or musician, or can improvise, or riff, off of a chorus or a break. The riff examines every aspect of the rhythmic theme, the seed-pattern, that the dancer's instru-ment is capable of, as well as every aspect of the dancer's feeling for the theme. The riff is the dancer's personal voice; it develops the experience of the melody in any and every way the experience of the rhythmic theme can be heard or perceived. Whatever is taken from the previous line and however the call of one statement is repeated, varied, extended, renovated, deconstructed, or de-formed, what signifies is to move the dance forward. As the jazz pianist Mary Lou Williams learned about a jam session she participated in, "Style didn't mat-ter. What mattered was to keep the thing going."[19] Even when the response in the challenge is not improvised, the performance of it must, as I have said ear-lier, have the effect of being in the moment, spontaneous, and "vitally alive,"[20] as it is a perpetually creative moment that will never again be repeated in the same way. It is the dancer's willingness to stay open to the possibilities of what the next moment may bring that allows the improvisational moment to stay alive and to thrive. This moment, Albert Murray so eloquently explains, is "the moment of greatest opportunity . . . the heroic moment . . . when you establish your identity . . . write your signature on the epidermis of actuality . . . come to terms with the void."[21]

Never have the improvisational operatives in the challenge been so boldly demonstrated as in the tap dance challenge between Colin Dunn and Savion Glover that took place at the 1997 Grammy Awards and was broadcast nation-wide on February 26, 1997. This staged challenge dance not only pitted Dunn, the star of *Riverdance,* against Glover, the star of *Bring in 'Da Noise, Bring in the 'Da Funk*—the two hottest musicals on Broadway that year—but also the per-cussive dance traditions (Irish step dancing and African American jazz tap danc-ing) that each represented.

The dancers from *Bring in 'Da Noise* had just finished performing the "Indus-trialization" number from the show when, over the applause, the master of cere-monies announced: "From the cast of *Riverdance,* Colin Dunn." Standing with his back to the audience, wearing slim black pants and billowy white shirt, Dunn spun quickly around to face the audience, stopping his turn with the sharp stamp of his high-heeled shoe. With hands placed neatly at the waist, he drew himself up onto the balls of his feet and clicked out neat triplets and cross-back steps in place; he then repeated the rhythmic phrase traveling sideways. The camera zoomed in on the flurry of Dunn's crossing his legs in the air and the speedy precision of his footwork, and then suddenly panned right to revealing the hulk-ing figure of Glover. Wearing black baggy pants and a black baggy shirt, Glover burst into a succession of flat-footed stomps that deadened Dunn's sweet-sound-ing trills. "Dara da DA / dara da DA DA," he thumped with the soles of his leather shoes, his arms and mop of dreadlocks gesticulating frantically.

As if Dunn were hard of hearing, Glover turned directly to face him and re-peated the throbbing thumps of the previous phrase by beating the insteps of his shoes into the floor; he then hunkered down further to deliver a tirade of paddle-and-rolls. Dunn heard him. Taking his hands off his hips, he turned to face Glover, answering the tirade with a pair of swooping scissor kicks that sliced the air within inches of Glover's face. Dunn continued with a fluid monotone of shuffles and cross-backs in place, which brought the volume down to a whisper. Glover interrupted Dunn's meditation on the *sssh* with short-cut, jagged hee-haw steps that mocked Dunn's beautiful lines and brought the conversation down to raw sound, not pretty look. Then they traded off, keeping the beat going by spit-ting out shards of rhythmic phrases that stopped dangerously short of interrupt-ing each other. Dunn offered sprightly jumps and heel clicks; Glover repeated them, jumping higher and adding the toes. Dunn rolled out an airy, melodic flutter of feet; Glover repeated the flutters from a crouched position. Tired of giving each other a chance to speak in turn, they staccatoed simultaneously. Tap-ping over each other's lines, their beats formed a polyrhythmic drumming or-chestra that sounded a fast and furious race to the finish line. When the audience screamed with excitement and Dunn broke his concentration to acknowledge the applause with a smile, Glover found his edge by perching on the very tip of his shoe. Dunn repeated the beat, but with a dig of his square heel into the floor, giving Glover the chance to pull the ace in his pocket—a flick-kick with the other dangling leg that brushed close to Dunn. Stopping short of each other, they slapped hands, turned away, and walked off the stage, never looking back.

To sum up the salient features of the challenge trope, as the Colin Dunn–Savion Glover tap challenge so vividly illustrates, a challenge predisposes a *referent:* something or someone one is mocking, referring to, or commenting upon. How do you refer to it? By mimicking, repeating, copying, and deforming it through the use of humor, invective, or satire. Why do you refer to it? To learn it, to pay respect and admiration, to own it in a different way, to put your opponent down, to gain respect; hence, it is a competition. The call-and-response form of the challenge provides the framework for *spontaneous interaction* between perform-ers, though this may not necessarily lead to the extemporaneous invention of new materials in the moment of performance. It is clear that Glover was in fact improvising new material in the dynamic interplay with Dunn, that he was ac-tively responding (and rather fiercely) to Dunn's steps by repeatedly mocking and deforming them, and then one-upping with his own flat-footed and blunt yet rhythmically propulsive style of hitting. Though Dunn did not directly ad-dress Glover's challenge steps, he answered instead from his own storehouse of virtuosic moves; he countered not by dealing in the currency of what Glover offered but by drawing on the authority of his traditional Irish step dancing, known for its speed, precision, and airborne grace. The dynamic exchange be-tween Glover and Dunn, then, was both spontaneous and practiced. Finally and perhaps most important, the challenge begs for and is fed by an *audience re-*

sponse. There must be some sort of recognition on the part of the audience as to what or who is being challenged or commented on because the challenge is performative; it reaches out to an audience and either includes them in the assault or forces the recognition of it. I think the audience's in-the-moment response to the challenge dance is what makes it the most dynamic of performance expressions, and also what aligns it most closely with improvisation. The audience, with its cheers or jeers, reinforces the feeling that whatever they are experiencing in the interchange onstage, illusory or not, whatever is going on onstage, and their reception of it, is vitally alive; and this bares the dangerously exciting unpredictability of the improvisatory moment.

Speaking with me about the Grammy Awards tap challenge some years after the event, Glover remembered that a few weeks before the airing of the show, Colin Dunn's manager phoned Glover's manager asking to schedule a rehearsal for the tap challenge. Dunn apparently wanted to *rehearse* the challenge dance before performing it for a live theater audience, cameras rolling. Glover says he was totally bewildered at Dunn's request. "How do you rehearse a challenge?" he asked me. He says he ignored Dunn's request. But after several insistent phone calls from the representatives of *Riverdance* (which included heated negotiations over what kind of flooring to stage the challenge on—*Riverdance* wanted marley, *Noise Funk* wanted hardwood tongue-in-groove; they settled on a stage that was half marley, half wood), Glover reluctantly consented to a walkthrough "rehearsal" of the challenge dance, in which they marked steps and places for their entrance and exit. On the night of the Grammy Awards, however, when the time finally came for Glover to face Dunn onstage before the live audience, Glover claims he completely dismissed what he had walked through in rehearsal with Dunn. Instead, says Glover, "I got all worked up [offstage] and came on ready to go anywhere."[22]

How do you rehearse a tap challenge? For Glover, clearly you cannot. It is that supreme moment of dangerous unpredictability, when you are face to face with your opponent, buoyed by the cheers and jeers of an audience wanting to be taken by surprise. Dancers excited by the potential of inventing something new and being able to share that discovery with the audience—that makes the tap dance challenge the most dynamic of performance expressions. Does not the challenge dance, with its improvisatory ethos, affirm that competition, repetition, mimicry, signification, and stealth can be some of our most worthy motivations in American dance making? Who could ask for anything more?

NOTES

1. Marshall and Jean Stearns, *Jazz Dance: The Story of American Vernacular Dance* (New York: Macmillan, 1968), 342–47; Whitney Balliett, "Groundhog," *New Yorker,* December 12, 1964, pp. 47–49, 51; J. R. Goddard, "The Night Groundhog Was King of the Gate," *Village Voice,* November 26, 1964, pp. 8–9; author's interview with Chuck, Green, New York City, May 25, 1991.

2. Gunther Schuller, *Early Jazz: Its Roots and Musical Development* (New York: Oxford University Press, 1968), 55–57. Schuller adds that in Africa, the improvisation of many lines at the same time is a typically African concept and is perpetuated in most forms of early jazz, a music marked above all by "collective improvisation."

3. Marshall and Jean Stearns, *Jazz Dance,* 15.

4. Kathy J. Ogren, *The Jazz Revolution: Twenties America and the Meaning of Jazz* (New York: Oxford University Press, 1989), 12–13.

5. See Anne G. Gilchrist, "The Song of Marvels (or Lies)," *Journal of the English Folk Dance and Song Society* 4 (1950): 113–21.

6. "*Sundiata:* An Epic of Old Mali," trans. by G. D. Pickett in Isidore Okpewho, *The Epic in Africa: Toward a Poetics of Oral Performance* (New York: Columbia University Press, 1979), 60–61.

7. For a lively example of a semi-improvised challenge song known generally in Brazil as *desafio,* and the retention of other challenge singing traditions in the Atlantic cultural triangle, see Peter Fry, *Rhythms of Resistance: African Musical Heritage in Brazil* (Middletown, Conn.: Wesleyan University Press, 2000), 1–4.

8. Quoted in Marian Hannah Winter, "Juba and American Minstrelsy," in *Chronicles of American Dance,* ed. Paul Magriel (New York: Da Capo, 1948), 44.

9. In his book *Modernism and Harlem Renaissance* (Chicago: University of Chicago Press, 1989), Houston Baker proposes that it is the simultaneous "mastery of form" and "deformation of mastery," or the filtering of Western standards in art through African American cultural expression, that led artists of the Harlem Renaissance to a so-called African American modernism. Baker's theoretical paradigm is extremely useful in discerning the rhetorical devices of the challenge form.

10. For discussions of signification see Henry Louis Gates, *The Signifying Monkey: A Theory of African American Literary Criticism* (New York: Oxford University Press, 1988), 89–124; and Mel Watkins, *On the Real Side: Laughing, Lying, and Signifying—The Underground Tradition of African-American Humour That Transformed American Culture, from Slavery to Richard Pryor* (New York: Simon and Schuster, 1994), 63–79.

11. Henry Louis Gates, *Signifying Monkey,* 52.

12. *New York Clipper,* April 11, 1868.

13. Fayard Nicholas, quoted in Constance Valis Hill, *Brotherhood in Rhythm: The Jazz Tap Dancing of the Nicholas Brothers* (New York: Oxford University Press, 2000), 150.

14. Shorty Snowden, quoted in Marshall and Jean Stearns, *Jazz Dance,* 322.

15. Shorty Snowden, quoted in Marshall and Jean Stearns, *Jazz Dance,* 323–24.

16. See Gunther Schuller, *Early Jazz,* 58 and 378; and Barry Kernfeld, "Improvisation," in *New Grove Dictionary of Jazz,* ed. Barry Kernfeld (New York: St. Martin's, 1988), 554–62.

17. Ornette Coleman, quoted by A. B. Spellman in *Seeing Jazz: Artists and Writers on Jazz,* ed. Elizabeth Goldson; comp. Marquette Folley-Cooper, Deborah Macanic, and Janice McNeil; introd. Robert O. Meally; with foreword by Clark Terry and afterword by Milt Hinton (San Francisco: Chronicle Books, in association with Smithsonian Institution Traveling Exhibition Service, 1997), 44.

18. Steve Lacy, quoted by Richard Scott in "The Man With the Straight Horn," in *Seeing Jazz,* 51.

19. Mary Lou Williams, quoted by Whitney Balliett in "Out Here Again," in *Seeing Jazz,* 29.

20. Robert Farris Thompson, *African Art in Motion: Icon and Act* (Berkeley and Los Angeles: University of California Press, 1974), 9. The concept of vital aliveness, which

Thompson identifies as inherent motion in African art, is communicated through the percussive attack (vigor, high intensity, speed, and drive) in musical and choreographic performance; the body parts as independent instruments of percussive force that entail playing the body parts with percussive strength.

21. Albert Murray, "Improvisation and the Creative Process," in *The Jazz Cadence of American Culture*, ed. Robert O'Meally (New York: Columbia University Press, 1998), 112.

22. Savion Glover, conversation with the author, Saratoga, New York, August 5, 2001.

THE WRITING ON THE WALL

Reading Improvisation in Flamenco and Postmodern Dance

Michelle Heffner Hayes

During the rehearsal process for a work titled *Detour,* choreographer Susan Rose designed a structured improvisation for me and another company member, Kelli King. The framework for the exercise emerged in a conversation about the difficulty of representing movement through writing. In what ways does dance write? Can we use these strategies to write about dancing? How do the two systems of representation "speak to" one other? And, how does improvisation figure into the discussion? The rehearsals and performances of this work have lent me insight into this project and serve as a point of entry into my discussion of improvisation in flamenco and postmodern dance.

Fig. J1. Flamenco students in rehearsal at the University of California at Los Angeles, 2000. (Photo: Ani Nahapetian. Courtesy Liliana de Leon-Torsiello.)

THE SETTING TO WORK

"Do you have enough chalk?" Susan asks before Kelli and I take our positions for the dance to begin. I look down. My hands, as well as the rest of my body, are covered with white chalk and the black residue of paint from the wall. Constantly rubbing against its surface, I slide, roll, and crawl as I chase Kelli and mark the black surface with scrawls. The wall leaves a map of my contact with it across my knees, elbows, belly, forearms, and fingers. I have a piece of chalk about three inches long grasped between the fingers of my right hand. I wince; it's risky using such a long piece of chalk. If I'm not careful, it will break off and fly in some undetermined direction, which means I will have to look away from Kelli's dancing figure and pick up the chalk, and then return to my task of contour-drawing her form across the surface as she dances. But if the piece of chalk is too short, it will quickly rub down to my fingertips as I draw, and then I might scratch my fingernails against the chalkboard, or smudge the chalk marks I have already made to account for her continuing movement. I sigh, snap off an inch-long section of the chalk, and nod that I am ready to begin.

Kelli initiates the first phrase of her improvisation. She swings forward, and red Nikes land on the ramp that intersects with the wall. I trace the outline of her profile. She moves suddenly; pelvis and torso arrive on top of sneakered feet.

I write a thick arc to indicate the path of her torso. She slides her body up the wall to arrive standing. I flop onto my belly against the ramp and outline the shape of her legs as she stands. Knees bend; I scribble and whomp! She sends her right foot to the top of the wall. With legs extended, she grasps with both hands the top edge of the wall, and retracts her standing leg from underneath her. I'm scrambling and struggling to account for each movement a moment after its execution. She continues to move, and I make split-second decisions to trace the torso rather than the legs, or the subtle movements of her head as her body writhes and changes direction. I capture the path of the movement rather than its shape. How do I write the moments when she hangs and swings her body away from the wall, suspended by her hands? On the lowest section of the ramp attached to the wall, I trace the path of her pelvis. How about her slow slide down the wall to arrive in second position, body cast forward? I draw a thick line by dragging the side of the chalk down the ramp as I stand beneath her. I find myself imitating her movements in an attempt to remember them as I draw the last moment, translate the new image and watch as she continues to move.

What becomes clear in this juxtaposition of bodies and their activities is the space of interpretation, the moment of writing. Innumerable details of the dancing are lost. Operating under a different system of representation, the written account indicates the decisions of the dancing scribe more than the movement performed. After several runs of the piece, the black wall eventually bears a series of markings that reflect the different choices of information privileged in each moment of interpretation. Along similar lines, the many drafts I have written to account for the improvisations I have performed or watched reveal the process of making sense of the events after the fact. And, as I write, I am marked by the process in the same way that the chalk and the paint from the wall stain my skin. Rather than pose these written texts as failures to capture the danced moment, I view them as a continued dialogue within the structure of the improvisation.

A tentative definition of improvisation becomes necessary in order to consider flamenco and postmodern events in the same space. It is a cautious consideration: how do I write it so that the differences are not lost, but some similarities are emphasized? Like the scrawls on the "blackboard," improvisation is in my view a citational process. In both flamenco and postmodern traditions, the performer refers to a "map" of possible choices determined by the structure of the form. The "map" must be recognized by a community of participants in order for the improvisation to "make sense," but the "map" does not definitively mark the entire terrain. Here is the paradox of improvisation: it is neither truly spontaneous nor fully choreographed. Performers learn to make rapid compositional choices based on their knowledge of a system of meaning. These choices encourage a dialogue within the community; the other performers make decisions in response to each dancer's contribution to the work. The dialogue (danced, written, spoken, sung, drawn, or otherwise represented) among dancers and other participants in the work adds to the "map." The different layers of representation, from the vocabulary used to compose a solo to the written account of the performance, combine to form an elaborate living textile, a tradition.

The definition of "tradition" in flamenco varies from context to context. For many practitioners of flamenco, "pure" flamenco is performed exclusively by gypsies in southern Spain. For nongypsy, or non-Spanish, practitioners of flamenco, the category of "traditional" flamenco refers to the study of forms that emerged in Andalusia during the late nineteenth and early twentieth centuries. *Bulerías* (Andalusian song and dance) is standard fare for traditional flamenco performance and allows for sections of improvisation in *brazeo* (arm movements) and *zapateado* (Spanish heel-tapping dance). The gypsy style is characterized by the closeness of the arm movements to the trunk, flexed hands that press out in the space surrounding the body, and fingers that curl and unfurl in sequence. By contrast, "classical" flamenco is informed by theatrical concert dance. The shapes are more elongated and "refined," the arms expand in long ovals away from the body, the hands are not flexed, but curved, and the fingers usually move in and out of a "bird of paradise" shape, with the index fingers and thumbs touching. Performances in the gypsy style feature short improvisational solos, while "classical" or concert flamenco dance is usually fully choreographed, often for groups of dancers.

Similarly, one would be hard-pressed to categorize a single "tradition" in postmodern dance. I discuss a specific kind of structured postmodern improvisation that does not speak for all of postmodern dance, but is shaped by previous dialogues concerning movement and authenticity. Generally, scholars trace the beginnings of postmodernism to the movement improvisations of artists such as Anna Halprin, the compositional theories of Merce Cunningham, John Cage, and Robert Dunn, and performances by the Judson Church Dance Theater and the Grand Union, which took place during the period spanning the late 1950s through the 1970s. The movement practices of these artists influenced the development of Contact Improvisation in the 1970s and 1980s. Contemporary choreographers such as Susan Rose do not necessarily belong to the first generation of postmodern dancers, but postmodern concerns and methodologies contribute to the "map" of possibilities for post-postmodern improvisations. These include spontaneous decision-making in the moment of performance, movement invention based on task structures, and the blurring of the line between the performer and the spectator. The isolated examples I have chosen for examination do not exist in a vacuum; they are informed by the traditions that have generated them.

In this particular discussion of improvisation, the distinction between spontaneity and the rapid composition of movement in performance is important. I find the absence of discussion about the learning process in the dialogues surrounding improvisation troubling; any representation of improvisation as a purely spontaneous event effaces the complexity of the decision-making process in the danced moment. The written or spoken narratives that attempt to capture the evanescence of the improvisational moment often romanticize the process as "natural." The uncomplicated discussion of "nature" in the context of improvisation has alarming repercussions in representations of flamenco and postmodern dance performance.

THE AURA OF AUTHENTICITY

Improvisation is associated with virtuoso performances of flamenco. According to many flamenco purists, a fully choreographed presentation of flamenco, like those often seen in tourist venues in Spain, does not qualify as "authentic" flamenco.[1] Gypsy performers are often credited with the most "authentic" flamenco, because of their "natural" abilities. Even in a fairly recent, highly progressive scholarly work on flamenco history, James Woodall insists that gypsies possess an "innate grace." He writes, "Natural grace is, I suspect, a rare phenomena in most people's experience; when confronted with it in certain sorts of gypsy mannerisms—their posture, their gesticulation, their dress-sense—it is arresting, sometimes heady, sometimes even ridiculous."[2] This description reveals the stereotypical, and often demeaning, associations with improvisation, flamenco, and gypsies. These associations cling to the dancing figure, and affect the signficance of her performance.

Part of the lore surrounding gypsy performance of flamenco supports the contention that gypsies do not "learn" flamenco; they are born dancing and singing. In ethnographic studies such as the one conducted by Bertha Quintana and Lois Gray Floyd in 1972, practitioners insist that the gypsy child begins hearing and feeling the rhythms of flamenco in the womb: "The babies come out dancing!"[3] Matteo, in his encyclopedia of Spanish dance, features a photograph of Andalusian children accompanied by the statement, "Children on a street in Seville improvise on rhythms that come as naturally as a spontaneous ethnic expression."[4] Certainly, the complex cultural contexts in which gypsy children are introduced to flamenco are different from the professional training of flamenco dancers in other areas of Spain or the rest of the world. To suggest, however, that gypsies perform flamenco as a spontaneous expression of their blood runs dangerously close to the myth that African Americans are born with the ability to dance. It is a racist assumption that ignores the specificity of the cultural practice of flamenco. This assumption is further developed and reproduced by those flamenco artists, Spanish and non-Spanish, who insist that "true" flamenco (always the desired goal of any performance) can only be accomplished by people with a specific racial heritage.

"Nature," in the context of holistic health practices, New Age spiritualism and environmental awareness, has played an equally powerful role in the history of postmodern dance improvisation. The development of Contact Improvisation, in particular, has been punctuated by dialogue concerning the metaphysical and the improvisational event. In an early issue of *Contact Quarterly*, Steve Paxton issued a cautionary statement about the direction of the dialogue surrounding the improvisational event:

I want to go on record as being *pro-physical-sensation* in the teaching of this material. The symbolism, mysticism, psychology, spiritualism are horse-drivel. In actually teaching the stand or discussing *momentum* or *gravity*, I think each teacher should stick to *sen*sational facts. . . . Personally I think we should guard our thoughts about auras and energyfields and E.S.P. until we can actually demonstrate *and* teach such matters. *Personally*, I've never seen anything occur that was abnormal, para-physical, or extra-sensory. Personally I think we underestimate the extent of the "real."[5]

Paxton emphasizes that physical sensation as a system of information is integral to the performance of Contact Improvisation. In a similar vein, Cynthia J. Novack describes the ideal state for the improvisational performer as "the responsive body." In this state, "[p]roperties often associated with mind in American culture— intelligence, judgment, communication—and with the emotions—tenderness, expression, spontaneity—are attributed to the body, thereby blurring commonly accepted categories of aspects of a person."[6] Novack's formulation of "the responsive body" unites the Cartesian split between mind and body in a specific improvisational context. Instead of viewing this transformative, and practiced, process as a return to a previous state of innocence, these authors call attention to the recognition of a system of information employed in performance by a community of participants. The discussion of postmodern improvisation as a mindfully embodied process counteracts the tendency to locate within "the body" a calculated naïveté, a "natural" state of being that stands at odds with the "artificial" process of acculturation.

Flamenco dance and postmodern improvisation forms do not share the same cultural history. They employ different uses of movement, syntax, space, and time. The ideal body that results from the training in each area has a specific configuration of gender attributes, racial identity, and class consciousness; however, improvisation figures prominently in both movement traditions, and the ways in which movement, meaning, and virtuosity are expressed can be compared as similar negotiations of improvisational structures. My interest in discussing these decisions as intelligent, and intelligible, choices stems from my desire to recognize the articulateness of the dancing body in the moment of improvisation without opposing the body to the intellect, or the natural to the artificial. To begin to see how these decisions are informed, I turn to the spaces in which these skills are learned.

THE PRACTICE OF FLAMENCO IMPROVISATION

Classes with Antonia Rojas begin when she moves to the front of the studio, draws her torso up with a breath, and sinks into her stance. The students fall silent. We stop fiddling with the flounces of a skirt or the elastic band on a shoe, and follow her example. Antonia turns her head to the accompanist and murmurs the name of a form: *soleares*.[7] The musician strums his guitar, and plays the signature opening for the form. She claps, with *palmas sordas*,[8] a rhythmic phrase, then begins a slow, repeating pattern of *brazeo*.[9] We watch her, and our own reflections in the mirror, as we follow her movements. At first, the patterns are simple: our arms move symmetrically from the level of the hips, with fingers spiraled in flowering shapes, out to the side and then extend up to form circular frames around our watchful and expectant faces. Gradually, the patterns become more complicated, with independent pathways for each arm, sudden attacks, and slow decrescendos. Antonia introduces changes in facing for the torso and head. She watches us in the mirrors and gently encourages individuals to deepen their stances, arch their backs, keep their heads in line with the horizon, curve their arms, and lift their elbows.

The introductory section of Rojas's flamenco class demonstrates several important aspects of the determining structure for improvisation. First, it reveals the codified vocabulary from which improvisations are formed. Second, it shows how these movements are practiced in measured sequences, in partnership with musical accompaniment. Students simultaneously develop the technical mastery for producing these movements as they practice different possible combinations of them. The entire process is mediated through several frames of reference: I watch my teacher, her reflection, the other students, myself, and our reflections as I listen to the guitarists and the sound of hands clapping. The teacher's movements serve as a guide, an original sequence that is endlessly permutated throughout the classroom on different dancers' bodies. She watches, altering her decisions to serve as an example for ours.

After several minutes of uninterrupted movement, Antonia chooses one of the advanced students to take her place at the head of the class and to improvise as we follow. Usually one of the youngest takes Antonia's place. The girl grabs her skirt in her fists, and leads the group in improvised patterns of *brazeo*. During this time, Antonia walks around the room and gives corrections to the other students. She places her hands on my waist, presses in and tells me to lift up through my torso. With her fingers, she instructs me to pull together my scapulae and press up through my sternum. My head falls back when I assume this posture; she tells me to lengthen my neck and fix my eyes on a point on the horizon. I try, and I feel the muscles surrounding my spine contract. She restores the pressure around my waist. For a moment I *feel it,* the integration of activities that support the flamenco posture. She smiles, congratulates me, and moves on to another dancer. After some time, she relieves the dancer at the front of the room, whose brow and upper lip are marked with beads of sweat. Antonia leads the class in another exercise, adding footwork. She continues the practice of bringing students to the front of the room to improvise so that she can give comments to the rest of the class. By the end of the hour, we are clapping out a breathtakingly rapid *compás* for *bulerías*.[10] Each dancer performs a solo as the other dancers support him or her with their *palmas* and *jaleo*.[11]

In the second section of the class, a child stands before a group of adults as an ideal example. Her skill and experience give her an "authority" in the classroom based on her expertise, not her age. She is insulated and protected within the community of the classroom; she is encouraged to take risks. Her challenge is to lead us, but also to surprise us with unexpected changes of direction, tempo variation, and patterning of the arms. Still, her decisions fall within the codified possibilities for improvisation in flamenco. My own focus turns inward, and I have access to different possibilities, a series of repetitive movements steeped in continuous time. As a performer, I recognize an internal voice as it emerges in the dialogue of bodies, the sensation that one particular organization of effort succeeds, then is lost. The class as a whole has a narrative structure that emulates the development of the improvised solo: a few movement possibilities are introduced, repeated, combined, accelerated, and varied until the speed surpasses the realm of the possible. The limits of the structure are explored and then exhausted.

For a skillful flamenco dancer, improvisation provides the opportunity to display both mastery and abandon in performance. Even in the most spontaneous gathering of dancers who play *palmas* for one another as they trade solos, the codes for improvisation are strictly prescribed. Yet dancers find innumerable ways to play in and around, to interrupt and recombine elements of traditional flamenco vocabulary. The solo is a community event: the group provides a rhythmic foundation for the dancer's choreography; the participants shout out words of encouragement; they tease and dare the dancer to take risks in performance. The dancer can signal to speed up, slow down, dance in silence, or change rhythms, but all of these decisions depend on clear communication within the group through coded steps, gestures, or phrase lengths. The decision-making process may be spontaneous, contextually defined by the situation and the members of the group, but a successful improvisation makes sense through the invocation and subtle disruption of traditional choreographic codes.

A POSTMODERN DANCE REHEARSAL

As the "blackboard" section of *Detour* progresses, another dancer attacks the ramp, followed by another scribe. The four dancers make their way from the left side of the board to the right, as if their movements are writing. When Kelli reaches the end of the "blackboard," I toss away my chalk and draw a measuring tape out of my pocket. She performs a series of non sequitur improvised movements, and I "measure" her. As I indicate the width of her torso, the length of her spine, and the height of her raised leg, I address the imaginary audience with a "scholarly" evaluation of the dancer and her performance. "Note the width and flatness of the dancer's torso, produced by several years of ballet training." "The length of the spine is directly proportional to the span of her delicately outstretched arms." "Aha! Here we have the arabesque! Above ninety degrees, the mark of the professional dancer!" When we reach the downstage corner, we switch our focus to the "blackboard" at the back of the stage. We each study a panel and stand with our backs to the audience, waiting for the other two dancers to finish their improvisation and join us.

Once all four dancers arrive, we continue to study the individual panels until the group breathing is in unison, and the collective rise and fall of our chests determines the tempo for our march up to the black wall. We advance in a line, until we arrive at the foot of the ramp. Then, each dancer begins a phrase of movement based on the script provided by the scrawls on the black wall. These phrases travel from the wall upstage to the line of construction cones downstage, close to the audience. The movement pathway captured from the horizontal passing of bodies across the "blackboard" is fragmented and reinterpreted along the vertical corridors of the panels and the stage. I interpret the high positioning of a scrawl on the panel of the "blackboard" as a movement initiated with the head, performed in the same quality as the chalk stroke: fluid and curved, with an abrupt accent on the end. Once each dancer has finished a version of her newly composed phrase, she runs back to the "blackboard" and begins again. This time, though, the phrases must move more rapidly, while attempting to maintain the same shapes and length of lines. The newest phrases are different from before; the speed, quality, and syntax change according to the demands of the improvisational structure.

In *Detour,* the original phrases performed across the "blackboard" serve as the template for a succession of new phrases. These new phrases constantly refer back to the original material, but they also disrupt and transform it through space. In addition, when the choreographer set up the structures for this improvisation, she called attention to the process of "reading" dances. As we rehearsed the piece, the "evaluation by measuring" became more comical, almost absurd, revealing the limits of my tools to capture Kelli's movements. What the audience sees is much more than the aspects I narrate. Kelli and I have satirized the relationship between the critical gaze and the object of evaluation, suggesting that "the chase" can never capture the fullness of the movement.

The flamenco classroom and the postmodern dance rehearsal space share certain compositional and pedagogical elements. The conventions of the flamenco tradition serve as a coded structure for improvisation. They provide a vocabulary, syntax, and style for exploration. Movement segments are combined according to a specific set of rules, then embellished according to the performer's design. Similarly, in *Detour,* the structure for the improvisation is dictated by a set of predetermined rules set up by the choreographer. The performers make decisions based on the limits provided by this structure. In flamenco, the shape of the improvisational event is contained by the rhythmic structure and a dynamic of building complexity. The architecture of *Detour,* the layout of the stage and the predetermined cues for the beginnings and endings of sections, serves to limit the movement in time and space. In both cases, a single thread gives rise to innumerable responses. The teacher's example causes ripples of interpretation to move throughout the flamenco classroom, while Kelli's journey across the "blackboard," first plotted by the choreographer, creates the raw materials for successive movement sequences. The improvisational process demands a dialogue among participants in the construction of a system of information and a field of possible meanings.

Up to this point, I have discussed only one side of the paradox of improvisation, the extent to which the event is already choreographed. I have also focused on the similarities between pedagogical settings that produce flamenco and post-modern improvisations. The other side of the paradox, the spontaneity of improvisation, demands recognition. Improvisation is valued because the compositional decisions happen in the moment; therefore, it is the most authentic and the least contrived kind of dancing. These moments are immediately, and joyfully, lost. Yet, the aura of authenticity clings to representations of improvisation, taking the place of what cannot be exactly duplicated. In the words of Walter Benjamin, "Even the most perfect reproduction of a work of art is lacking in one element: its presence in time and space, its unique existence at the place where it happens to be."[12] The continuing traditions of improvisation attest to both the absence of the original event and the repeated attempts to conjure it through a community dialogue.

In flamenco, improvisation allows the opportunity for the arrival of the *duende,* the spirit of inspiration that overcomes the dancer and endows his movements with a sense of "authenticity" lacking in fully choreographed productions. The ideal setting for this kind of performance is the flamenco *juerga,* an informal gathering of musicians and dancers. According to Doris Niles, "The climax will be the emergence of *el duende.* Any dancer *en serio* [serious dancer] knows that there is nothing to compare with dancing for a select few, as this becomes your personal dance in which your emotions touch those close to you in this intimate and secluded exhibition of fine art."[13]

In his essay, "Theory and Play of the *Duende,*" first delivered at a conference before the Institución Hispanocubana de Cultura in Cuba, the poet Federico García Lorca defined *duende* as "a power, not a work; it is a struggle, not a thought."[14] Though the *duende* can inhabit the arts of any culture, Lorca maintains that "the great artists of the south of Spain, gypsies or flamencos, that sing, dance, play guitar—they know that it is not possible to have any emotion without the arrival of the *duende.*"[15] For Lorca, the *duende* seems always to invoke a sense of loss, a momentary surrender of the self in the moment and the potential eradication of the self through a proximity to death. The transformative power of the *duende* was particularly visible in the dance: "The *duende* operates on the body of the dancer like the air on sand. It converts, with magical power, a girl into a lunar paralytic, or fills with adolescent blushes a broken, old man who begs in the wine shops; it gives a woman's hair the smell of a nocturnal port, and in every moment it works on the arms with expressions that are the mothers of the dance of all time."[16]

The invocation of the *duende* within written narratives of flamenco appears as a phantasmic visitation of what is unrepresentable, the ephemeral dancing body. Upon closer examination, however, the *duende* actually functions as a means of representing the complex and intricate decision-making process of the practitioner who operates within the parameters of the tradition. The *duende* as a sign, a written representation of the unrepresentable moment within improvisational performance, again raises the following questions: In what ways does dance write? Can we use these strategies to write about dancing? How do the two systems of representation inform each other? Improvisation in flamenco constantly refers to and rewrites the structures of the tradition, preserving certain elements as inviolable while others remain flexible. The movement choices influence the narrative organization and syntax of the written description, moments of accent and subtlety. The two systems are never quite so separate as the distinct categories of writing versus dancing would imply; however, the fullness of improvisation also serves as its limit-text. It can never be repeated in dance or writing as it was specific to that moment in time. The *duende* marks that moment of simultaneous plenitude and loss.

The notion of "the responsive body" and the importance of improvisation within the history of postmodern dance speak to a similar variable, the function of the *duende*. In accounts of postmodern improvisational performances, very often artists will emphasize the importance of an intense focus, an awareness of many physical sensations and movement possibilities. Simone Forti refers to this phenomenon as the "dance state":

> Maybe I could compare it to certain meditational states, or states in which you arrive at a certain concentration and then it's not an effort to do what you're concentrating on doing, because your whole system is flowing in that direction. You're acting almost—I wouldn't say in a state of no-mind, but your system is geared to *performing*. It could be adrenalin, it could be theta waves, it could be what Castanedas writes about: a state the warrior can be into when his powers are awakened. Enchantment comes from the root *to chant*. I think of it as a musical state, a state in which the musical centers of the mind are in focus, in operation, and all your motor intelligence is blossoming.[17]

Forti's description of "the dance state" reveals the difficulty of containing and naming the moment of improvisation, "It could be . . . it could be . . . it could be. . . ." The possible analogies refer to something outside the mode of everyday existence: meditation, excitation, or the challenge of the warrior. She alludes to the intoxication of the *duende* through the use of the term "enchantment." Forti also articulates an important alignment of balance: the mind and the body are not divorced from each other in the improvisational process. The use of labels such as "the responsive body," and "the dance state" serve a function similar to the term *duende*. They indicate a heightened moment of "presence" that is specific to a single moment in time, unrepeatable in its exact configuration through dance or writing.

Despite the similarities of structure and representation in the comparison of flamenco and postmodern dance practices—the ways in which they are simultaneously choreographed and spontaneous, the modes by which they read and write themselves—the traditions differ in their evaluation of the improvisational event. The rigors of improvisation in flamenco demand that the internal structure and outer appearance of the event resemble established flamenco. Departures from the form must follow specific guidelines, or they are simply *not* flamenco. Improvisation in flamenco enervates established codes, but rarely changes those codes. While structured improvisations in postmodern dance may be strictly organized, movement invention is often recognized as an important component of the improvisation. The mark of "success" within a postmodern improvisational performance depends largely on the communication of its specific organizing principles to the intended audience. The expectations of the participants in each form are different, but both practices rely on the dialogue between performers and spectators. The exchange of information is always already at work in improvisation. A dialogue is the result of the play within a system of movement. This play happens within specific conventions, and is supported by a particular training. An informed community of participants interprets the gleeful citation of these codes, and creates or inscribes "meaning" in the performance.

The writing on the wall provides the opportunity for future improvisations based on the map of marks left behind. When we "read" the scrawls, we begin to "translate" the markings into new choreography that constantly refers to the codes of a tradition, yet manipulates them in unexpected ways. These machinations celebrate contradictions: moments of plenitude and loss, an ephemeral presence that is also concrete, and the confusion and distinction between the written and the danced. Caught up in the complex matrix of activities are mindful bodies, written by the danced event even as they perform it. The "success" of the improvisational event lies not in the capture of the "original," but in the generation of new possibilities, through community dialogue, within each performance.

NOTES

1. For a discussion of "true" flamenco versus commercial flamenco, see Madeleine Claus's "Baile Flamenco," in *Flamenco: Gypsy Dance and Music from Andalusia,* ed. Claus Schreiner (Portland, Ore.: Amadeus Press, 1990), 89–120.
2. James Woodall, *In Search of the Firedance: Spain through Flamenco* (London: Sinclair-Stevenson, 1992), 89.
3. From an interview conducted by Quintana and Floyd, in *¡Que Gitano! Gypsies of Southern Spain,* ed. George and Louise Spindler, Case Studies in Cultural Anthropology (New York: Holt, Rinehart and Winston, 1972), 94.
4. Matteo (Matteo Marcellus Vittuci) with Carola Goya, *The Language of Spanish Dance* (Norman: University of Oklahoma Press, 1990), 99.
5. In Cynthia J. Novack's *Sharing the Dance: Contact Improvisation and American Culture* (Madison: University of Wisconsin Press, 1990), 82.
6. Ibid., 185.
7. *Soleares* is a song and dance form that belongs to the category of *cante jondo* (deep song), sometimes referred to as *cante grande* (important song). It has a characteristic metrical structure of $\frac{12}{4}$, with emphasis on the beats 3, 6, 8, 10, and 12. Usually danced as a solo for a female dancer, *soleares* is marked by seriousness and, often, pathos.
8. *Palmas* serve as the rhythmic accompaniment to flamenco. Participants clap hands in time with, or against, the *compás,* the accented metrical structure of the form. *Palmas sordas* are muted handclaps, which are distinct from *palmas claras,* sharp handclaps.

9. *Brazeo* refers to the movements of the arms in flamenco, very much the same way that *port au bras* describes the patterns of arm movement in ballet.

10. *Bulerías,* like *soleares,* belongs to the category of *cante jondo* or *cante grande,* and shares the same $\frac{12}{4}$ metrical structure. Unlike *soleares, bulerías* occurs at a high speed and involves the use of footwork. It is not uncommon for a solo to change from the sober *soleares* to the fiery *bulerías.*

11. *Jaleo* is the spoken or shouted encouragement to the performer.

12. Walter Benjamin, "The Work of Art in the Age of Mechanical Reproduction," in *Illuminations* (New York: Schocken Books, 1968), 220. It could be argued that even fully choreographed productions cannot be exactly duplicated from one performance to the next; in improvisation, however, the unrepeatability of the event contributes to its value as an "authentic" object.

13. "El Duende," *Dance Perspectives* 27 (Autumn 1966): 47.

14. In "Theory and Play of the Duende," *Obras Completas* (Madrid: Aguilar, 1967), 110.

15. Ibid, 112; translation mine.

16. Ibid, 118; translation mine.

17. Simone Forti, in Sally Banes's *Terpsichore in Sneakers: Post-Modern Dance* (Middletown, Conn.: Wesleyan University Press, 1987), 35.

IMPROVISATION AS PARTICIPATORY PERFORMANCE

Egungun Masked Dancers in the Yoruba Tradition

Margaret Thompson Drewal

Scholars and dancers have pondered why Western dance critics do not write about improvisation. The reason, I suggest, is that Western viewing conventions position critics as distanced observers. As such, they have no access to the inner workings of the improvisation. Especially when viewing another culture's improvisation, the critic will not automatically understand the improvisers' techniques, codes, signifying practices, or the myriad contingencies they play out. For Western critics, the improvisation is an object of their gaze. In actuality, what they witness is an inaccessible conversation among improvisers. The pleasure of experiencing improvisation is the discovery, the frisson, of divergences and differences played out temporally against the performers' common stock of shared knowledge. To assess improvisation, the critic must share this common stock of knowledge. Thus the participant and viewer alike must be in the know.

In West Africa, where performance is participatory, that is, where there is no neat distinction between spectator and spectacle, the community shares some level of knowledge of, and competence in, performance traditions. Doing research in Yorubaland taught me the value of participation as a mode for acquiring knowledge about the give and take of improvisation. I remain a novice when it comes to the very specialized dance styles involving irregular rhythmic patterns. Nevertheless, my hosts all across Yoruba country brought me into their performances to contribute at my own level of proficiency and engage with the drummers and other dancers. In my experience, Yoruba performance practitioners do not take researchers seriously who do not show a willingness to participate. Reflecting on this experience made me aware of the need for full participation in the processes of production to learn about the poetics of improvisation, whether dance or other creative forms.

Periodically repeated, unscripted performance, including ritual, music, and dance in Africa, is improvisational. Most performers—maskers, dancers, diviners, singers, and drummers—have been trained from childhood in particular techniques enabling them to play spontaneously with learned, in-body formulas.

Fig. K1. Egungun masked dancer, village of Imewuro, Ijebu area of Yorubaland, August 1986. (Photo: M. T. Drewal. © 1986 M. T. Drewal.)

This kind of mastery distinguishes a brilliant performer from a merely competent one. Improvisation can be parodic; that is, it can signal ironic difference from the conventional or the past, a past experience, the past performance. In one Yoruba performance, for example, a woman puts on a man's garment to perform a male-style dance signaling just this kind of ironic difference from the conventional. I do not assume that improvisation derives either from the unconscious or from rational choice.[1] Rather, I propose improvisation springs from an ensemble of learned, embodied knowledges about the social world in which the improvisers operate, the techniques and skills to deploy them, and imagination.

Performance, broadly defined, is the performers' exercise of learned, embodied skills and techniques to create a particular activity, whether it be dance, music, oratory, or even sports. Performance may be a bounded event with a precise beginning and ending, such as in theater productions or basketball games. Alternatively, it can be an ongoing activity, as in the performance of everyday life, in the contingencies of people meeting and greeting each other at a very mundane level. Thus performance may be predetermined and fixed with little opportunity for improvisation, or it may be completely open-ended and highly improvisational.

What is most critical about improvisation is that the past is always already manifest in the embodied techniques that ground it; equally important, improvisation is never an exact reproduction of that past. The practices performers embody are resources, or capital, for transaction and transformation in the very process of the doing. In this way, improvisation is an interpretive strategy for negotiating the present as well as the embodiment of skills and techniques that have withstood the test of history. Improvisations are thus synthesizing practices that apply embodied knowledge to new situations. They are hybrid and nomadic.

Such synthesis is the case with improvisation among Yoruba peoples of southwestern Nigeria and southern Benin (fig. K2—map). Yoruba-speaking people number approximately twenty-five million and constitute Nigeria's second-largest language group.[2] Composed of some twenty-five distinct subgroups that extend approximately three hundred kilometers from the Atlantic coast, the Yoruba have a certain linguistic and institutional coherence, despite their cultural diversity. Improvisation, indeed, is part and parcel of all kinds of Yoruba performance. Conceptually, it is linked to the Yoruba notion of spectacle, which is different in significant ways from spectacle in Western traditions.[3] In brief, spectacles for Yoruba are otherworldly phenomena

Fig. K2. Map of Yorubaland (Courtesy M. T. Drewal)

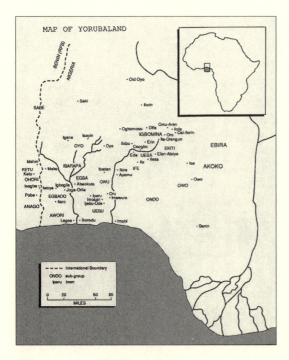

whose worldly manifestations are temporary and periodically reintroduced or re-generated. They are permanent, otherworldly dimensions of reality that, until *revealed* by knowledgeable performers, are inaccessible to human experience.

Intrinsic to the meaning of the Yoruba word for spectacle (*iran*) is repetition and transformation.[4] *Iran* derives from the verb radical *ran*. Yoruba use this root for the verb "to remember" (*ranti* [*ran eti*]) and "to recite Ifá verses" (*ranfá* [*ran Ifá*]) as well as "to send a message by way of a messenger" (*ranse* [*ran ise*]). In the latter case, the message delivered is the messenger's interpretation of the original. Each repetition is a revision of the initial material, an improvisation, if you will. The Yoruba word for a visual representation (*awòràn'*) is likewise based on the same root, as is the Yoruba term for spectator (*awòran*).

It is the role of knowledgeable performers to bring spectacle into this world periodically from its otherworldly domain so that the entire community can ex-perience and contemplate it. Thus, spectacle in the Yoruba context highlights the agency, or power, of the performers, rather than the impact of the experience on the spectator. The idea that spectacles are temporary, worldly manifestations of permanent, metaphysical realities is evident in various types of dance perform-ance, such as possession trance, during which the deities become manifest in the bodies of their priests through dance, song, and prophecy.[5] Another example of temporary manifestations of the ordinarily invisible occurs in masked dances honoring ancestral spirits known as Egungun. Their amorphous cloth forms evoke the spirit realm.

Yoruba spectacle is in many ways similar to the Western understanding of spectacle, yet maintains significant differences. Here I draw on John MacAloon's identification of four characteristics of spectacle: (1) visual sensory and symbolic codes are primary; (2) the event is grand and monumental in stature; (3) it en-genders excitement in the audience through the heightened dynamism of the performance, and (4) spectacle institutionalizes separate roles for the audience and the performers and thereby establishes distance between them.[6] There is a presumed distinction between active performers and passive spectating. Such spectacles tend to present a seamless, linear, unified representation for audience consumption.

Yoruba improvisatory performances meet all but one of MacAloon's criteria. Insofar as Yoruba spectacle is participatory, it does not divide audience and per-former into two categories of experience. Rather, participatory performance breaks down any possible differentiations between spectacle and spectator; they collapse into each other. Participants we might presume to be spectators continu-ally interrupt the performance to become part of the show, sometimes leading the dance for brief periods of time. Likewise, the Yoruba critic is part of the spectacle, never at a remove. Olabiyi Yai makes this point about oral poetry. Taking issue with dominant performance theories, he has argued,

> by portraying oral poetry [and I can easily substitute dance here] not as one moment
> in its mode of existence but as the absolute event they [scholars] unconsciously reify it

and endow it with attributes of finiteness typical of written literature. Oral poetry [dance] is thus equated with an "oeuvre" and a monument, an attitude which blocks the way for perceiving critical activities outside *the* "event." The truth is that a literary work in oral form [likewise, an improvisational dance work] is never "bounded" and that we can grasp oral criticism . . . before, during and after "performance."

He goes on to say, "we know . . . [oral tradition] by practicing it and by contributing to its making."[7] In the above quote I have substituted dance or dance work for oral poetry or literary work in oral form. Yai points to a necessary shift in critically engaging dance improvisation, and other oral forms, as ongoing production rather than individual products.

In its broadest sense, Yoruba dance expresses the vitality of existence and the well-being of the individual (*iwapele,* literally, gentle or prudent character).[8] Thus, one of the most valued traits of a Yoruba dancer is composure, registered in a highly kinetic and rhythmic lower body over which presides a calm, often expressionless face and a held head. This characteristic of Yoruba dance is what Robert Farris Thompson has called "the aesthetic of the cool."[9] For Yoruba, a collected, controlled outer appearance reflects a composed, prudent inner state. Technical proficiency combined with improvisatory flair communicates this ideal inner state. When this state begins to slip away through the rigors of the dance, a participant will likely interrupt the dance and take the dancer away to cool her down.

The stress on technical mastery and improvisation means that the formal and stylistic properties of Yoruba dances override any concern for telling a story. Indeed, taken together, rhythm and style are the primary content of Yoruba dance. Dancers performing simultaneously play with the rhythms of the music in the particular style appropriate for the dance and musical accompaniment. Their danced interpretations of the musical framework are spontaneous so that no two dancers will necessarily be doing the same steps. This is in marked contrast with traditions in Western-based choreography when there are segments of unison dancing or when unity is the primary value (as in chorus lines). Yoruba performers dancing simultaneously do not necessarily do the same steps, nor are they concerned with facing in the same direction. There is little concern for strict spatial, dynamic, or even rhythmic uniformity among dancers. What is most crucial is the communication between each dancer and the musicians and/or other bystanders within particular stylistic bounds.

Another important element of Yoruba dance is the dancers' use of cloth and clothing as a kinetic element of their performance. Dancers improvise with their cloth garments, because costuming has visual, kinetic, tactile, and audible attributes that contribute dramatically to the dances' expressive qualities. Men use their large flowing robes improvisationally to shape, texture, and punctuate the body's movement. Both masked and unmasked dancers use their cloth garments as visual and rhythmic components of the dance, suggesting the social and aesthetic importance of cloth to dance styles and movements. In one performance, for example, an elder pulled a woman from the crowd and instructed her to dance, giving her his outer garment (*agbada*) to put over her head before she began. Afterward, when I asked why, people explained that this type of dance is more appealing in men's garments. The male dancers used their voluminous flowing garments to accentuate large leg and arm gestures and twirling movements. These values also obtain in the Yoruba-derived Candomblé dances of Bahia, Brazil, as well as in Santeria in Cuba and the United States.

Another factor that makes loaning cloth for a dance culturally significant is gender. Yoruba conceive men's dancing as typically "hard," forceful, and energetic, while women's dance is typically "cool," fluid, contained, and delicate.[10] The high kicks, the large leg swings, and the percussive shoulder movements are kinetically more forceful and dramatic in loose-flowing men's robes that transform shape with each step. Tightly tied women's wrappers, on the other hand, hug the body. During dance or other kinds of activity, wrappers loosen up and begin to fall off during movement, and women are constantly retying them. These garments enhance the delicate, contained movements associated with women and the retying gestures become part of the women's dance improvisation. Thus when a woman danced this male style, the man generously offered her his garment to enhance her performance.

Yoruba dance is composed of discrete rhythmic units. Through improvisation, the dancer may elaborate, repeat, delete, or condense these units. The outer features of Yoruba dance include spatial and temporal segmentation, discontinuity, asymmetry, repetition, spontaneity, and diverse actions and dance steps performed simultaneously in the same space. The more specialized dances are also rhythmically irregular. Dancers may perform relatively simple rhythms as long as each works up to his or her own capacity; drummers respond to the level of the dancers' proficiency, either progressively increasing the complexity and sophistication of the music or simplifying it. The dancing is inseparable from drumming. In fact, the most frequently mentioned criterion for good dancers is that they understand the musical structure and phrasing of the drums and match their stepping to their staccato rhythms. One grandfather said of his dancing grandson, "He's the best dancer. In all-around course—beating, everything—he can catch everything easily—beating, stopping, all sorts of dancing. He is the best."[11] People speak of "catching" the rhythm. "Catch" is a key word here. Within the corpus of oral Ifá divination texts, there is a popular verse that concludes:

> He [made a sacrifice].
> He did not die.
> He started to dance,
> He started to rejoice.
> He started to praise his Ifá priests
> While his Ifá priests praised Ifá.
> As he opened his mouth [to sing],

He uttered forth his song to Ifá,
As he stretched his legs,
Dance caught him.[12]

The idea is that dance "catches" the dancer as the dancer begins to "catch" the nuances of the music. The Yoruba metaphor of dance "catching" the dancer, or the dancer "catching" the drumbeats, reflects the contingent and spontaneous experience of improvising. This catch-as-catch-can approach to dancing means at the same time that the dancing often appears rough and ragtag; the dancers sometimes seem off-balance. The ultimate effect of being taken over by the rhythms of the music is illustrated when bystanders (or, in one case, a masker himself) rush forth to grab captivated dancers, shut down their dancing, and pull them out of the dance arena.

I use Egungun masking in honor of the ancestors to demonstrate improvisatory dance practices. The masks manifest the spirits of ancestors. As such, the masks are nonfigurative. Their synthesis of costume and movement totally transforms the human body into an abstract kinetic sculpture (fig. K3). These masks allude to the nonhuman qualities of spirits. In their movement, the dancers strive for a more thoroughly integrated dancing image in which legs and arms are often imperceptible.

To communicate their liminal states, Egungun use altered voice qualities, wear amorphous cloth forms conceived and sewn in ways to obscure or to alter human features, carry dangerous medicines on their person that prohibit outsiders and the uninitiated from touching them out of fear of sickness or death, and perform highly stylized dances. The dance sequence I concentrate on in this essay was performed in the context of the 1986 Annual Rally to raise money to install electricity in the small Ijebu hamlet of Imewuro in southern Nigeria.[13]

There are four dances I describe: one masked and three unmasked. The unmasked dancers, however, are performing the same style of dance as the masked performers. Because of the radical difference in costuming, the dances appear different, and indeed there *are* differences in the individual interpretations of the genre and in the tempo of the music and dance. Particular attention to the relation between the dance movements and the drumming can help the viewer comprehend *how* each dancer "catches" the rhythms.

DANCE 1.   An elder in Imewuro's Egungun society dances unmasked. First, he tosses the drummers money for their accompaniment and begins to warm up as he feels his way through the music. Singing a song to cue the drummers, he begins with a slow spin shifting from foot to foot. Turning to face the camera, he folds the long cloth of his outer garment over his shoulders as he begins a low-key stepping pattern to work his way into the music. He continues slowly placing his feet on the earth in rhythm to the drums, holding the front of his cloth waist high. As he gets more into his dance, he gestures and yells for some small Egungun to get out of the way of the camera. All of a sudden, he jumps into a wide stance, knees flexed; pulls one foot in with a back flick of his right lower

Fig. K3. Egungun masked dancer performing at the Imewuro Annual Rally in an amorphous cloth costume that obscures human features to evoke the realm of ancestral spirits, village of Imewuro, Ijebu area of Yorubaland, August 1986.
(Photo: M. T. Drewal. © 1986 M. T. Drewal.)

leg, changing feet; and does a high kick forward with his left leg. The phrase does not end here, however; he immediately begins to step backward to position himself to move forward again. This time he raises each knee and crosses his foot over the midline of his body so that his hips twist back and forth, and each foot turns out just before being placed on the ground in a loose fourth position, creating a stylized walk. He finishes this sequence with another jump into a wide, parallel, second position (fig. K4), repeating the large forward kick, this time on the opposite foot. With a few quicker steps forward, punctuated by a smaller kick, he jumps high, straight up into the air six times, turning clockwise. On the

final turning jump, he lands, kicks forward across his body with a twist at the waist, and plunges right in the opposite direction into a wide stance. After several small steps to get in sync with the drums, he falls backward and repeats the large jump into second and the step kick, but this time he puts more of his body into the sequence, adding to it large twists of the hips and upper torso working in opposition. Out of this sequence, he spins, torso tilted, with little mincing steps three times clockwise, holding his cloth up and out in a disclike shape (fig. K5). He ends this spin dramatically with a high staccato right knee kick, extending his entire leg very emphatically sideways; his torso leans to the left (fig. K6). Freezing this extended, angular position in space for an instant, the dancer then breaks into some tiny mincing steps that work their way into hops forward, first on one foot, then on the other. Beginning another sequence in front of the drums, this time he combines all these movements into a more complex, irregular sequence, bringing subtle shoulder movements more forcefully to bear on the whole: jumping into wide second, high kicks forward (fig. K7) and sideways, backward hops, and spinning on one leg. Figure K7 shows the drummer and dancer carefully watching each other to coordinate the final beat of the rhythmic sequence, highlighting the contingency of their performance. The drummer's stick rebounds from the drumhead and the sound reverberates just as the dancer's high

Fig. K5. Unmasked dancer whirling with tilted torso and little mincing steps, his cloth garment held out from his body as he turns to shape the movement, Ijebu area of Yorubaland, August 1986. (Photo: M. T. Drewal. ©1986 M. T. Drewal.)

kick reaches its peak. In the next two sequences, the dancer subtly marks the rhythm: instead of hitting the final beat of the sequence with a high kick, he raises his arms high and throws them downward; the second time, his cloth flies up and over his head as he thrusts his arms down.

At this point, participants interrupt him to give him money for dancing well. Meanwhile, a man runs along the perimeter of the open space as if to draw a boundary. A drunken youth carrying a ram's skull wanders through the elder's dance space. The elder dancer continues with variations based on the movements described above. Finally, the elder pays the youth to leave, and another elder escorts the drunkard away as the dancer continues more forcefully into his improvisation. The same movements reappear with greater intensity, at the same time incorporating larger shoulder movements. I do not know the dancer's intention, but it appears he stated the basic elements of his dance during the warm-up, laid them out clearly in a couple of variations, and then concluded by combining them all in a longer, nonrepetitive sequence. His dance ends abruptly as a woman throws her arms around him and pulls him away from the open stage.

DANCE 2.   Another elder leads a young woman wearing a red head tie into the dance space. She kicks off her shoes. The audience cheers as she puts on a man's garment (*agbada*). The elder gives his garment to her so that the dance will "be good." She adjusts the garment, folding the long sleeves over her shoulders and warms up for dancing. Throwing her arms up to stop the drummers, she redirects them by singing a song that in effect dictates the dance rhythms and pivots around to survey the entire crowd around her. The woman dances what Yoruba consider to be a man's dance, with large percussive kicks across her body that turn her torso into a spiral, leg swings, and jumps, accompanied by more subtle shoulder movements. As she gets into it fully, she tosses her head tie off into the crowd. Just as her energy builds to its peak, an elder woman moves in to pull the dancer out of the dance space, but the dancer resists and persists in concluding her dance. Throwing her right arm straight up into the air, she punctuates the final beat. The crowd roars with vociferous excitement. The woman then takes off the man's garment and returns it as the audience cheers.

People begin yelling, "don't do that, don't do that." The audience's attention goes to the second story of a two-story house, from which an Egungun masker exits and drops to the ground. Another appears in the window holding a framed photograph of an ancestor, whom the Egungun honors in manifesting his spirit in expensive cloth garments. People tell him to go back. It does not appear the Egungun masker is as much at risk as the portrait of the ancestor.

Fig. K6. Ending his spin dramatically with a high emphatic kick to the side, the dancer holds this angular position for an instant before breaking into tiny steps that work their way into hops (Photo: M. T. Drewal. ©1986 M. T. Drewal.)

DANCE 3.   Meanwhile, another Egungun begins to dance. He whirls; his lappets of colorful cloth fly out on the wind. Other Egungun greet him in turn. He whirls again, first clockwise and then counterclockwise, steps, hops, and jumps, all in coordination with the drumming. A female chorus joins in with a song as the dancer and two other Egungun greet by flipping the front lappets of the costumes forward toward each other. The drummers continue to guide the dancer rhythmically as he continues to whirl, step, sway, whip his shoulders around, and jump. Finally, in a flurry, the dancer runs off into the house as a young unmasked man begins to dance.

DANCE 4.   The next sequence reveals a much more rigorous, high-energy performer unmasked. It is possible to observe more clearly the energy that animates the amorphous Egungun garments as the young unmasked man steps, spins, kicks, jumps, and thrusts his shoulders percussively forward, backward, and sideways. This time an Egungun masker grabs him to restrain his energy and pulls him off, but not before, still enveloped in the Egungun's cloth, he punctuates the last beat of the drums with a forward kick. The segment ends as Henry Drewal, the videographer, compliments the performer for having danced well. He responds with a polite acknowledgment, "eh-oh," and smiles.

Fig. K7. In the final segments of his dance, the dancer punctuates the end of the phrase with a kick over his head, maintaining eye contact with the drummer (*left*) who guides his rhythmic interpretations. (Photo: M. T. Drewal. ©1986 M. T. Drewal.)

CONCLUSION

Improvisations are difficult to recognize unless the observer is knowledgeable, that is, unless participants are familiar with the inner workings of the improvisation, the difference that marks similarity, the shared stock of performance knowledge. Each improvisational move is, in Linda Hutcheon's sense, a "formal analogue to the dialogue of past and present" in which the past is modified and imaginatively re-figured.[14] Each instance is production as opposed to bounded product. Conventional or mainstream Western theater practice, at least since the nineteenth century, has treated performance as product. It does so by maintaining a system that privileges the distanced, critical (mind's) eye of the spectator/director at the same time that it subjects the bodies of the performers as objects to his gaze.[15] Products of this sort value fixity and are thus not conducive to improvisation. In the rigid division between spectator and spectacle, the audience sits neatly in rows side by side in the dark, and the etiquette for viewing is complete silence. This arrangement positions art, what is onstage, as life's Other, where seeing (the audience's position) is associated with mind and the body under scrutiny is tidily contained onstage. The objectivist or rationalist approach to representation stresses integration, coherence, uniformity, and similarity against a background that is in actuality constituted by difference.

By contrast, improvisation features divergence, difference, and departure set off from uniformity or similarity. Improvised participatory spectacle, such as that of Yoruba people, does not set up fixed, unequal power relationships between the gazer and the object of the gaze. Rather, the participatory nature of Yoruba spectacle itself means that subject and object positions are continually in flux during performance. Participants move in and out of the action, moving at the same time between autotelic and reflexive experience. The Yoruba case provides a model that collapses distinctions between audience and performers in which participants are at the same time both spectators and spectacle. Furthermore, the roles and positions of the participants are continually in flux through improvisatory practices. It is also a model that incorporates that which remains unseen or invisible as part of its ethos. Finally it attributes agency to the performers, rather than to some disembodied eye of a distanced critic. Indeed, critique is part of the performance itself and is never removed from it. In contrast to a visualist or objectivist paradigm inherent in the distanced gaze of the critic, Yoruba dance improvisation entails the following:

1. Knowledge is produced through embodied techniques and skills in collaboratively improvising spectacle. Participants share these techniques and skills unevenly. This contrasts with forms of knowledge produced through the distanced gaze.
2. Power, according to Yoruba conceptions, is in the performer's ability "to bring things into existence," "to make things happen"; thus they fully engage themselves in the social construction of reality.
3. People understand explicitly that reality is only partially visible. Vision, or visuality, as the singularly legitimate mode of knowing in Western thought precludes our understanding any social system in which reality is constituted as much by what is not manifestly visible, but can be rendered visible through the performance of spectacle by knowledgeable performers.
4. Yoruba place value on difference, or rather repetition with infinite distinction, rather than fixity in the performance.
5. The give and take of the collaboration produces transformations and shifts, in which subjective and objective positions are continually in flux or collapse altogether. I call these fluctuations in the participants' experiences of the collaboration at hand *nomadic subjectivities*.

Egungun dance improvisation thus is open-ended, malleable, and participatory. Through collaborative, participatory practices, it signifies divergence, difference, and departure from a common stock of performance knowledge. Reciprocity in the collaboration produces fluctuations in subject and object positions. Ever changing and migratory, Yoruba improvisation engenders nomadic subjectivities.

NOTES

1. I began to articulate the issues in this paper as preceptor of the Institute for Advanced Study and Research in the African Humanities, Program of African Studies, Northwestern University, in 1995–96. The topic of inquiry for the entire academic year was improvisation in Africa. I am very grateful to the Program of African Studies for its generous support and, in particular, to Jane Guyer, its director.

I understand the unconscious and rational choice to represent two poles from which scholars have theorized human action. For recourse to the unconscious in theorizing human action, see Pierre Bourdieu's theory of *habitus,* developed farthest in Pierre Bourdieu and Loïc J. D. Wacquant, *An Invitation to Reflexive Sociology* (Chicago: University of Chicago Press, 1992). Rational choice theory has been popular in economics and political science to explain microeconomics. See, for example, Anthony Giddens and Jonathan Turner, *Social Theory Today* (Stanford: Stanford University Press, 1987), 78. Neither of these scientific theories of human behavior can deal adequately with dance improvisation, or with any kind of improvisation for that matter. Both imply certain constraints or the imposition of structures that do not necessarily hold for collaborative processes at once indeterminate in their very constitution, but based in the practical, embodied skills and techniques that define knowledgeable performers.

2. Rowland Abiodun, "The Future of African Art Studies: An African Perspective," in *African Art Studies: The State of the Disciplilne, Papers Presented at a Symposium Organized by the National Museum of African Art, Smithsonian Institution, September 16, 1987* (Washington, D.C.: National Museum of African Art, 1990), 64.

3. I have discussed the Yoruba idea of spectacle (*iran*) elsewhere; see Margaret Thompson Drewal, *Yoruba Ritual: Performers, Play, Agency* (Bloomington: Indiana University Press, 1992), 13–15.

4. This discussion is based on information provided by linguist Olabiyi Yai, Department of African Languages and Literature, University of Florida, personal communication, 1990.

5. See, for example, Margaret Thompson Drewal, "Dancing for Ogun in Yorubaland and Brazil," in *Africa's Ogun: Old World and New,* ed. Sandra Barnes (Bloomington: Indiana University Press, 1989), 199–234.

6. John J. MacAloon, "Olympic Games and the Theory of Spectacle in Modern Societies," in *Rite, Drama, Festival, Spectacle: Rehearsals Toward a Theory of Cultural Performance,* ed. John J. MacAloon (Philadelphia: ISHI, 1984), 243–44; for further analysis of the ideology and politics of spectacle in the Western tradition, see Margaret Thompson Drewal, "From Rocky's Rockettes to Liberace: The Politics of Representation in the Heart of Corporate Capitalism," *Journal of American Culture* 10, no. 2 (1987): 67–80.

7. Olabiyi Yai, "Issues in Oral Poetry: Criticism, Teaching and Translation," in *Discourse and Its Disguises: The Interpretation of African Oral Texts,* ed. Karen Barber and P. F. de Moraes Farias, Birmingham University African Studies Series 1 (Birmingham: Centre of West African Studies, University of Birmingham, 1989): 63 and 68.

8. Rowland Abiodun, "Identity and the Artistic Process in the Yoruba Aesthetic Concept of Iwa," *Journal of Cultures and Ideas* 1, no. 1 (1983): 16.

9. Robert Farris Thompson, "The Aesthetic of the Cool: West African Dance," *African Forum* 2, no. 2 (1966): 85–102.

10. I have elaborated on this dimension elsewhere; see Henry John Drewal and Margaret Thompson Drewal, *Gelede: Art and Female Power among the Yoruba* (Bloomington: Indiana University Press, 1983), 136–51. These contrasts between male and female dance styles parallel the construction of the gender of Yoruba deities, and their respective dance styles, although female deities may take on male characteristics, such as aggressiveness and volatility and certain male deities may manifest gentleness and calmness. See Omófolábò S. Àjàyí, *Yoruba Dance: The Semiotics of Movement and Body Attitude in a Nigerian Culture* (Trenton, N.J.: Africa World Press, 1998), 38–39.

11. Unidentified Egungun elder attending the Imewuro Annual Rally. (Field video footage record no. 86.13, village of Imewuro, Ijebu area, Wednesday, August 27, 1986.)

12. 'Wande Abimbola, *Ifa: An Exposition of Ifa Literary Corpus* (Oxford: Oxford University Press, 1976), 61–62.

13. I have written on the circumstances that initiated the rally and its history in some detail in my *Yoruba Ritual: Performers, Play, Agency,* 160–71. For those who would like more detailed sociological and historical information on the Egungun society in Yorubaland, see "Egungun Bibliography" in *African Arts,* special issue, 11, no. 3 (April 1978): 97–98.

14. Linda Hutcheon, *A Poetics of Postmodernism: History, Theory, Fiction* (New York: Routledge, 1988), 25.

15. Recently, there has been much written critiquing occularcentrism and objectivism in Western thought and practice, primarily by philosophers and social scientists concerned with issues of gender, sexuality, class, hegemony, and ideology. See, for example, Michel Foucault, *Discipline & Punish: The Birth of the Prison* (New York: Vintage Books, 1979); Susan Buck-Morss, *The Dialectics of Seeing: Walter Benjamin and the Arcades Project* (Cambridge: MIT Press, 1989); Renato Rosaldo, *Culture & Truth: The Remaking of Social Analysis* (Boston: Beacon, 1989); Randy Martin, *Performance as Political Act: The Embodied Self* (New York: Bergin and Garvey, 1990); Martin Jay, *Downcast Eyes: The Denigration of Vision in Twentieth-Century French Thought* (Berkeley and Los Angeles: University of California Press, 1993); David Michael Levin, ed., *Modernity and the Hegemony of Vision* (Berkeley and Los Angeles: University of California Press, 1993); Rosalyn Diprose, *The Bodies of Women: Ethics, Embodiment and Sexual Difference* (London: Routledge, 1994); Elizabeth Grosz, *Volatile Bodies: Toward a Corporeal Feminism* (Bloomington: Indiana University Press, 1994); and David Halperin, *Saint-Foucault: Towards a Gay Hagiography* (New York: Oxford University Press, 1995), among many others.

AGAINST IMPROVISATION

A Postmodernist Makes the Case for Choreography

Victoria Marks

I often find myself in the position of defending choreography, whether to dancers who improvise, or to myself at moments of choreographic self-doubt. Why would anyone want to spend long hours in the studio choosing between using a straight arm and a bent one, a right leg or a left, when either choice would do? Each time I face this argument, however, I come to the conclusion that I place great value on being an author who stands in the wings while other people do the dancing—an impossibility for an improviser—and that I like studying the way meaning is affected when one makes carefully predetermined choices about what happens onstage. To be honest, and precise, I do not actually care whether something is on the right or on the left, or if it goes inside or outside. Not unless it affects meaning. And then I care a lot. Which is why, at the outset of this essay, I admit that when confronted with the option of improvising or choreographing, I choose to choreograph.

Recently, in the studio, some dancers I was working with spoke about how much they preferred improvising to setting material, and I immediately wondered if this was because improvising offers immediate gratification whereas choreography implies a long-term relationship. To choreograph, you must already be holding in your mind the thought that this thing you're making will be part of something that will go on for a while, and that eventually and *only* eventually will it be apprehended by an audience. This extended commitment is what I aspire to. It is very rare that one comes across a performed improvisation that can control this much material, or whose dancers can think in such large terms.

This is not to say that I am against improvisation entirely. In fact—true confession—when composing a dance I actually start with improvisation. I use it as a kind of net, spreading it wide, watchful for what I might catch. The improvisation is the place for things to happen between people, or between the dancers and the dance. It is a way to discover what the dance will be about. The dance is found in between the people, in the moment, and often in the places where I least expect to find it. It is not ever performed as an improvisation, however. Before I present the work, it has been transformed into carefully worked and reworked choreography, down to the smallest details. That is the way I like it.

Fig. L1. Becky Bryant and Steve Bryant in *Fathers and Daughters*, 1999, choreography by Victoria Marks. (Photo: Carol Petersen. © 2000 Carol Petersen. Printed with permission.)

I started making dances in the early 1980s, approaching dance making with a twenty-something's urge for pure movement. At that time, choreographed dances purred out of me. Working intuitively from a combined emotional and kinetic source, I usually discovered much later what I was dancing about. I simply exalted in the sensuality of moving and the ability to make choices about action. Like a gold miner I would work until I found something that stood out from the rest. The next day and the days after, I would return to my little gems, to "polish" and embellish my finds. It wasn't meaning I was concerned with, but the experience of doing, of finding new orchestrations of motion in my body.

The desire to find new ways of moving and to disturb my habitual patterns soon led me to a workshop with Sara Rudner that required us to compose "on the spot." A postmodernist, Rudner goaded us to expose intuitively made movement phrases to mathematical and kinetic challenges. These composing "procedures" allowed a world of new movement possibilities to unfold. (My favorite was to attempt to do two very different movement sequences fully and at the same time.) I liked the way these processes required diligence and thorough investigation, and that, because they required every cell in my brain to be on full duty, there was little room for worrying if the resulting movement wasn't pretty. I was hugely interested in the kinetic and visual surprises the work yielded.

In my own subsequent rehearsals, rather than attempt to teach the results of my efforts to others, I learned to create movement procedures for my dancers to work through. I created recipes for the dancers to follow and reveled in the results, which were fascinating combinations of similarity and dissimilarity, counterpoints and cross images. These procedures were the early antecedents of improvisation in my choreographic process. It was here that I began to value the surrender of control and planning to the here and now of a creative process.

Gradually, my interest in the sheer sensuality of dancing gave way to a curiosity about the way dances conjure meaning. During the 1980s I formed a small company whose dancers had an especially large appetite for movement. Though I greatly appreciated their virtuosity, I wanted to move away from the anonymity of their excellence, away from the disguise of contemporary dance, so as to reveal each individual and the particular contributions each dancer made toward process. In *Dick* (1986), for example, I asked company members to put themselves on the line by engaging with a challenge greater than that of dancing: to locate themselves, personally, in relationship to an issue (in this case, the bravura of war) and within that the connections between physical aggression and desire. My own interest in making dances that take an activist or political position created unrest among some of my company members, but I soldiered on. My instructions for the creation of *Dick* went something like this:

> Could the two of you work with force together? Try pushing against one another, as if to send each other back to the wall. Can you try to find a handhold that allows you to push harder? And if you play with lessening the force . . . yes, like that, but keep searching for a handhold . . . . You know this is starting to look like an embrace. Could you do it again, starting with as much force as you can muster and allowing it

to dissipate or become rarified? As your physical connection becomes softer, would it be okay to kiss?

I think the dancers loved this piece. And I did too. Afterward I couldn't go back to making work that was just about dancing. It wasn't the kiss, it was the process, and I began to feel that I was onto something. Gradually I ceased working with a coherent regular group of individuals in favor of being a "freelance" choreographer. *Dick* had served as a choreographic turning point for me, as I moved away from a studio process engaging movement procedures and toward the use of improvisation as a way of letting the dance unfold.

During the same period that I worked with my first company, I enjoyed a regular relationship with a group of high school girls through an after-school dance program in Eastchester, New York. Each year, during a three-day retreat, we addressed identity issues that the girls were confronting. And each year, in response to these issues, the girls learned how to improvise so that they might find voice and address one another body to body. It was at this time that I began to discover improvisation as a way of making a place for nonverbal discussion. These improvisations also served as groundwork for choreographed as well as improvisational performances. For example, I would say:

> We're going to play follow the leader and anyone can be a leader. You may also be a follower if you choose. Work on making swift and invisible choices between following and leading. (*After some time.*) How many leaders can we have before the improvisation becomes too chaotic? (*A little later.*) Notice if you have a preference for leading or for following.

This interchange might be followed by a discussion with the girls about social issues related to standing out and disappearing, passivity and agency (without assuming that following in the improvisation meant passivity), and the perils of cliques.

In 1993 and again in 1994, I had the opportunity to make dances for the camera with film director Margaret Williams for national broadcast in the United Kingdom. The first project was a collaboration with CandoCo, an integrated mixed-ability company, and the second, a film for mothers and daughters. It was in the making of these pieces that I realized that I was most fascinated when simply getting to know the people I was working with; I wanted to "represent" people through a dance in ways that challenge conventional representations of performers. I began to situate my work outside the confines of a typical dance audience, working toward greater accessibility and toward the possibility of participating in a larger social discourse. From this and other choreographic experiences I learned that dancing was never only about dancing; it was never neutral and always rich with meaning.

I particularly noticed the way movement began to sing, sometimes just because one had information about who was doing the moving. For example, it makes a great deal of difference to know that a real mother and daughter are dancing together. I don't believe that the same set of meanings could be generated if the dancers were unrelated trained actors performing a relationship. It is not that I am against acting. I am the first to take the imaginative leap of faith that theater often asks of us. But to me, when a mother and daughter are dancing a piece made for them, I get a thrill knowing that a real, and not imaginary, transaction is taking place for the two on stage. We are then not only audience members, but witnesses as well. From this point, I began to think of my choreographic process as one of portraiture, with a large debt to the revelatory processes made possible by improvisation. Here began my utter reliance on improvisational structures as a means of locating the material for a dance.

These days I cling to improvisation, even in the face of my choreographic proclivities, because it is a place of discovery. I do not walk into a room knowing what a dance will be about, but instead allow it to be discovered in the underbelly of the rehearsal process. In fact, it seems that my dances are about who we are and what we bring with us as we go into a studio to work. I also like the fact that improvisation offers the performers an opportunity to stay in dialogue with me, to exercise agency, to plunge forward into the stuff they find most engaging. For me, it also relieves enormous pressure: it doesn't matter so much what I do; if nothing interesting happens, the whole thing is disposable. I can throw out the day's work and try another improvisation score on the morrow. But that is seldom necessary. I find that things spring to life in the studio when dancers begin to improvise, and I consciously try to set improvisational structures that allow us to come upon ourselves in surprising ways. I work to create a kinetic situation where something unexpected will be revealed, where we will "give away" who we are as we work together. I find that one can go to risky places in the context of an improvisation, in part because it is a disappearing act.

For unaccustomed movers, who are not used to memorizing movement, it is important that the dance be easy to remember. From improvisations, a sequence grows that comes out of the original logic and reality of relationship. These are not decorative embroideries, but homespun stories based on real relationships. These, for example, are improvisations that led to a set of dances titled *Fathers and Daughters:*

> You are the leader, and you, the follower. Could you initiate actions, shape the body of your partner, much like a sculptor works with his material? Let's swap roles. Let's work so that either of you can initiate and "sculpt" the other's actions. Let's add that that you can either be receptive or not. You can "argue" with your partner's suggestion.

> Let's play a game in which you simply stand in these places, across from each other. You can either look at your partner or look away. You can turn, but you cannot travel off these spots. Take as much time as you want in any one place.

> If you could map out your lives together, as if this stage were a road map, where would it begin? And what happens along that map?

When I ask the dancers to repeat something they've just done, I say, "Do you remember what happened? Let's try to go back and have that happen again." In this way, initially, we are talking not so much about the physical details of what and where and when, as we are about the internal experience of an event, the "eventness" of what happened. Gradually we (the performers and the choreographer) make an equation between an analysis of action and the richer (and more difficult to articulate) sensory, emotional, relational experience that those actions have yielded. For me, one cannot exist without the other. "Feeling" has quantifiable correlates in action.

In creating portraits, it is essential that the performers participate in, if not direct, the fashioning of their own representation. That said, I think of a piece of choreography as an inquiry. I peel back layers to burrow under the surface and find provocative contradictions. At the same time, I recognize how delicate this process is, especially as we work to push the edges of our comfort zones, my own and those of the performers. What would be the point of making a dance that felt comfortable?

The father looked as though he had been an athlete. He said he'd been a wrestler in college. I asked if he and his daughter had ever played or wrestled together. I asked them to show me what it had been like. I taught them a command sequence, "Go! Stop! Go back (repeat)! Slow motion!" so that either one could shout instructions to the other as they wrestled. When a command was shouted, it either served to lead the dancers further into or out of intimate or uncomfortable places. Saying "slow motion" caused the two to embrace as though locked in a wrestling-match takedown, tracing a path, usually downward toward the floor, but softly and with a sense of endless time. Somehow for this father and daughter, wrestling made room for a dance about the threat of imminent separation, about more affection than either of them could manage, and about the way it feels to lie back, trusting one's weight to another's arms.

I notice that such things are never the same when you go back and do them again. A choreographed dance is a living thing. It is a place where things happen. When you are dancing, if you are alive, you are improvising. You can make choices and observe the way the dance is different this time, than ever before. A dance is like a house. It's a place in which things happen. You can go back to the house, but you can't occupy it in the same way you did earlier.

I maintain that a piece of choreography gathers substance over time as the immediate gratification of improvised dancing gives way to repetition and detail, thoughts about parts and pieces, and the way it will conjure meaning for an audience. I like laboring over a moment and a connection. It is as if I could fix things, reorganize the world, change myself, and make a more perfectly imperfect place. Of course all dancing, improvised or choreographed, goes away. Perhaps it is this conundrum, of honing something that will shortly and most assuredly disappear, that I treasure most. Especially in a time of change, in a time when people, places, and things disappear too quickly, I want to choreograph so that, for even a brief moment, I can find something, anything, to hold on to.

MULTIPLE PLEASURES

Improvisation in *Bharatanatyam*

Avanthi Meduri

The phenomenon of improvisation in *Bharatanatyam,* a form of South Indian classical dance, is epitomized in the expressive unit known as *padam,* which is embedded within the seven-part repertoire of the traditional *Bharatanatyam* recital. Perhaps the greatest exponent of the *padam* in this century has been T. Balasaraswati, a legendary dancer admired by both Western and Indian dance critics. For me, having been immersed in the learning of *Bharatanatyam* from childhood, Balasaraswati manifests herself not just as a great dancer but as the polar star of Indian dance history itself. I shall discuss here Balasaraswati's improvisations as realized in the *padam* and show how her improvisations do not break with the received tradition of *Bharatanatyam* but actually build upon and extend the traditional form. Improvisation in the *padam,* then, can be described as a codified, paradoxical phenomenon in which the dancer negotiates her artistic freedom from within traditional parameters. The dancer, in other words, is not stepping out of or rejecting tradition, but rather engaging with it creatively.

The *padam* is a lyrical, poetic, melodic composition sung in a leisurely manner. In any given rendition of the *padam,* the female dancer draws upon the text verses of the *padam* composition and revisualizes the textual composition. The dancer does this by amplifying and explaining the text lines with the help of mimetic expression known as *abhinaya.* The poetic composition is also explicated with the help of *mudras* or codified hand gestures constituting the rudimentary alphabet of the nuanced language of *Bharatanatyam.* The poetic text of the *padam* is repeated again and again and serves as a vehicle for the creation and realization of an emotive mood brought forth and visualized through embodied *abhinaya* or mimetic expression. The mood of the *padam* is usually that of love, but it is love expressed in its myriad, changing, nuanced dimensions and endorsed by the spectator able to revel in the cascading shades of emotion dramatized in the piece.

Balasaraswati was particularly celebrated for her rendition of the *padam* known as *Krishna ne begane baro.* The opening text phrase, "Krishna, hurry into

Fig. M1. T. Balasaraswati, 1974. (© Jan Steward.)

my embrace," is repeated numerous times. Yet each rendition of the opening text phrase is interpreted differently by the dancer. While the words of the text remain the same, "Krishna, hurry into my embrace," the dancer attempts appropriate gestural variations, and thus elaborates on the thematic sentence. Now her eyes plead with Krishna—suddenly she is angry! She coaxes, she rejects, she punishes, thus embellishing and developing on the thematic phrase. Balasaraswati, critics tell us, was not only a consummate actress; she was also able to imagine infinite variations of a single poetic text phrase, especially in *Krishna ne begane baro*. Indian critics also tell us that Balasaraswati did not re-present a rehearsed *padam* but actually improvised her variations extemporaneously.

Even Western choreographers such as Merce Cunningham, Martha Graham, and Ted Shawn apparently came under her artistic spell and were moved by Balasaraswati's rendition of *Krishna ne begane baro*. Narayana Menon, a well-known dance scholar and impresario, tells us that Balasaraswati performed this dance in her Edinburgh concert recitals of 1963. On that tour, she offered eight recitals, all of them to sold-out houses.

> Merce Cunningham, the great avant-garde dancer and choreographer, who has little respect for "traditional" forms, said that watching Bala was one of the great experiences of his life. Ted Shawn described her performance at Jacob's Pillow festival as a "unique experience" and said at the end of the performance: "You are in the presence of greatness. Tonight has been a historic night." Martha Graham came under her spell the first time she saw her dance. At the end of one of her first recitals at the Edinburgh Festival, one of the most eminent dance critics of Europe whose review appeared on the center page of one of the leading newspapers, started his piece with the words: "Krishna came." The reference of course was to her rendering of *Krishna ne begane baro*.[1]

Balasaraswati was, in fact, monumentalized for her rendition of this *padam*. After her landmark 1963 performances in the United States, she and her family of musicians were offered teaching residencies in Western universities, and they lived in the United States for long periods of time. Balasaraswati passed away in 1984, but her dancing grandson continues to live in the United States, and her students keep the memory of her artistic practice alive here. A film version of *Krishna ne begane baro,* which catapulted Balasaraswati on to the international stage, is archived at Wesleyan University.[2] Another version of this *padam* is also preserved in the documentary film entitled *Bala,* which is available in the National Archives in India.[3] Directed by renowned Indian film director Satyajit Ray in 1976 and sponsored by the Government of Madras and National Center for the Performing Arts, the documentary film is used as research material in the world arts and cultures department at the University of California, Los Angeles, and in the dance department at the University of California at Riverside. As a video version of the documentary film is available for viewing here in the United States, I shall refer to it and critique it later in this essay. But first, I shall situate the *padam* within its performative milieu, describe how it is performed, and show how integral it is to the *Bharatanatyam* concert repertoire.

PADAM IN PERFORMANCE CONTEXT

In live performances or concerts of *Bharatanatyam* presented in metropolitan cities in India and in the United States, the dancer is usually accompanied by a musical ensemble comprising a singer, percussionist, flutist, violinist, and *nattuvanar* (one who keeps time). The ensemble is seated on the right side of the dancer facing the audience, framing the stage-right portion of the proscenium stage. The accompanying ensemble is usually male, but the dance itself was traditionally performed exclusively by women dancers, known as *devadasis*. The *devadasis* were symbolically married to temple gods and performed their dancing as part of the ritual service of the Hindu temple. According to Balasaraswati, women traditionally performed the dance because the dynamic power of the self (*Sakti*) is itself always considered to be feminine and its static source is masculine.[4] While it is true that men perform *Bharatanatyam* today, I believe the dance is better suited to women: in its ideal form it represents the yearning of the woman dancer for self-completion with godhead—Krishna, Vishnu, Shiva—conceived in male metaphors.

The seven-part structural sequencing of the *Bharatanatyam* concert repertoire underscores the spiritual aspirations of the dance mentioned above. The traditional *Bharatanatyam* concert begins, for instance, with the invocation known as *allarippu,* an item of pure rhythm, followed by *jatiswaram,* in which there is the added joy of melody. This is followed by *sabdam,* a composition with words, then by *varnam, padam, tillana,* and *sloka.* Balasaraswati describes the structural format of the *Bharatanatyam* recital as follows:

> The *Bharatanatyam* recital is structured like a Great Temple: we enter through the *gopuram* (outer hall) of *alarippu,* cross the *ardhamandapam* (half-way hall) of *jatiswaram,* then the *Mandapam* (great hall) of *sabdam* and enter the holy precinct of the deity in the *varnam.* This is the space which gives the dancer expansive scope to revel in the music, rhythm and moods of the dance . . . *padas* now follow. In dancing to *padas,* one experiences the containment, cool and quiet, of entering the sanctum from its external precincts. The expanse and brilliance of the outer corridors disappear in the dark inner sanctum; and the rhythmic virtuosities of the *varnam* yield to the soul-stirring music and *abhinaya* of the *padam.* Dancing to the *padam* is akin to the juncture when the cascading lights of worship are withdrawn and the drum beats die down to the simple chanting of the sacred verses in the closeness of god.[5]

PADAM AND ITS RELATIONSHIP TO MUSIC, RHYTHM, AND POETIC TEXT

The *padam* is performed after the intermission, and is featured as an important piece in the second part of the concert recital. Having experienced the rhythmic elaborations and intricate metric patterning of the first half of the concert, the spectator is ready to let go and relax his mind in the second. The slow cadences of the *padam* emerge as if from the wings of the proscenium stage and begin to play on the spectator's imagination. But it is, in fact, the singer seated on the stage who is actually rendering the opening text line of the *padam.* Still, the spectator is confused because the dancer emerging from the wings appears to be singing the song rendered in fact by the singer seated on the proscenium stage. The ensemble then joins the singer and the dancer, and all prepare to embark on a creative adventure: interpreting the opening text line.

While some in the audience might perceive the dancer as taking her cue from the singer or from the melody of the text line, others might perceive the singer as taking her cue from the dancer. It is, in fact difficult to identify the agent or subject in the dancer-singer dialectic, or to separate one from the other: in the words of Balasaraswati again, the *padam* in its "highest moments, is the embodiment of music in visual form, a ceremony and an act of devotion. For more than a thousand years, the *shastras* (rules) have confirmed that an individual dedicated to dance must be equally dedicated to music and must receive training in both the arts."[6] The dancer thus is singing the melodic line and rehearsing the song in her mind even as she is embodying the text line with the help of *mudras* and mimetic expression. According to Balasaraswati,

> Only if the artist is a true musician and enters into the spirit of the song through the music, can she interpret the song to perfection by simply keeping the movement of her hands and eyes in consonance with the ups and downs, the curves and glides, pauses and frills in the melody, irrespective of the actual words of the song but in keeping with the dialogue that she has gesturally woven around them.[7]

The dancer's mimetic expression and her hand gestures, in other words, fold into the cadences of the melody and rhythm and lose their singularity and distinctiveness. An intricate dialogue has been forged between dancer and singer, between song and *abhinaya,* facilitating the misrecognition of the one in the place of the other.

The percussionist and other musicians now join the singer/dancer in collaboration. They do so as if without cue and proceed to amplify and embellish the text line, each in his own way. Thus begins the phenomenon of simultaneous improvisations: the innovations or elaborations begin to take shape in the musical, rhythmic *(tala),* emotive *(bhava),* and melodic *(raga)* registers of the performance. Balasaraswati writes: "for the perfect evocation of *rasa* or aesthetic satisfaction, all three performative elements must be kept in balance."[8] Although the *tala* (percussion) provides a strong and steady backbone, for the collaboration, it is undoubtedly the *raga-bhava* (melody/emotion) combination that evokes *rasa* or aesthetic satisfaction, both in the spectator and dancer. We should never forget, says Balasaraswati, "that in deriving *bhava-raga-tala* from the component syllables of *Bharatanatyam,* there is an underlying concept of the equality of these three elements."[9] (One of the several explanations for the name of this dance form is that *Bharata* derives from the amalgamation of the initial letters of *bhava, raga,* and *tala.*) With the percussionist and other musicians joining in the artistic collaboration, the *padam* gathers momentum and begins to integrate itself at the multiple levels of gesture, emotion, melody, and rhythm. Integration of sound with emotion, gesture with rhythm is profoundly cathartic; it helps unify, extend, and expand the consciousness of the spectator. In the ensuing state of expanded creativity, the ensemble members begin to improvise one with the other.

It is the repetition of the poetic text line, the phenomenon of spontaneous or multiple improvisations being shaped in the *padam,* that creates the conditions for a unique kind of catharsis or enjoyment. In any given live performance of the *padam,* the opening text line is repeated at least twenty times (not so in the truncated version of the *padam* presented in the Bala documentary, where the opening line is repeated seven times). But it is, in fact, the repetition of the text line, returning differently in each repetition, embellished now by percussionist, then by singer, and then again by dancer, that creates the hypnotic effect that is achieved in any successful rendition of the *padam.* While the poetic text merely reiterates the phrase, "Krishna, hurry into my embrace," the dancer has the freedom to interpret that text phrase in a variety of ways. She could, for instance, describe how Krishna was conceived, or describe his amorous escapades with the women of Brindavan. *Krishna ne begane baro* can be interpreted erotically, that is, as a woman seducing Krishna, or can be explicated as Balasaraswati does in the documentary film, as a composition embodying maternal love. The poetic text remains the same in any given rendition of the *padam.* Yet the textual composition does not dominate or overwhelm the performance. Instead, it facilitates numerous kinds of interpretations, and structures the improvisational process taking shape in the visual, aural, and embodied registers of the live performance.

TEXT AS CRYSTAL BALL

To understand the uniqueness of this kind of improvisation, we might begin by conceiving the poetic text through the metaphor of a many-splendored crystal ball that the dancer examines by using hand gestures, eye movement, mimetic expression, dance movement, and emotive feeling. The dancer takes the crystal ball in her hands, examines it, and throws it playfully into the lap of the accompanying musicians. What we have here is a subtle code, signaling that the dancer is ready to play the ball game. All who desire to play the ball game must keep their eyes focused on the invisible ball, the textual and/or poetic composition. They have to watch it travel from musician to dancer, to percussionist, and back again. While the poetic text is the constant unit in the dance recital, shared by dancer, singer, and accompanists, it is also the most dynamic and fluid unit in the performance. All members of the ensemble can improvise and play with the crystal ball, but they all equally share the collective responsibility of not letting the poetic text or crystal ball disappear from the spectator's imagination. All must, in other words, return to the text phrase, *Krishna ne begane baro,* the structuring and unifying theme of the piece. In the words of Balasaraswati, "while the dancer is gesturally enacting monologues and dialogues that are far removed from the actual words of the song, she must keep repeating the actual words of the song text. That is, whereas she is gesturing a myriad of changing moods and environments, she must vocally adhere to the same changing phrases in the text."[10]

What the *padam* offers then is the experience of innovations that take shape in the musical, rhythmic, and visual registers of the performance all at once. It is perhaps because the *padam* offers this experience of simultaneity (what I describe as "the return of the different in the structural tract of the same") that Balasaraswati described the *padam* as the pinnacle of the *Bharatanatyam* technique. It is the one item in the *Bharatanatyam* repertoire in which we see musicians forging a dynamic relationship with the dancer, in which textual composition is linked with embodied gesture, movement, emotional expression, and musical improvisations.

PADAM AND AUDIENCE APPRECIATION

The slippery, interlocking kinds of improvisations taking shape in the *padam* pose some interesting questions in terms of audience appreciation. The informed spectator/listener is undoubtedly compelled by the nuances in the improvisational process, and is called into the piece. Yet the spectator seems unable to describe precisely the shape of this artistic phenomenon even as it impinges on her consciousness. The spectator is hard-pressed to objectify the experience as the innovations are being enunciated by the singer, the musical accompanists, percussionists, and/or by the gestures and moods that the dancer portrays, all at once. Is the dancer's body supplementing the text, or is the singer's rendition of the text line supplementing the dancing body? Where, in fact, is the dancing body? Is the body residing in the textual composition or in the gestural language of the dance? The spectator/listener is confused, unable to speak about the experience or objectify it; she is in the flow of the experience, somewhat like a syncopated beginning. The spectator is participating in an artistic phenomenon that delivers satisfaction to only that singular person who is willing and able to play the ball game. This implies, of course, that the spectator cannot assume a detached, distanced position while watching. The spectator has to enter the performance and the improvisational process, play by the rules of the game, and recognize the codes of the different improvisations being shaped in the multiple registers of the performance. The spectator, in other words, must consent to being located inside the frames of the performance and not outside them.

WHERE IS THE CRYSTAL BALL?

The trained spectator/listener watching or listening to the unfolding of the *padam* has learned to enter the piece and to hear, see, feel, and participate in the subtle innovations taking shape in the multiple registers of the *padam*. He has learned to follow the trail of the invisible text (which I have referred to metaphorically as the crystal ball, one that is passed among singer, dancer, and musician). Yet the spectator is unable to give voice to his experience of the *padam* because in every act of repetition priority was given over either to the percussionist, singer, or dancer. In other words, the spectator is unable to articulate precisely who has the crystal ball, who is passing it, from where, to whom, and where the ball is at any given moment in the elaboration of a *padam*.

The dancer, on her part, experiences the same perplexity. She, too, is on the trail of the invisible text line that is now with her and then suddenly in the hands of the singer who is embellishing it. The dancer, like the spectator, is unable to mark the initial moment of her innovations, to inhabit that place, and to name or claim it as her own. Perhaps that is why Balasaraswati chose not to speak of her artistic elaborations as improvisations but rather as imaginative embellishments that were coterminous and continuous with the traditional repertoire. Balasaraswati was unable to name her improvisations as such because they were embedded deeply within the folds of traditional form, linking mimetic expression with traditional gesture, with text, with melody, and with rhythm. Balasaraswati's artistic body, her embodied gesture, her mimetic expression, were always already in motion, and always already being modified.

Having discussed the traditional template of the *padam* and its improvisational process, I shall now examine Balasaraswati's truncated rendition of the "Krishna" *padam* visualized for us in Satyajit Ray's documentary film entitled *Bala.* We shall see how and in what ways the film version falls short of the live re-presentation of the *padam* as performed on the concert stage.

THE DOCUMENTARY VERSION OF BALA'S *PADAM*

In the documentary *Bala,* a male narrative voice guides the viewer and sets the context for the unfolding of the piece. The male narrator, speaking in the English language, describes the *padam* as one of the most beautiful pieces in Bala's repertoire, one that displays both her singing and mimetic accomplishments. The narrative voice tells us that the piece is a song about the childhood of the god Krishna. Krishna has strayed from home and Balasaraswati, impersonating Krishna's mother, Yeshoda, implores her god-child to come back. Immediately after this brief introduction the camera cuts to an image of Balasaraswati photographed against the backdrop of the Indian Ocean.

We hear the melodic rendition of the text line, *Krishna ne begane baro,* played on the flute; the camera, instead of zooming in on Bala, continually focuses our attention on the Indian Ocean. Wave sounds clash with the tonal qualities of the melodic refrain, dash against it, and create a strange dissonance that provides the musical and structural backdrop for the unfolding of the piece. Then we see Bala. There she is, a rather tall woman by Indian standards, standing alone and looking extremely vulnerable against the magnificent backdrop of the roaring sea. We see Bala with her sari billowing in the wind, and the wind itself pushing at her body, threatening to sweep her off her feet. How can a dancer dance in the shifting sands of the ocean, in the shifting sands of time? What if her feet suddenly disappear into the sand, or if her sari unravels from the impact of the gushing wind?

The omniscient eye of the camera, however, seems unconcerned with these little details, and moves back and forth between Bala and the ocean, attempting to harmonize the sound of the waves with the melody of the song. And then slowly, and from somewhere within the womb space of the ocean, we hear the flute rendition of the text line, *Krishna ne begane baro.* Where is her musical ensemble? How is she going to improvise the *padam* without the ensemble? The drums then join in on the melody and set the rhythm for the piece. The camera zooms in again on Bala and we hear her sing the line *Krishna ne begane baro.*

In the first repetition of the text line, Bala simply calls to her imagined godchild. She uses her right hand and calls Krishna into her embrace. In the second repetition she uses hand gestures to describe her relationship with her child, and in the third she shows us how she loves Krishna, the one who carries the flute in his hand, and entreats him to come back to her embrace. The opening text line is repeated several times. But I cannot isolate the renditions for the reader because the camera, with its desire for the feel of the ocean, chops up the different repetitions and keeps returning us again and again to the ocean, to the roar of the sea. I have often thought that it was the Indian Ocean, not Bala or her rendition of the *padam,* that was the subject matter of this documentary film.

Because the opening text phrase, which might have been repeated at least twenty times in a live concert, is truncated, the camera fails to provide a unifying theme or mood for the rendition of the *padam.* The initiated viewer would have liked to see more renditions of the text line, which would then have established the narrative plot for the song. His desire is further frustrated by the ocean backdrop and the wind gushing from the ocean that is always already unsettling Bala's hair and billowing her sari. The unsteady, restless gaze of the camera, shuffling between Bala and the ocean, does not enhance our aesthetic pleasure in any way. Did the director situate Bala against this backdrop as a way to naturalize and essentialize the dance, to evoke notions of cosmic plenitude, timelessness, and infinitude? Or did he desire merely to spiritualize and idealize both the dancer and the dance? The director's good intentions notwithstanding, the juxtaposition fails because both the dancer and the dance are lifted out of their performance contexts and presented ahistorically, that is, as timeless, never changing images. The ocean backdrop is so imposing in its magnificence that it manages to effectively subsume, efface, and abstract the quotidian details involved in the rendering of the *padam.*

Separated from immediate engagement with her musical ensemble, which had always supported and accompanied her live performances, Bala appears forlorn in this film. Without the musical ensemble she seems vulnerable, caught off guard, and incomplete. The imposing ocean backdrop seems unable to compensate Bala for the lack of the ensemble, and actually supplements her performance in dangerous ways. In this piece, we see Bala trying to grasp at something eluding her own imagination. Yet Bala was always able, we are told, to hold her own on the concert stage. In the Ray film, we behold not a confident but a distraught Bala, one trying to manage her fly-away hair and sari. We also behold a dancer valiantly trying to respond to musical cadences and word phrases emerging from an ensemble that she is unable to see or interact with.

Deprived of her musical ensemble (her right arm, so to speak), we see a fumbling Bala re-presenting the piece as if it were rehearsed. There is a certain poetic poignancy to all this, because Bala spoke against mechanical, commodified performances of this kind that sever the integral links connecting the dancer with music. It is ironic that Bala's performance itself was subjected to the gaze of the camera. The disembodied instrument successfully penetrated her performance and was able to sever the intricate, symbiotic relationships that had already existed between music and dance, text, hand gestures, and mimetic expression. What is preserved then in Ray's documentary version and held as artistic treasure in the National Archives in India is a somewhat wooden presentation of the dance that had long secured international recognition for Balasaraswati.

When I compare Satyajit Ray's version of the documentary film with another rendition of the same piece archived at Wesleyan University, I find the latter to be more satisfying. In the Wesleyan version Bala is seen dancing on the proscenium stage, located firmly within a mechanized form of reproduction. Yet this version, in comparison to the other, seems more able to communicate the spiritual qualities of the dance. Why? In the Wesleyan version, Bala is not idealized as some timeless symbol but is presented as one engaging in a dialogue with her musical ensemble, and vice versa. The presence of real people sitting at the right-hand corner of the proscenium stage improvising with Bala's dance, not only enhances the spectator's enjoyment of the piece, but actually demonstrates the intricate interconnections between the spiritual and the material. It is worth remembering that Bala herself always spoke of the spiritual elements in *Bharatanatyam* without eschewing the sensuous. She said, "the spiritual quality of *Bharatanatyam* is achieved not through the elimination of the sensual but through the seemingly sensual itself, thereby sublimating it." *Bharatanatyam,* Bala used to say, "was divine as it is, and innately so."[11]

The dance did not require that it be placed within the backdrop of the Indian Ocean in order to be perceived as spiritual. If Satyajit Ray desired to underscore the spiritual values of *Bharatanatyam,* he could have achieved this by simply locating the dancer and the dance within the live sensuousness and materiality of her ensemble, the artistic context or locale that enables the process and phenomena of multiple improvisations described above. The Wesleyan videotape provides a broad context for understanding Bala's performance and makes it possible for us to discuss the questions of improvisation that the Ray film forecloses rather arbitrarily. We can begin to understand the process of improvisation in the *padam* only by locating the performance within its artistic context, the broad network of musical, rhythmic, and textual significations that define the meaning of the *padam.*

CONCLUSION: ARTISTIC INTERDEPENDENCIES

The artistic context itself will not help us understand the complex kinds of improvisation being negotiated in the *padam.* The film director/critic/student has to do more. She must begin by asking about the complex forms of interdependencies forged between form and content, between text and dancer, between musicians and percussionists. We have seen already that the *mudras,* or gestures, depend equally upon the melody (*raga*), upon text (*pada*), and upon the dancer's use of her imagination in filling out these in-between dependencies. If the film director/critic focuses selectively on the musical composition, the dance patterns, or the narrative text as a way to objectify the dance, she is sure to miss questions relating to improvisation, as one half of the meaning of a particular *mudra* resides in the melody of the song and vice versa. The *padam* then has been structurally conceived as an open-ended form, wherein one unit acquires meaning only when combined with another unit. It is a form composed of minute parts or units, *bhava, raga, tala,* that conjoin to create the whole, the *padam,* with its structural coherence. It is perhaps because the *padam* embodies complex notions of inter-dependence that Balasaraswati described it as the pinnacle of the *Bharatanatyam* technique.

In summary, improvisation in a *padam* seems always to be in a perpetual state of emergence, something that could happen any time and anywhere in the performance. Yet the improvisation seems to operate on internal cues and codes that an uninitiated director/viewer cannot break into from the outside. To understand this unique phenomenon, the film director/critic has necessarily to enter the performance text and to follow the trail of the invisible text line, the crystal ball of time as it travels through the various performative registers. What is required is not an interdisciplinary but multidisciplinary approach, one that can engage with the literary, poetic, musical, movement, gestural, and facial expressions of the dance. What is also required is a holistic consciousness on the part of the spectator, one that can see, hear, and respond to the multiple forms of improvisation taking shape in the *bhava, raga,* and *tala* registers of *Bharatanatyam,* the quintessential dance of the Indian nation.

NOTES

1. Narayana Menon, "A True Symbol of Dance Tradition," in *Balasaraswati (1918–1984),* ed. Louise Elcannes Scripps (New York: Balasaraswati School of Music and Dance, 1986), 4–6.
2. *Balasaraswati,* 1962 (housed in the film archives at Wesleyan University, Middletown, Conn.).
3. Satyajit Ray, *Bala* (Government of Madras and National Center for the Performing Arts, Bombay, 1976).
4. T. Balasaraswati, *Bala on Bharatanatyam,* trans. S. Guhan (Madras: Sruti Foundation, 1991), 14.
5. Ibid., 10–11.
6. Ibid., 12.
7. Ibid., 14.
8. Ibid., 13.
9. Ibid., 13.
10. Ibid., 13.
11. Ibid., 14.

RECONSIDERING CONTACT IMPROVISATION

A SUBJECTIVE HISTORY OF CONTACT IMPROVISATION

Notes from the Editor of *Contact Quarterly*, 1972–1997

Nancy Stark Smith

Nancy Stark Smith has lived at the center of the cultural ethos surrounding Contact Improvisation since the dance form's birthing. Not only was the nineteen-year-old Smith a witness to the performance at Oberlin College in 1972 of Steve Paxton's now-legendary *Magnesium,* a piece that was pivotal in the development of Paxton's ideas about improvisation, but later that year, while still a sophomore at Oberlin, she was invited by Paxton to participate in the New York performances that were the first to be called "Contact." Thus, Smith's keen intelligence, her famed kineticism, and her long straight plait—practically a fifth appendage—have been literally imprinted on the form.

All this would suffice to place Smith in a unique position from which to chronicle the more than twenty-five-year development of Contact Improvisation (CI for short), but Smith is also an accomplished writer with a gift for rendering movement and ideas in words. Others have written with eloquence on key aspects of Contact, notably Cynthia Novack, whose *Sharing the Dance: Contact Improvisation and American Culture* (Madison: University of Wisconsin Press, 1990) has become a classic text for students of both dance history and anthropology. But Smith, so particular in her point of view, and admittedly so subjective, provides an alternative account. She has taken her readers deep inside the world of Contact since 1975, first as founder and editor of the *Contact Newsletter* and then as editor of *Contact Quarterly,* the journal that evolved from it. Her writing is both intimate and searching, so much so that, at times, it is difficult to know whether she is writing about herself or the dance. Perhaps there is no difference.

Smith and I first met as fellow Oberlin College alumni. I was on campus to debrief following a two-year stint in India funded by a college association and Smith had returned to her alma mater to teach Contact and prepare a special "College" issue of the *Quarterly.* As a member of the group preparing the magazine, I often hitched rides home with her and became fascinated with the way she navigated that little Midwestern town. When checking traffic she didn't just stare out her windshield like the average driver, but rather seemed to sense everything that was going on around her. I have

Fig. N1. Nancy Stark Smith (*left*) and Nita Little, Re-Union performance at the San Francisco Museum of Modern Art, 1976. (Photo: Uldis Ohaks. Courtesy Nancy Stark Smith.)

since heard her refer to this phenomenon as "telescoping awareness," indicating a shifting between narrow and wide views, from up-close sensation to perceptions of the wider world. At Oberlin I became Smith's assistant on the "College" issue and, ultimately, enjoyed the rare and daunting privilege of penning a *CQ* Editor Note of my very own.

Smith has chosen the excerpts that follow from among the dozens of beautifully crafted Editor Notes she has written over the past quarter century. These Notes begin with her recollections of *Magnesium* in 1972, written a quarter century after the fact, and run through the celebrations marking the twenty-fifth anniversary of Contact Improvisation in 1997. A few of these writings are excerpted but most appear in full, to preserve the Notes' unique format. One is cowritten by Smith's coeditor, Lisa Nelson, who gradually became integral to the magazine after its inception. Several of Bill Arnold's strikingly original photographs, which have illustrated the Editor Notes page since the mid-1980s, are included, in part because they served as inspiration to Smith and in part because they reveal Smith's wry sense of humor in dialogue with visual imagery.

Smith confides that these paragraphs were almost all written under extreme deadline pressure, just as an issue was going to print, but also with great pleasure in the sensuality of the written word and its potential to transmit the experience of dancing — and living — to the page. She describes each Note as "a kind of distillation," akin to a snapshot in scale but more like a poem in intensity. Thus, Smith's writings are a lingual counterpoint to Contact itself, displaying an improviser's sense of curiosity, openness, and split-second timing in response to her world.

> *David Gere*
> *UCLA*

CAUGHT BY SURPRISE

Contact Quarterly 22, no. 2 (Summer/Fall 1997) (CI's 25th anniversary year)

Sometime during the Grand Union's January 1972 residency at Oberlin College, Steve Paxton showed what he had been working on with his men's class. "The extremes of disorientation," he called it. Men following the "small dance" of balancing out into big reeling spills, falls into rolls, following momentum back up to their feet. Soft collisions, slides, a fountaining of men on a giant old canvas mat; "Magnesium," he called it. We audients on the circular track overhead watched spellbound, stirred, in love, with the beauty of this . . . phenomenon, followed by five minutes of quiet standing "to draw a great distinction in the scale of movement," Steve later wrote. "If you ever work like this with women, I'd love to know about it," I said. Three months later I got a call. Come to New York in June.

About fifteen people, a few of Steve's dance colleagues, and the rest dance students he had taught as a guest artist at the University of Rochester, Oberlin College, and Bennington College. Two weeks: one week rehearsing in a downtown loft on a blue wrestling mat. Next week performing "contact improvisations" five hours a day at the John Weber Gallery on West Broadway, in SoHo.

At Lisa's suggestion, I went digging into my closets yesterday for some record of my first exposure to Contact. Here it is. A Sierra Club engagement calendar with each day's box jammed with tiny scribbled notes. Some excerpts:

Sat. May 27, 1972: Little did I know what I was in for. Into NYC in usual shorts and little T-shirt. Find Steve. Intro: Oberlin meet Rochester and Bennington. Steve's stuff. Interesting way to meet people. Beautiful. Tired.

Sun. May 28: to Battery Park. Nice work-out all day. Ouch knee. Burns, etc. Hot sun. OK improv. Work. Tired! Statue of Liberty!

Mon. May 29: finally find rehearsal. heavy weight today. do catching, throwing weight, standing, then massages. nice.

Wed. May 31: felt really good about rehearsal today. more flow. more trust. Saw Grand Union performance tonight. Tired.

Thur. June 1: First performance day. evolution of the group is fantastic—likes and annoyances jelling—understanding needs, know how far can go, who you'd like to work with. Home. Video. Sleep.

Sat. June 3: working today felt ok. I have so much to learn. saw videotapes. I want to work on this stuff for a long time.

For the performances, we brought the mat over to Weber. Its perimeter marked our playing area, so usually no more than one duet danced at a time. The rest of us watched closely, observing the phenomenon, taking it into our nervous systems, new synapses being provoked by the unpredictable movement relationships, the initiatives, the consequences. We were willing subjects, testing and trying the forces of gravity, momentum, centrifugal, friction, that played us and us each other within them, in dialogue, body to body, face to face, force to force. What would happen if . . . Oh, did you see that? When he tucked his head, when she dipped her shoulder under his waist and pushed up, just when he slid and wrapped around, as he turned over in her arms and ended up on her shoulder. Or the tiny physical/energetic exchanges at the other end of the scale—slow, sensing through a very light touch, the skin operating "in all directions at once," Steve might say, and us inside its operation, going along for the ride.

I think it was in a parking lot in Los Angeles the following January, 1973, during our first tour of Contact in California. Something to do with a parking meter. Something to do with realizing, as we swung and leaned on it, angled against it, slipped and slid all over its erect and supporting mass that we . . . certainly that I, was in a radically altered and rather blissful state. A state of assumed physical coordination and union with all things. Weight in a chair, rolling off a bed onto your feet, leaning against a wall to put your shoes on—the usual things—not to mention the glancing touches shoulder to shoulder in elevators, the instinct to reach for someone as they begin to falter on the escalator at the airport. Partners were everywhere.

After this first immersion at Weber, I definitely came out the other side altered. And I liked it and didn't want to stop. This dance is a paradox of unity and separateness and, still, after pretty much every dance, I feel awe, love, at such a pure meeting; so beautifully set against the crudeness of such raw physical activity. Such a physical and energetic meeting seems to touch the soul along with the body. No wonder so many of us continued.

When we left New York, we carried a seed with us. A seed that, like certain cryptography codes, like the regeneration of life itself, needs two parts to activate it. And so, we went off to find more partners.

NOTE FROM GROUPS ISSUE
Contact Quarterly 3, nos. 3–4 (Spring/Summer 1978)

At some point in the growth of Contact Improvisation there was a call for definition, rules, a clear way to identify what was (or wasn't) Contact Improvisation. ("There are no lines, only edges"—Ansel Adams.) Only a few years after its inception, Contact seemed to be spawning generations of contacters so quickly as to be involved in some kind of "telephone game." John tells Sally who shows Sue who passes it on to her brother who tells his wife who shows their kids who bring it to school the next day for recess. If John were walking by the schoolyard at noon, would he recognize anything familiar going on in the playground? For all the interest in defining Contact Improvisation, the answer to that quandary is in watching a contact duet between two dancers who have just met. The definition is in the doing.

Contact bases its language on the natural laws that govern motion (gravity, momentum, inertia, etc.). With these laws as our constitution, we have no need for legislation. The natural world enforces its own laws—drop a book, consciously or not, and it will fall. Clearly Contact Improvisation is not the beginning or the final stage in the opus that relates the body and its movements to the earth and the other movers on it. The truths we find in Contact, whether basic or elevated, are truths that exist with or without Contact Improvisation as a means for revealing them to us. Often in the enthusiasm of the work it is possible to forget that bodies moving in contact are not new. It is, however, the continued focus on the elements involved in that contact, techniques for it, applications of it, that is specific to Contact Improvisation.

Making a magazine (*Contact Quarterly*) for the exchange of information and viewpoint instead of making a congress, allowed the various subtexts that existed to emerge and be shared. As a technique for moving together, Contact resonates in the lives of the practitioners. Those resonances are personal and varied, and though they enrich the work, the basic practice seems unchanged.

After six years, Contact Improvisation continues, with or without music, in twos, threes, in groups with a name or without. Contacters have gathered in bodies, regional families, to corroborate and continue. A context has developed similar to social dancing wherein people can come together and "jam." Through *Contact Quarterly* a network exists, making known places where Contact can be found. When a poker player comes into a new town, he looks for the game.

Nancy Stark Smith
Lisa Nelson

NOTE FROM HEALING ISSUE

Contact Quarterly 5, no. 1 (Fall 1979)

When I first started falling by choice, I noticed a blind spot. Somewhere after the beginning and before the end of the fall, there was darkness. And then the floor. Luckily, there were mats at first. Soon I learned that the end of the fall was the beginning of another move, usually a roll. That gave me somewhere to go. So I rolled. At the end of that roll was another roll, and at the end of that, another. Then, I noticed another blind spot. Somewhere after the beginning and before the end of the roll, there was darkness. In that darkness, however, I noticed a body moving, a body that knew just where to go.

The blind spot in the fall is the moment when the fall and faller lose synch. The faller falls asleep and her body falls without guidance to the floor. Truly lost in space. Ever fall asleep at the wheel? You're so tired your eyelids stick together each time you blink until they pop wide open as you realize you've just been driving 60 mph on the highway with your eyes closed, for how long? The same sensation occurs while falling. You wake up shortly before reaching the floor, just in time to hastily steer yourself to safety. Adrenaline makes your hair stand up.

The more I fell, the more familiar the sensation of dropping through space became, the less disoriented I was during the fall. Staying awake from the first moment of balance loss, I found that falling was in itself a dynamic balance. One in which the forces at play—gravity, momentum, and mass—were all operating in their natural order and if my mind was with me I could gently guide that fall toward a smooth landing. Confidence came with experience and soon enjoyment took the place of fear and disorientation. In the course of a Contact Improvisation duet, I found myself taking every possible option to fall. I would slip out unexpectedly from under my partner just to take the ride: head first, feet first, horizontally, diagonally; falling became irresistible.

It has become clear; there is no where we can stay put. As Ann Woodhull has written, "Even standing, we execute a continuous fall." The expression, "fall from grace," becomes an impossible statement when falling itself is experienced as a state of grace. This is not to say that disorientation, confusion, and dis-ease have no place in the geometry of balance. They, in fact, stimulate the balancing mechanism. Stimulate us to ask questions: what is dis-ease, what does healthy mean, how do we recognize and maintain it? How can we stay awake during the fall; this is the healing issue.

WHERE YOU GOIN' WITH THAT GUN/SETTING OUR SIGHTS

Contact Quarterly 5, nos. 3–4 (Spring/Summer 1980) (Sports Issue)

Ready. Aim. Fire. On your marks. Get set. Go.

The starting gun fires. To the runners in position, heels backed up against the running block, that shot opens a floodgate of kinetic energy, turning the still figures into a blur of movement, all headed in the same direction, "pouring it on" full tilt towards the finish line. With baton in hand, they race towards the next runner who, tracking his man, matches stride so the passage of baton from one running body to the next can occur seamlessly. Together they are going somewhere.

The daily jogger, on the other hand, is focused more on internal movement sensations: the rhythm of breath, the beat of heart, the sweep of momentum, the impact of earth. Where s/he is going is not on the map—though s/he has to cover ground to get there. Though it is the movement and not the direction that is significant, a direction must nevertheless be chosen in order to proceed.

For a long time it appeared that Contact Improvisation was an activity without a goal. That we, like the joggers, were more concerned with sensation than achievement and could therefore feel free to choose any direction for our practice of the work. There is the sense in practicing Contact that any physical interaction that doesn't intentionally injure you or your partner is "right." Anything goes. Yet there is a limit to how broad an activity can be before it has no parameters at all and dissolves into the collection of experiences one could simply call life, or in this case, human experience. When, in 1977, Steve Paxton was asked, "What is the point of Contact?" he replied, "Just the pleasure of using your body is, I think, maybe the main point. And the pleasure of dancing with somebody in an unplanned and spontaneous way, where you're free to invent and they're free to invent and you're neither one hampering the other—that's a very pleasant social form." However, it was by first establishing priorities that Contact was able to provide its particular kind of pleasure.

Contact can be seen as a means for communicating through physical contact. Dialogue proceeds, using the exchange of weight between partners to tune them to the physical forces that effect their motion and to tune them to each other. At the outset of Contact Improvisation, a choice was made to minimize the social content of the contact and to work, initially, with the physical elements involved in the exchange. Stated or by example implied, this choice, along with others, brought depth to the practice of Contact by limiting its scope. By narrowing the focus of the activity, subtle information was made visible: the experience of gravity; the "small dance" of the skeleton balancing erect; the flow of weight through the body as it rolls across the floor; the exchange of weight between partners during lifting, throwing, and catching; the sensation of sharing a dynamic center of balance with another mover.

It has been eight years since the decision to work with these specific physical elements. In this time, practice has revealed many principles that, serving as anchors, allowed the scope of partner exchange to widen. The practice of CI continues to suggest ways in which its principles and skills can be applied. Following these suggestions leads to fascinating work in dance, theater, therapy, and education. As the concern with physical contact and weight exchange becomes less of a focus in their work, many Contactors wonder whether they are still doing "Contact Improvisation." Others continue their studies regardless, not caring one way or the other what it is called.

Contact, as an evolving system, tends to attract the forces that work to open what is fixed, change what is static. Ever since its formation as the *Contact Newsletter* in 1975, *Contact Quarterly* has reflected this eagerness to find relevance in a broad range of sources. In considering the direction of our interests, as editors we ask ourselves, "What does shooting guns have to do with Contact Improvisation?"[1] In shooting, one tests the accuracy with which a message of energy (power) can be delivered to a distant point (moving or still). As a "vehicle for moving ideas," *Contact Quarterly* shares that aim.

JUDSON/CONTACT RELAY: A LEGACY OF AMBIGUITY [EXCERPT]
Contact Quarterly 7, nos. 3–4 (Spring/Summer 1982) (CI's 10th Anniversary Issue)

And so it is ten years since the first public performances of Contact Improvisation. People are talking now of producing historical Contact Improvisation events, writing books about Contact, and this issue of *Contact Quarterly* is CI's 10th anniversary issue.

At least one baton that seems to have been passed from the Judson world of the '60s to Contact in the '70s is a resistance to being solidified—the sense that to stay in one place too long is to freeze there. But whether you stay or go further, a "place" has inevitably been cleared by your passing, and that point of reference exists. Every day more trails are blazed to, from, through and around that place, with other landmarks forming along the way; and so it becomes increasingly difficult and in fact pointless to fix its outer limits.

There does seem, however, to be a center—a downtown, as it were—to this sprawling Contact metropolis. But that center isn't exactly on the map. It's more implied than stated, suggested by the overlapping spheres of experience that the work produces. The activity of Contact itself is remarkably straightforward and recognizable, but the experience of it is relative. An atmosphere of curiosity has made the work a currency of exchange rather than a place to go—awkward for those who had expected to someday arrive somewhere. The way is the going itself; we remember what we are left with, but not always where we left from.

One night at the Vermont Movement Workshop in Putney a few summers ago, about fifty people gathered for a discussion about Contact. No particular subject was slated. So, we started from scratch and asked, What is this thing called Contact Improvisation that people are so hot to do? What *is* it? Some people said it was about communication, a code of sorts; others said it was about sharing weight, getting a rigorous workout, acquiring new skills; and others said it was about developing sensitivity. And the list went on. After the discussion, on our way back to our rooms, a few of us were walking past a cabin where some of the students were living and I heard through an open window as we walked past, "They *know* what it is, but they just won't *tell*. That Steve Paxton has passed on a legacy of ambiguity that keeps everyone from saying what it is, but they know." I laughed when I heard her, but I've thought about what she said a lot since then. And I think she's right. Not only did Steve offer a dance, but a built-in way of keeping it alive. Thanks, Steve, for that one.

MAKING CONTACT [EXCERPT]

Contact Quarterly 9, no. 2 (Spring/Summer 1984)

Having breakfast the other day with a longtime practitioner, teacher, and performer of Contact Improvisation, it occurs to me that he probably hasn't seen the new issue of *CQ* and I eagerly reach down for the one in my bag. But he's squirming uncomfortably and I hesitate and look up. "You know I really don't read the *Quarterly* any more," he says, "Maybe I should tell you why." "Please," I say, slipping my hand out of my bag and onto my lap. In short, he says that as the mouthpiece for Contact Improvisation, *CQ* isn't getting to the substance of what people are doing, but only printing superficial, undeveloped reports. Sympathetic and amused to see the magazine in this strangely inverted position, I agree with him (almost) completely, *and* ask him why he hasn't written about the great workshop he's just spent the last hour telling me about.

It *is* true that people are busy doing, perhaps too busy to be telling of it. And perhaps it's also true that their tales, were they to be told, might no longer fit comfortably—in form *or* content—into the format of the *CQ Newsletter,* now slated for Contact exchanges. More important, is there really a call for this kind of exchange? Judging not only from my recent breakfast talk, but from the number of charged conversations that found their way into and around the busy schedule at St. Mark's Church during the two-week Contact At 10th and 2nd festival in New York last June, it is clear that the appetite is there to talk and hear about how people are working in and from Contact.[2] The real hands-on stuff. As is said, "It furthers one to have somewhere to go." So, as of this issue, we've opened a new column, "Still Moving," to make room for that rich flow of ideas to run through.

But let it be said that *Contact Quarterly* is not the final word on nor the official mouthpiece for Contact Improvisation. If anything, we're simply a mouth, changing shape to fit the words that you put in it. So go ahead, put words in our mouth.

DEALING WITH THE HEAT

Contact Quarterly 9, no. 3 (Fall 1984)

This is about friction, about two things rubbing up against each other, and the value of that heat. I'm the kind of person who tends to harmonize opposing forces. When faced with a conflict, I'm always eager to jump to a perspective that encompasses both sides, one in which they are no longer at odds—a view that renders each side valid and useful and yet, as a result, often impersonal, removed from the initial charge that formed it. But I'm beginning to see what I've been missing.

There's something to be said for two things rubbing each other the wrong way. The friction between them wears each side down to its undercoat, its framework, thus testing its strength and revealing its ground. True, the way the friction is used and why are important factors. Sometimes when sharpening an edge, it is

Fig. N2. Photo: Bill Arnold. Printed with permission.

possible to cut off completely what you're just trying to hone down. But that's what practice is for. In Push Hands, a T'ai Chi Chuan sparring form, for instance, one is looking through the touch, arm to arm, for the resistance to the push. The partner tries to "empty" wherever the other pushes, to offer no resistance, thus hoping to draw the pusher off balance. The pusher perseveres with a delicate but relentless touch, to search through the other's inner space for their resistance, trying to force the question. Having finally backed the partner into a corner, so to speak, inside his/her own body, the pusher has only to push lightly (no more than 8 oz. of pressure) to send the partner flying backward against the wall. They resume starting positions eagerly—facing each other, body centered in a low, grounded stance, forearm to forearm—ready for another go at it. Like hide and seek, it's only really fun to play if someone's out to get you. And the more heated and skillful their search, the better the practice.

The Studies Project discussion between Bill T. Jones and Steve Paxton, printed in this issue of *CQ,* is a juicy and personal play, full of edges, pushes, falls, and fakes.[3] Several times during the talk, I felt myself wincing at the action as one might while watching a boxing match when the swing connects. I noticed myself subtly backing off from their verbal sparring when it seemed to be getting the most heated. But luckily, I couldn't change the channel. What I saw light up in the heat of that friction was each man as an individual; his unique perspective came into focus as it was forced to narrow from a more general *field* of vision to a distinct *point* of view, teased and poked and pushed into the light. And though I squirmed in the heat of that confrontation, I was at the same time struck by the commitment behind the stand.

I've learned a lot from doing Contact Improvisation about coordinating with the forces-that-be: accepting gravity, falling, following momentum, blending with a partner's movements—i.e., "going with the flow." But lately, I've been feeling feisty. I'm a little too comfortable now with the dizzy of flipping horizons, torquing pathways and unexpected chutes, and more and more I find myself playing *against* the forces—making myself heavy instead of light when a lift starts, adding a splash to the easy pouring of weight, insisting instead of yielding, adding fierce to gentle, no to yes. It's a start. I've been in the harmony business a long time now. It might take a while to really get the hang of holding my ground instead of so gladly letting it slip out from under me. As much as I love running around, I think I'm going to try running *into* things more often, or at least up against them.

STILL IN THE MIDDLE [EXCERPT]
Contact Quarterly 10, no. 2 (Spring/Summer 1985)

In the past few years, disorientation has reemerged as a central theme for me in teaching and practicing Contact Improvisation and in performing improvisation. What began as a physical survival skill for Contact has become for me a keystone—not only for the survival of the bodies in contact, but for the vitality and heart of the improvisation.

One of the earliest exercises in physical disorientation for Contact Improvisation, and still at the heart of the work for me, is Steve Paxton's "small dance of standing." Relaxing erect, the intelligence of the body is revealed as it fires the appropriate muscles just enough to keep the body mass hovering within range of its vertical supports. The micromovements that occur to keep me balanced are so tiny and yet so magnified, and arise from such a deep feeling of stillness and space, that I get giddy, tickled by the impossible magnitude of such subtle sensations. The disorientation in the stand comes from the feeling that inside the apparent solidity and stillness of standing, there is nothing but movement and space! Each time, I come to feel as precarious standing on the floor on two legs as I might on one leg on a trampoline.

Without the willingness to risk one's point of view, to be temporarily at a loss, improvising can become a sleepy exercise in restating what's already perfectly clear. When nothing is really at stake, one's survival is assured, but some deeper satisfaction, both as a watcher and as a performer, is lacking.

But it's tricky keeping the cutting edge sharp—the body/mind adapts incredibly fast to unfamiliar circumstances. What is attempted and survived with hesitation the first time, is approached with more courage the next, until soon it is done automatically. After a while the real challenge changes from "how can I survive this disorientation" to "where do I find the next one?"

NOW AND THEN
Contact Quarterly 10, no. 3 (Fall 1985)

Practicing improvisation in the '80s is not the same as it was in the '70s. But then, it isn't altogether different.

In the '70s, when Contact Improvisation began and was first developing, the time was ripe for risk and discovery. The '60s had shaken so may basic assumptions, that by the '70s, it was almost impossible *not* to approach things with a fresh look, ready for news. The times not only supported but *demanded* an ability to improvise. Contact Improvisation offered a movement practice that developed physical and mental flexibility and strength within a state of constant flux. Its invitation to extend one's limits—physically, conceptually, aesthetically, psychologically—was welcome and well taken.

The enlivened state of being that resulted from this movement practice created a strong motivation and reference point for its practitioners. Just knowing that such freedom was possible generated tremendous willingness to engage in the process. The work was fed by its practitioners' recognition of and faith in that possibility. And it was largely because of that nourishment that it continued and grew.

In 1977, Christina Svane wrote "In Praise of Bad Dancing" for the *Contact Newsletter*. In it she said, "I value this work not only for the rare glimpses of in-touch, in-time, in-tune, but for the companionship of the ever-present indications of what is possible. The form itself, if one exists beyond the instances of attempts to experience it, is none other than the existence of the possibility of a dance in which wills, instincts, and verges merge. Emergency, emerge, merge. It amounts to having to believe in a possibility which one may never have experienced. All this is to say I am devoted to something which I rarely feel, the possibility of which I never leave. We extend to ourselves an invitation which we rarely accept, but the extension of it is what matters. Living for so long on the verge of that acceptance, I figure it's time to call it home."

Contact Improvisation has always been compelling work for me. I've invested a lot in it, and I've gotten a lot in return. It is a generous form in that way. Smitten as I was by the enlivened state it had the capacity to induce, for a long time it seemed to me that the form existed totally independent of our insatiable pursuit of it. It gave but didn't need.

I've since come to realize that the freedom improvisation offers doesn't come without bidding. Its pleasure is a discipline. In the practice of Contact Improvisation, one is constantly faced with one's tendency to make the same choices over and over again. Within the form, this tendency is countered by working in close contact with a partner who is in a position to remind you that there are options you hadn't considered. Appreciating that invitation is one of the basic challenges improvising offers.

I've also come to realize that it's possible to practice the physical techniques of Contact Improvisation and never make the choice to improvise. Is it because one hasn't been shown the possibility, doesn't see it, or simply doesn't choose it?

Though they greatly encouraged it, it was not only the climate of the '70s, nor the improvisational forms it gave rise to that enabled us to appreciate the value of staying open to unexpected possibilities. The potential for openness is human, and can be chosen and actively cultivated any time, by any individual, through any form. It is the desire for it that makes it possible. Like the fairy godmother said to the destitute woman in a theater improvisation I once saw, "I can make your wish come true. But *you* have to make the wish."

BACK IN TIME [EXCERPT]
Contact Quarterly 11, no. 1 (Winter 1986) (Space/Time Issue 1)

Within the study of Contact, the experience of "flow" was soon recognized and highlighted in our dancing. It became one of my favorite practices and I proceeded to "do flow" for many years—challenging it, testing it: Could we flow through *this* pass? Could we squeak through *that* one, and keep going?

I used to have a partner that I called the Flow Machine. His considerable mass streamed through the channels of movement, sometimes like a rushing brook, sometimes like molten lava, but always ongoing. I would get euphoric and giddy as the end of the phrase never arrived—always there was a new curve, and we'd bank off the edge of that one, going on and on. There is great pleasure in this. And it is in large measure through establishing and maintaining a mutual flow that the trust is formed between partners which supports further risk-taking, as from this baseline one can quickly sense changes in the flow as they occur—changes in direction, modulations in timing—and be ready to adapt to them.

The kinetic pleasures and soothing rhythms of time-in-flow can be hypnotic and often go unchallenged in Contact. Why rock the boat now that we've finally gotten it steadied? As I've said, I've always loved "doing flow" and still do, but the time came when I began to wonder what else was possible. What other kinds of time could be played out in the dancing, and where might that take us?

What I'm finding is that it is there, in the departures from the established time frame, that new aspects of the dancers' personalities emerge and new risks are taken. Taking the lid off the flow container, time can move in new ways, reflecting not only the dancers' mutuality but their singularity, in time, and in space.

Challenging any established order is a risk, and can come with a fair amount of disorientation and awkwardness. But Contact trains us so well in *spatial* disorientation—with all its whirling about, off-center and falling—surely our practice can welcome a little confusion in time as well.

ALL IN GOOD TIME [EXCERPT]

Contact Quarterly 11, no. 2 (Spring–Summer 1986) (Space/Time Issue 2)

When I teach beginning Contact Improvisation, there are a few principles I come back to over and over—some for safety reasons, others for flavor. Some have to do with expanding one's orientation to space—experiencing space as spherical, dealing with disorientation, being able to fall, roll, and ride momentum, alone and in physical contact with another mover. I suppose this could be called spatial conditioning.

Then there's time conditioning, which I'm just beginning to take particular notice of. A lot of the meditations on physical sensation (e.g., Paxton's "small dance") that have always been a part of Contact training are actually as much about inducing an experience of expanded time as they are about the physical sensations they point up.

This sense of expanded time is a subjective state, one where time feels mutable and there are slippages—where a 45-minute dance can feel like five minutes, while a two-second fall can feel luxuriously long. It is a relaxed state, one where time seems to have been released from is inexorable unit-to-unit march and allowed to roam in an open field with wide horizons and no fences, a time whose divisions and textures vary according to the moods and perceptions of the people moving through it.

As with spatial training, this new temporal experience may be puzzling at first. All too often you lose your place in the dancing, but you find out through experience that if you just hang on a few seconds longer (*those* seconds feel like *hours!*) your place will come floating up under you like a pair of lost footprints. You come to trust and in fact look forward to those gaps because in them you're as vulnerable and available as you can be, and from there come new perceptions and some of the more surprising and refreshing movement material.

But how do we get there from here? Especially when we're coming in to the studio from Chemistry or Shakespeare or Ballet or a 65 mile drive.

The transition from clock time to internal time can begin during the personal warmup—a period of time I often give at the beginning of class to relax and "arrive," to get ready physically and mentally to dance with others. It deepens during the periods of extended duet improvising. Absorption in the moment expands the feeling of time and you come out of it enlivened no matter where you've been. It's this state of absorption and enlivening that I aim for in my own dancing and teaching.

INTELLIGENCE [EXCERPT]

Contact Quarterly 11, no. 3 (Fall 1986)

Early in its short history, Contact Improvisation's duet dances were often referred to as physical dialogues, conversations. We talked about the movement form as a language, and even named certain moves that recurred often enough to be identified, like "58" (or was it "42"?), a throw, or "orbits," where one body circles around the other's shoulder girdle. But, for the most part, these names were made

up and used only for a short time, never really achieving the stature of "vocabulary," just convenient ways of referring to a movement for awhile. As the movement language evolved and our perceptions became more articulated, the word images would change too, attempting to remain as flexible as the movement to which they were referring. It was important and fun to be able to discuss what was going on in the improvised dancing, but it also seemed important not to stifle the form's growth by oversolidifying the terminology surrounding it.

Last November I had a special opportunity to experience Contact Improvisation as a language. The First European Contact Teachers Conference, held in Amsterdam, attracted twenty-five Contact teachers from nine countries. Though English was quickly established as the common language, there was need for translation into at least one other language almost all the time. So it was with great relief that we moved into the studio to dance. In contrast to the choppy nature of our verbal exchanges, the dancing seemed smooth as silk. Contact Improvisation was, as it turned out, our most common language. In the dancing, each person's humor, intelligence, and spark were not only recognizable but accessible. It was clearly there, in the movement, that the wealth of our experiences as Contact dancers and teachers was being exchanged. That's where the conference was taking place.

Similar to learning any foreign tongue, once you can make and hear the key sounds, words, and constructions, you can begin to talk with anyone else who knows the language. The initial training in Contact is at best a preparation for being able to safely and intelligibly set out on your own as soon as possible. And like most languages, Contact can only really be learned by using it. Actually, the true test of Contact teachers' success has always been if their students could do Contact with someone who learned it from another source.

In Contact, movements are born all of a sudden and are two-sided. You bring to the exchange your half of the story and your partner brings another. The beauty of being able to dance with many different people is that each partner has a different piece to the puzzle and they don't automatically fit together. You have to improvise to make them mesh. . . .

But what gets a tired dancer up off her back is not the chance to conjugate a few movement verbs. The movement language we call dancing isn't just a way of efficiently transferring information. It's an opportunity to make contact, not just with the partner or the physical forces at play, but with the creative forces that make words into poetry and movement into dance.

CROSSING THE GREAT DIVIDES

Contact Quarterly 17, no. 1 (Winter 1992) (Dancing with Different Populations Issue)

The first time I experienced Ishmael Houston-Jones's score, "The Politics of Dancing," was in Berlin at the 1988 European Contact Teachers Conference. In his afternoon workshop by the same name, he asked us to imagine a railroad track running diagonally through the room from corner to corner, dividing the room in half. Gathering in the middle of the room upon the invisible track, the group met for instructions: "All those people who have both parents alive, form a group on the right side of the track; all those who do *not* have both parents alive, form a group on the other side." To the image, he added a fast-approaching train and with it the need to make a quick decision, one side or the other, which way to go.

Once we were divided, Ishmael said, "Look at your group." Eyes to eyes, eyes to bodies, eyes to floor. Eyes certain, eyes shy, eyes teary, eyes wide. After some minutes he said, "Now turn and look at the other group." Across the length of the studio, across the invisible track, we look at "the others." What we see: how many of them there are, who's there, the visual design of the group—heights, colors, postures; mood. What we feel: anything, everything. We are nervous, proud, curious, bored, uncomfortable, sad, amused. It depends of course on the category.

After several more minutes of looking at the other group without talking (the whole exercise was done in silence), we are asked to move towards each other slowly, to mix again in the middle and wait for the next instruction: "All those who were raised in a Jewish household, go to the right side; all those who were not, go to the other side."

Some categories were easier to respond to than others, either because the answer was indisputable or the subject less charged. Sensitivities varied greatly from person to person, and subject to subject, whether questions of age (under 35/not under 35); social/sexual issues (homosexual/not homosexual; living with mate/not living with . . .); self-image (those who consider themselves above-average intelligence/those who do not consider themselves . . .); money (those who make above $20,000 a year/those who do not . . .); politics (those who voted in the last election . . .).

As I remember, we basically stuck to the score in Berlin. There was, however, always recourse in interpretation: some people decided to lie, or at least play "the facts" in their own way; other people agonized over every decision, trying to be absolutely honest: did having had an abortion place you with "those who have had children" or "those who have not"?; and then there were people who chose to get run over by the train rather than make an impossible decision or acknowledge an unacceptable categorization.

"The Politics of Dancing" came back around last summer when it was led by Daniel Lepkoff, an old friend and former collaborator of Ishmael's, as part of a "group morning" at the A Cappella Motion workshop in Northampton, Mass. The exercise was conducted, as before, in a very straightforward manner—the instructions simple and clear, the categories ranging from mildly to extremely sensitive. This time, the response was stronger than I remembered: more soul-searching, people crying, and more people choosing to stay on the track, even for questions like "those who are women on this side, those who are not women on the other side." Gradually, new spatial categories of response were invented as people placed themselves in the room on a continuum between the two extremes, until on some questions the group was completely scattered from one end of the room to the other rather than divided into two distinct groups. Emotions ran high, bonding among participants strong, and by the end we were all a bit dazed.

I remember going through a range of emotions as the categories came and went and I dutifully plumbed my depths for the truest answers. Among my feelings were suspicion and irritation, as I wondered what made this The Politics of Dancing, what this had to do with dancing at all, and what it had to do with me. I went away from the exercise stirred up and confused, my consciousness obviously raised, or at least on edge.

I am reminded by this writing that I have always loved facts about people. I often like to ask workshop participants for a fact about themselves. Anything: I ate an English muffin this morning; I like to play golf; I'm grieving the death of my boyfriend; I learned something new about leverage in my last dance. I don't exactly know what it is about these details, the particulars of their lives, that moves me. I do know they add a dimension that wasn't there before.

And what exactly did we mean by an issue of *CQ* about "dancing with different populations"? What does "different" mean? If Ishmael had said, "All those who are different go to this side, all those who are not different go to the other side" who would have gone where and why?

Common denominators among people are many, yet differences remain. They help to distinguish one thing from another, provide contrast, and with it, dimension. Using movement to communicate across boundaries—cultural, age, experience, gender, etc.—is a challenge that can teach us a great deal, about ourselves, each other, the nature of nature, and the power and complexity of the language of movement. Overcoming prejudice, ignorance, and fear through dancing with "other" people is awkward, outrageous, liberating, and can be quite a lot of fun.

There seems to be a first flush (does it continue?) that accompanies this opening to another person, where the reservoir of human compassion and humor is tapped and we are deeply moved by an unimpeded flow of—is it love?—to someone once distanced from us by definitions and circumstance. At these moments we might feel we are truly dancing beyond ourselves.

I honor and have felt this effusion and glow. And now I wonder what will happen next, as the novelty of crossing borders gives way to other curiosities aroused once inside the new territory. What will be found as we continue to make our way through this complex world, deciding to turn right or left, following our instincts and desires into the dancing we love the most?

WHO DO WE THINK WE ARE? [EXCERPT]
Contact Quarterly 21, no. 2 (Summer–Fall 1996) (Sexuality and Identity Issue 2)

Once upon a time . . . I came in to teach a contact class feeling a little blue—nothing really wrong, just a little slower, not as upbeat and outgoing as usual. After some warm-up, I proposed a head-to-head dance. One man didn't have a partner, so I stepped in. He was a bit of a punk, this guy—spiky hair, black leather jacket with studs (not in class), and a pretty cool, indifferent attitude. We stood facing each other, the crowns of our heads bowing toward one another to touch, to lean in slightly, bridging our skeletons, our weight, up from the ground under our feet, through bones and joints, through the spine then skull, through the point of contact, and through the partner's skeleton back down to the ground.

We stood quietly, balancing together, noticing the small reflexive movements our bodies were making, floating in the balance, losing it, catching it. Like putting your ear up to the wall, a point of physical contact amplifies the movement on the other side. So, between our two "small dances" of balancing, there was a lot to notice, be in, dance.

I don't know what triggered it, maybe some tiny synchronous shift of weight, some micro-support offered for an impossibly obscure internal fall, a meeting point, but sometime during our moving, I felt my emotions release into the body of our dance. An ease and a fullness flooded in. The dialogue of our balancing became finer, deeper, subtler, and more personal as it went on. I was touched, inside and out, by his attention to our physical detail, and I felt myself expressive and responsive in every shift of my weight—my humor, my imagination, my humanity, and my sexuality, all evident in the dancing. Dancing is not a literary language, it isn't written or read across a page, but on some invisible membrane that, like fascia, runs in between all our parts, and can travel in many directions at once. That day, this dance was a sexy affair, and our touch never left the crown of our heads. I came away from the dance silently stunned, smitten.

In the remaining weeks of the course, we politely avoided contact with one another. In the end, my student was stronger and more forthright than I in con-

Fig. N5. Photo: Bill Arnold.
Printed with permission.

fronting our situation, and approached me on the last day to talk. When we told our stories they were the same. Except that he was avoiding me for fear that the contact wouldn't be the same, and I, because I was afraid it would. . . . We decided to have another dance. It was altogether different.

This is our second issue focused on "sexuality and identity." I was hoping to not only be moved by it but to learn something. What I have learned is that the issues of sexuality and identity in dance arise and are played out anywhere from in a casual encounter at a Contact jam, to a full-blown cross-dressed performance piece. And that the issues raised have to do with many things—the kick of hormones, the profound and simple opening of hearts, the investigation of what it is to be a woman or a man, and the play of all this research and experience as it moves through the body, through the dancing, through performance, and back out into the world.

STRETCH OF TIME
Contact Quarterly 22, no. 1 (Winter–Spring 1997) (CI 25th Anniversary Year)

Bottom of the lung, a very good place to start. In Oberlin, Ohio, with Steve Paxton leading, in a dark predawn gymnasium in January 1972. Bottom of the lung. The smallest stretch you can still feel. Standing. Fresh air coming in, old air out. A slight sensation there at the diaphragm as the dome flattens down, causing lungs to draw in air, filling the new volume. And then following the air out through the back, or sides, feeling three-dimensional.

Just inside the door to the big dark gym (smell of old wood, canvas, leather, plenty of good steam heat on this frigid morning), the three or four of us who generally showed up for class noticed an old wooden chair. On the chair, a box of Kleenex and a plate of cut-up pear. Take one of each, it seemed to say. Hmm, I thought. Fun. Mysterious. Dance class? Taking one of each, I entered, sleepy, fresh from the cold walk over from my dorm room across the square.

Steve's Soft Class woke me up; the Soft Class put me to sleep. The Soft Class met every weekday at 7 a.m. that January. Snappy short exhalations all in a row, followed by a few slow deep breaths, followed by twenty more short attacks on the diaphragm, three long slow deep ones. Sitting, standing, watching mind watch sensation: feeling gravity, my standing body's "small dance" of balancing, the tiny shifts of weight, of bones, etc. "In the direction that your left arm is hanging, without changing that direction, make the smallest stretch you can still feel. Go ahead. . . . And, relax it. Can you feel less? Can you . . . feel . . . less?" Rhythmic, to the point; I could almost, always, feel less. Steve's voice was low, slow, hypnotic, but at the same time easygoing, matter of fact. A nearly sublimi-nal story told directly to my body, to follow along and feel.

I floated, standing, in the seeming solidity of skeleton and structure. And just when I thought I had myself lined up perfectly, all at rest, in balance, something would take me just that hair off center and I'd drift until I'd feel my muscles fire and contract, just enough (well, sometimes a little too much) to catch and send me back over my legs, my center line, "arms hanging like plumb lines to the cen-ter of the earth," and so on. Observing my reflexes at work, feeling sensation, di-rected by Steve's words, presence, images, I met my body as it arrived into breathing, standing, and the day.

By the end of the hour-long class, the sun had come up, shooting a rich honey golden light horizontally across the gym from left to right from where I usually stood. A profound and personal sense of peace and beauty flooded me, daily, followed by an inexplicable sadness. I didn't know what I was feeling.

Sometimes, actually often, in the middle of "a stand," in the flow of balanc-ing in and around my bones, I would be dreaming. And I would carry on in my dreaming as I stood, for some time. And then the nod that goes too far and trig-gers the snap back up suddenly breathlessly erect, heart beating, like being on the road driving, hands gripping the wheel hard as I swerve back into the lane, heart pounding, suddenly seeing the road, realizing that my eyes had really been closed, that I was actually dreaming, that I am driving and am alive and just how lucky I really am to be so.

I quote Steve verbatim now when I teach the small dance in Contact class, hoping to transmit as directly as possible what I received first in the expectant calm of a predawn winter day in 1972 and many times thereafter. Something about the human condition, observing and being its physical intelligence, and meeting sensation where it lives in the mindbodymind. Being so simply in sensations—of breathing, stretch, rearrangement of bones, balancing of forces, tuning of senses (at some point we ate the pear). This body. This time. This place. So simple. So exalted.

Twenty-five years later, I am still feeling that smallest stretch, less and less of it, more and more. How could something so little last so long?

NOTES

1. This is a reference to a guest editorial by visual artist and marksman David Bradshaw in the previous issue.
2. The festival was organized to mark the eleventh anniversary of Contact Improvisation.
3. The Studies Project was an ongoing series created and hosted by Movement Research, Inc., New York.

DRAFTING INTERIOR TECHNIQUES

Steve Paxton

How awkwardly we are damned if we don't or if we do, I thought to myself after the European Contact Conference in Berlin in 1988. During a lecture event I had been asked, "Just what is Contact Improvisation?" and I had muffed the answer. I was being asked by a woman with an aggressive attitude, in the presence of a number of veteran Contactors, the general public, and students, and I hesitated in order to decide how the question should be answered for the whole group. The discussions up to that point had been full of historical revisions, elisions, pointed remarks about Americentric heavy-footedness. In short, the European Contactors considered themselves second-generation users of this form and wanted to know if they had to go through every step the Americans had gone through. A few people who had come to the conference without prior experience just wanted an explanation of what this whole thing was and how it was run and how did one improve and get recognition—reasonable questions in a normal organization.

The journal [*Contact Quarterly*] had, among other things, been working for fifteen years to elaborate on the basic answer to "What is CI?" As time has gone on, the answer has shifted: away from an experimental dance phenomenon and toward a physical practice allied with a number of complex new body and mind studies. I have come to think of Contact Improvisation as a physical event best described negatively: not art, not sport, not most of the things that characterize dancing in this century.

But I hate to describe things in the negative. It is accurate, but the mystics used it first and I don't like using their devices, which were used to inform students in conversations about the ineffable. We, on the other hand, are trying to describe the corporeal. But it is no longer easy to do so. It is, in fact, getting more difficult. We now know too much, or think we do; the corporeal seems to be a complexity of social, physical, geometric, glandular, political, intimate, and personal information that is not easily renderable.

Once things were relatively simple. I thought I knew how this then-nameless work should not be described. It was to be an improvisation without any ambiguous appeals to the imagination, because I did not know precisely what "the imagination" was (in fact, I thought doing this work might educate me to the meanings of imagination, improvisation etc.). For the same reason I would omit mention of sexuality, psychology, spirituality. These I would leave in the hands of the experts, and proceed with what seemed more immediate: the senses and the physical body.

It did seem that before I could begin to train the senses of students, something had to happen in their brains. In recognizing that we do not begin to move from zero, that first we have a desire or image to launch the system into action, I decided that I had to work in the area of images, though cautiously. The images were to be, well, "real." That is, they were not to be obviously unreal.

The effect of obviously unreal images upon the body is fascinating. For example, if you are told to imagine (that word!) your head is filled with a gas that's lighter than air, it is difficult not to respond with neck extension and postural straightening. Why should this be so? It may be related to the sort of mobilization that happens when we are searching for a lost object—first, the thought of the object, then the eye movements, the head turning, standing up, facing in different directions, a tentative walk to a new viewpoint or a possible site of the object. All this prompted by the mental image of the desired object. The responsiveness of the body to the image is innate, apparently, and with this innate connection the body may be responsive to any image the mind holds. But this is speculation about things that should be the subject of investigations. Without a theory of imagination to support our investigations, it seemed to me, we would have to improvise without fictitious gases in the head—if that were possible.

At any rate, I had only about a week to convey the central idea before we, a group of apt students and myself, would be doing it in public at the John Weber Gallery in New York City each afternoon. This time pressure meant that this effect of images on the body would be essential in transmitting the initial states of this physical duet/improvisation as directly as possible. The first job was to point out this image-action connection. Then, exercises that demonstrate it in various parts of the body had to be produced. For instance, a mental exercise I gave while people were standing, in which they were to "imagine, but don't do it, imagine that you are about to take a step forward with your left foot. What is the difference? As you were. Imagine . . . (*repeat*). Imagine that you are about to take a step with your right foot. Your left. Right. Left. Standing."

At this point, small smiles sometimes appeared on people's faces and I suspected they felt the effect. They had gone on an imaginary walk and had felt their weight responding subtly (but really) to the image; so when "Standing" was said, the smiles revealed that they got the small joke. They realized that I knew about the effect. We had arrived at an invisible (but real) place together.

The stand was useful. The basic event was standing and observing the body. This was an exercise in itself, though a very reductive one. What gets exercised in there, inside the standing body, is the habit of observation; a noticeable movement of consciousness through the body. Within this exercise there are encounters with parts of the body that tick along or breathe along as we watch. It clearly seems to be one subsystem, consciousness, examining others. The other subsystems are not obviously connected to the wandering consciousness, except that the encounter happens in what one calls "my body." The consciousness-as-observer regards the other subsystems as separate from itself.

The consciousness can travel inside the body. It is analogous to focusing the eyes in the external world. There is also an analogue for peripheral vision, which is the awareness of the whole body with senses open. Knowing these things and practicing them are different things, of course. We know far more than we can practice. We had to decide what to practice. One choice was the tiny movements the body makes while standing. I felt they were examples of reflex actions. They were not directed by the observing consciousness. Observing them might train the consciousness to understand reflex speed without going through an emergency experience, which is when we're most often aware of our reflexes.

We would be provided with many examples of reflex action when we began improvising in contact, but they might be of little use, because the consciousness can easily turn off to the experience of these reflexive moments. In other words, we can do something without "knowing" it. This turning off successfully preserves the integrity of the body but does not train the consciousness; it leaves a hole in the knowing of the experience. Could the consciousness learn to see these gaps of awareness? Or, if not, could it at least learn to observe reflexive action calmly during the highly adrenalized moments?

Why is *full* consciousness so important to me? Because consciousness can be felt to change according to what it experiences. If a gap of consciousness occurs at a critical moment, we lose an opportunity to learn from the moment. A blackout lasting fractions of a second during a roll is not acceptable as full consciousness of the roll, and the gap will remain embedded in the movement as part of the overall feeling of the movement. If consciousness stays open during these critical moments, it will have an experience of them, and will enlarge its concept to match the new experience. This expanded picture becomes the new ground for moving.

My speculation is that the gaps are moments when consciousness goes away. I don't know where. But I think I know why. Something is happening that is too fast for thought. For instance, the navigation of space is normally done with head erect and visual impressions comfortably constant, with the horizon's horizontality remaining an important reference for orientation. When this visual reference changes too rapidly for our (rather slow) consciousness to comprehend, as in spinning, rolling, and other "disorienting" movement, something reflexive and much faster than consciousness takes over. We play with this dual aspect of ourselves on carnival rides, or when learning to turn in dance.

Dizziness and nausea are, I think, signals that we have reached the borderland between these two aspects of physical control: conscious and reflexive. When we linger in the borderland on purpose, we become our own experiment. We are subjecting the reflexes to stimuli so our consciousness can watch them jump. Normally, consciousness easily slips out, reflexes step in, and then step aside again, as in the blink of an eye where most of the time we are unaware of any gap in our visual continuity.

Visual continuity is one of many ways we know "where we are," and not knowing where we are is experienced as an emergency situation. How many times a day, or an hour, do we reorient, I wonder. At any rate, Contact Improvisation constantly challenges one's orientation: visual, directional, balance, and where in the body the consciousness is positioned. The challenge to orientation is not just in the more acrobatic aspects of the movement. Students were sometimes made nauseous by noticing their internal space while standing still. This, oddly enough, is probably a form of motion sickness, which has been described as having a moving deck under one's feet but a steady horizon. In the stand, one experiences still feet and moving consciousness inside the body. In rolling or turning, the room seems (from the point of view of the eyes) to move, while the floor remains stable to the touch. What I had to do was resolve the problem of orientation so that the consciousness could stay aware of the movement. A chicken and egg problem.

Everyone in this group was athletic and many of them were dancers, so presumably their consciousness had already been informed by body movement. But they weren't being asked to do what they knew how to do. They were being asked to improvise; to do (or allow themselves to do) what they didn't expect to do. Under these circumstances previously learned movement techniques often hamper rather than help the desired sort of manifestation. Movement techniques are useful for other reasons, of course, but not for examining gaps of consciousness during unexpected movement.

Consciousness, supported by a collection of images and internal observations that reinforced each other, had a job. It should not press the body, nor engage in time travel out of the body into memories or schedules because these bring images that will also affect the body, distracting from the improvisation at hand. In this improvisation the consciousness was to hang in with the body, during real time, and stay alert. It should be a witness. This sort of consciousness—awareness of the present physical reality—is familiar to all of us. In fact, it is useful because it is commonly understood, although employing it requires choices. Without a process of sorting we are confronted with such a variety of current physical images that we are inundated rather than guided into a practice.

As the right kind of images were found, a *working model* began to emerge in my mind. The working model was based on aspects of an experience that I'd had while working with another person, in which an interesting event occurred and was confirmed by both of us. Moments of the duet, typically manifesting as "accidental" and flowing streams of movement, were for both of us pleasant, highly stimulating, and elemental. With other partners, more confirmations. It was worth pursuing. The working model was predicated on this experience and a desire to articulate the experience so others could find it. If others did find it, we were perhaps examining a basic mode of communication between the reflexes of people in physical contact as they moved. It was an idea that took two people to have. It wasn't wrestling, embracing, sex, social dancing, though it was an element of all of those. It needed a name, so we could refer to it without unwanted connotations. Contact Improvisation . . . ?

To envision the exercises, I took the working model to be a simple imaginary person with no physical, sensorial, or social inhibitions. It was a generic person with positive elements I had observed in many students, dancers, martial artists, and children. I had met such a being in my partners when we were doing "it," the duet phenomenon. I had been such a being to them, apparently, when they too confirmed the moment. It had to be a fairly simple model, because the users (the students and I) were actually functioning human beings with more possible neuronal connections than there are particles in the universe. I could not cope with that, of course, nor with other evident human complexities. In terms of the safety of the body in interaction with another body, though, I saw I could ask the students to concentrate on their movement and how it feels, and then suggest concentrating on the sensations of their weight, momentum, friction, the touch of their partner, the sensation of the floor under their body, and to learn to maintain their peripheral vision of the space. The working model had these characteristics and others equally easy to understand.

These were aimed at security, not at improvising. I recall saying that improvising could not be taught, though it could be learned.

But I did think that safety could be taught. "Keep your knees over your toes," for instance, is taught to students of dance. With the characteristics of the working model developed and understood by the students, I hoped they would be safe even if they were ass-over-teakettle. I pressed on. I made assumptions. I assumed I could explain things directly to the body ("notice gravity"). I assumed the body knew what I was talking about (gravity, usually ignored, moves into focus as a sensation of weight). I assumed that the body, having evolved for millions of years on this planet, was tuned first by planetary things that create our potentials, and second by cultural things that develop select parts of the potential. This notion of dual formation is in line with some current theories about how we acquire language; we are born with the potential to make the variety of human sounds and language connections, but are guided into the specific language of our culture, and the unused potential withers with disuse.

For the working model, the basic question was: potential for what? What had the culture physically suppressed or selected out that we might reclaim? We may, with a bit of experience of subcultures of our own, and other cultures, understand something of what our culture requires of us for inclusion: certain gestures, modes of posture and behavior (body language, as they say) that constitute proper social activities and communications, as well as the accompanying mental attitudes we acquire or aspire to for proper presentation of our "selves." Indeed, the very idea of a "self" is probably a cultural construction.

In sports and dance the rules of physical behavior are altered from the basic social behaviors to encompass activities understood to be outside the social norm but allowable in a controlled way. These activities require different sensing modes than does the usual body language we must learn for eating in company or attending school. The working model and its characteristics were like sports and dance in that they were altered. However, they depart from one another in how they are learned. Contact Improvisation behavior evolves from sensing movement; dance and sports, from attempting movement and then letting the senses fall into line, or not.

As to how we are educated . . . Not to become too embroiled in this, we may simply note that most of us learn to sit still and focus our attention for hours each day. The missing potential here is obvious—movement of the body and varieties of peripheral sensing. Our alterations involved the investigation of space, time, and mass with senses in peripheral sensing mode: space becomes spherical, time is the present, mass is a changeable orientation to gravity.

In devising an approach to this working model of the body, I skipped blithely by constraints and taboos of touching, because people are accustomed to ignoring them on the subway, during sports, or in the doctor's office. And I did not emphasize the unpredictable nature of the improvisation, akin to dancing on constantly shifting ground, but suggested instead a *steady state* of watching the reflexes. Let the reflexes figure out how to deal with the unpredictable. This method aimed to reclaim physical possibilities that may have become dormant, senses we have been trained to disregard. What would this lead to, really? It sounds very nice, this reclaiming and opening, but where would these changes take us? Who would we be?

When we began, in 1972, I went boldly into all this. The people in the group were young, healthy, and alert. I assumed that if we didn't consciously focus on problems we wouldn't create them; at least such difficulties as surfaced would not have been projected. As I said, things seemed simpler then.

It was to be assumed that some of these students would eventually teach something of what they were doing to others, and I felt the need to develop this material in such a way that the students were aware of the teaching mechanisms. It boiled down to making the principles—physical, mental, and cultural—known to them as they learned them. We had the services of Steve Christiansen and his video camera and spent hours, when we were not working on the mat, examining the movement and ourselves, the movers.

This was very useful. Video was, in those days, a new tool for witnessing the body/mind, and for letting us see points in action when we were operative but not conscious. Such moments, noticed with the help of the videotape or close observation by a partner, could later be examined in action. Clues about the nature of the gap might be noticed. We began to notice where the gaps appeared, at any rate, and something of their frequency. We also noticed high unfettered moments (and recalled the accompanying feelings). And we observed fettered duets where reflexive movement was not to be seen. Sometimes people seemed wary, unable to let go of conscious control. Disorientation, fear, or fixed habitual responses would be noticed.

In the working model, events of the emotions and disorientations that were felt in conjunction with a gap in awareness were considered to be symptomatic that the senses were not quite ready to report what was happening to the consciousness, that instead they were reporting to the reflexive part of the mind and body. I couldn't understand the wary duets. Obviously trust was missing. With some other partner or on some other day, this tended to change. All I could do to cope with this mode was to have partners change regularly. Eventually everyone found a duet that led her to her reflexes.

The movement techniques I proposed sometimes contravened ingrained movement habits: for instance, the Aikido roll, which is a diagonally forward roll that arrived on our shores from the Orient. At the very attempt at this roll, students translated it into a somersault, the symmetrical forward roll we learn in Western movement. This misunderstanding could persist through any number of repetitions of examples and attempts and was seriously frustrating to both the students and me. If they couldn't put their finger on what was going wrong, I decided, it was perhaps because nothing in previous movement experience had prepared them for the movement principles that were developed in the Eastern martial arts. These repeated attempts at the aikido roll provided the first gap I noticed. The act of propelling the body into the roll is slightly scary: many people have open eyes before and after the roll, but in the moment when they are taking weight on their neck and shoulders, they have their eyes squeezed shut, and they are not aware that this is so.

I did not solve this two-part problem in time for the first performance, nor for many years after, though the students did perfect their somersaults. I learned that before the body could find the new rolling pattern it was useful for it to learn the sensations that an aikido roll creates. The new sensations, and the parts of the arm, shoulder, and back where the sensations arise in the roll, could be explored without committing the whole body to the roll. This changed the position of the consciousness relative to the exercise. Instead of an unknown action versus a habitual known action (so similar that it subverts the attempt), the student has two knowable actions. One is new, tentative, but understood through the sensorial model. The other is habitual. Having remedied the first difficulty by establishing the difference between the two concepts of rolling, the gaps of consciousness in either could be ferreted out.

These explorations evolved into new technical approaches. It was noticeable that the approaches required the student to work with helpful mental attitudes as well as directly with the physical body. In the aikido-roll example above, it was less helpful to know the pattern mentally and try willfully to do it than it was to become an observer of the sensations and to work calmly on each emotional, orientational, or habitual block as it arose. The quality of consciousness was coming into focus. It wasn't all of consciousness and all possible interactions, of course. A working model for consciousness in this case is Swiss cheese. We buy it as a lump, and don't attend to the holes because we don't use them. I was trying to point to the holes, assuming that if a Swiss cheese could be aware of itself, then the cheesy part was one sort of consciousness and the holes were another sort, integral to the shape, the nature of the whole cheese. We can't take this model much further, I realize—so let's get on with the movement and its interaction with the consciousness.

As we began work on opening up the senses to their larger potential, it became clear that each of the senses has images of differing natures. The Swiss cheese above, mostly a visual image in that I am concentrating on how the cheese looks, occurred in my brain and was transferred to another person by my voice, so it was a verbal transmission of a visual image. What was most needed in our work was kinetic imagery that was both appropriate to the movement mode and true (unlike the speculation about the consciousness of the cheese).

The small movements of standing "still," which formed the basis of this sort of investigation, are true; they are really there. But are they images or sensations? If we observed them, would they filter through the observing mind and affect the body as images do? Does the nervous system and its mediation of posture relative to gravity have the possibility of teaching the consciousness? And does the consciousness have the property of amplifying or strengthening that mediation?

I assumed this reciprocity did exist. I decided that sensations are what we feel to be happening at the moment, and they can become images when we take notice that we are observing them. This suggests that the consciousness can be aware of itself—a defining characteristic—and that there is a positive use for this ability to split into self-regard. However, consciousness doesn't work very well with the unknown, as was revealed in the Aikido roll. Apparently it needs to know or to be noticing in order to direct itself and the body. The attitude of "witnessing" may change this internal awareness/control issue. The search for internal sensations reveals that "I can feel the small movements." Then our attitude begins to shift toward "the body is kept upright by constant reflexive muscular actions around the skeleton." First we feel the movements, then we can objectify the feelings into images. The moment between these perceptions can be as short as a hyphen. All the above suggests that there is an important difference between knowing-noticing and noticing-knowing.

These are the sorts of thoughts that came to mind during the working period from January to June 1972. Or to say it in terms of the work: from *Magnesium* at Oberlin College through the spring term at Bennington College where we further identified the premise, the phenomenon, to the presentation of the work in New York City that I called "Contact Improvisations." Students from those two institutions (plus members of the downtown dance community in New York who "sat in") were joined by students from the classes of Mary Fulkerson at the University of Rochester. The Rochester group was least familiar with the proposed movement and, as Fulkerson was teaching them Release Technique via intensive *image work,* it was in order to reach these students quickly in the approach outlined above that images were developed beyond what had been necessary at Bennington College.

At Bennington, I had begun by introducing these students of Western dance to Aikido techniques. However, I soon abandoned teaching Aikido and started work on specific tools for the interior techniques. Although physical techniques could be found for specific movement training, what those students required was a vision of the Eastern martial arts philosophy underlying the techniques (or a viable replacement for that). This re-visioning laid the ground for introducing an improvisation that requires a state of personal involvement and physical responsibility with/for another person. (It must be pointed out that many of the ideas about moving that I used existed before this study. The teachings of Release Technique, Aikido, and several other physical and mental disciplines were influential, and were adjusted according to my understanding at the time in order to convey the movement principles described by the words *Contact Improvisation*.)

To enable the movement to be accomplished safely, physical exercises were designed to introduce sensations that arise during "flying" (lifting and being lifted), and to physically strengthen the body for these energetic extremes of the form. Physical strength was seen as the result of finding the right (that is, the easiest, most efficient) inner "pathways." Stress was discouraged. We were starting to work on the technical method, a work that continues today, in an effort to describe what Contact Improvisation is (1) on its own terms as a phenomenon of duet movement, and (2) on the personal terms of a student. Some students, for instance, have physical strength but spatial weakness; some possess solo improvisational skills but refuse to trust their weight to another person.

To summarize: images were used to concentrate the mind and then give the mind foci within the sensations of the body. The words were to be unambiguous, unthreatening, informative, and generally understood. The statements were to be true, obvious, relevant.

To speak was also to set the tone. I tried to simplify the issues of the body for transmission to another body. I moved the mind of my mouth into my body, located issues, and reported the issues speaking (I assumed) directly to another body. The student's consciousness was enlisted to manage attitudes and observe the effect of image on the body—and to derive from these effects, and others observed within their bodies, images that could be named, objectified and discussed, and fitted into the improvisational structure.

I made a number of assumptions. To study something like improvisation, which is defined as you go, everything you assume is going to affect the result. I tried to be aware of what the assumptions were and to let the phenomenon we explored—the narrower field of improvisation when communicating via touch with another person—guide the definitive imagery into appropriate areas.

This guidance caused us to consider all sorts of things, such as communication, emotion, psychology, sex, education, childhood development, culture, taboos, space, time, and the self. It is all very well to say that one takes responsibility for one's self in improvisation, but it is indeed a staggering job in its details. An improviser's job is never done. All this to explore the ability of the consciousness to cleave to the body's moment and remain there as the moment changes.

NOTE
This essay was originally published in *Contact Quarterly* 18, no. 1 (Winter–Spring 1993): 61–66. It was dedicated to John Cage.

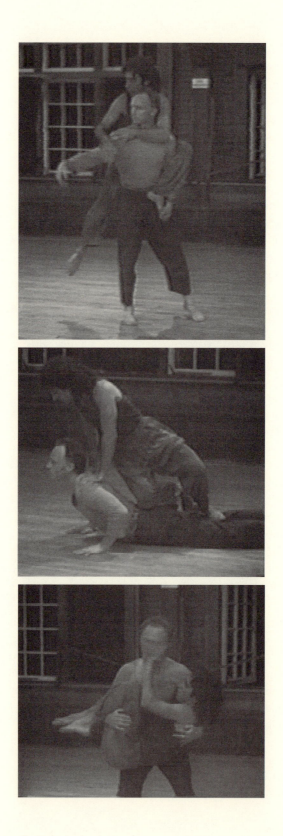

EMBODIED MEANINGS

Performing, Interpreting, and Talking about Dance Improvisation

Raymond W. Gibbs, Jr.

What can dance improvisation tell us about how people think? There are many reasons why people participate in, observe, and talk about (or write about) improvisational dance. The analysis of the improvisational process is of great interest to me as a cognitive psychologist because it directly explores the boundaries of the body/mind interface. Dance improvisation shares many qualities with improvisation in other art forms such as music, painting, and theater. At the same time, like other art forms, dance improvisation shares many features with how people think, speak, and move in everyday life. Although cognitive science (the fields of cognitive psychology, linguistics, philosophy, neuroscience, and computer science) can offer profound insights about the improvisation process from its empirical understanding of how people think and imagine, I believe that the study of improvisation in dance can also play a central role in our contemporary understanding of the human mind. The essential link between improvisation in dance and the mind is found in the body.

My interest in meaning as an embodied experience differs considerably from cognitive scientists' traditional concerns with how people think and act in rational, planned situations. The traditional view in Western intellectual history is that the mind and body are separable.[1] Much of contemporary psychology thinks about the mind as disembodied—one reason it seems easier to study the mind as a kind of computer than it is to study how we think, reason, and imagine in our everyday, embodied experience.[2] Most scholarly work on human creativity, a key feature of dance improvisation, focuses on how the mind can break away from constraining patterns of thought to facilitate divergent thinking.[3] The body, far from being the source of many creative ideas, is recognized more as a limiting force both in how we think and act creatively and how students of the mind think about cognitive processes.

In recent years several psychologists,[4] anthropologists,[5] linguists,[6] and philosophers[7] have started to challenge traditional dualist views of mind and body and have begun to explore the embodied nature of human experience. Consideration

Fig. P1. Alito Alessi and Julyen Hamilton in *Hilary*, video stills from a performance at A Capella Motion, Northhampton, Massachusetts, 1993. (Printed with permission of Alito Alessi.)

of how individuals make sense of their experience as dancers and as observers of improvisational dance nicely complements these other studies. No one can participate in or observe dance without immediately recognizing meaningful patterns of movement that communicate something about how people think about aspects of their experience. Just as two people must coordinate their actions as they improvise in spoken dialogue, Contact Improvisation, as the name implies, requires dancers to coordinate and cooperate as they lean against and balance each other, give support or are supported by each other, roll on the floor and over each other, jump up, fall, and perform various other solo and shared movements. Dancers and observers might not be consciously aware of these meaningful patterns as they move and watch. Yet a few moments of reflection on the aesthetic pleasure we get as dancers and observers clearly suggests that dance, especially improvisational dance, summons up important aspects of embodied cognition.

In this essay, I shall explore some of the relationships between dance improvisation and everyday language to show how each reflects significant aspects of human embodied meaning. My main argument is that Contact Improvisation illustrates an important part of our ability to conceptualize human experience in terms of metaphor. Metaphor is not merely a linguistic device to facilitate communication, but a specific mental mapping in which we attempt to better understand one, usually vague, abstract aspect of knowledge in terms of more concrete knowledge from a different domain. Most important, various mental, or conceptual, metaphors are rooted in recurring bodily experiences. We use our embodied understandings as source domains to better structure more abstract domains of experience. It is exactly here where the parallels between everyday language and Contact Improvisation seem most powerful and inviting to explore.

A CONTACT IMPROVISATION PERFORMANCE

The power of embodied metaphor in the performance and interpretation of Contact Improvisation is best demonstrated in terms of an actual performance. I consider my own response to the first few minutes of a Contact Improvisation duet by Julyen Hamilton and Alito Alessi, originally presented as part of A Cappella Motion, (1993).[8]

Julyen and Alito's performance begins with the two dancers walking onto the stage and Julyen lying facedown on the floor, arms extended in front; Alito moves over to squat on the back of Julyen's thighs. Julyen then raises his head and shoulders and looks behind to observe Alito, simultaneously extending his arms in front of him. Julyen lies back down and Alito moves upward onto Julyen's back, balancing himself, arms extended, then standing on Julyen's back as Julyen once more rises, this time to his hands and knees. Alito sits on top of Julyen, riding him. Soon Julyen couples his hands around Alito's feet as Alito wraps his legs around Julyen's trunk. Julyen stands, walks around the stage, and twirls Alito around in circles as Alito twists on Julyen's back, extending arms and legs outward in different directions, sometimes using Julyen's one extended arm as a guide. Julyen then stops his walking and slowly pulls Alito around in front of him, and, while still standing, cradles Alito in his arms. Alito lays back, arms extended over his head, legs extended outward. Julyen then forcefully attempts to pull Alito up and Alito jerks spasmodically (which causes the audience to laugh). Julyen again makes the same attempt, and again Alito jerks spasmodically (again the audience laughs).

Even within these first few minutes of Julyen and Alito's duet, I am struck by several specific movements and several general themes that suggest the influence of embodied metaphors. Through a number of movements and positions, the dancers, both individually and in concert, exhibit great symmetry, balance, support, linkage, emotional involvement, and independence. As the performance proceeds, the dancers appear to be on an improvisational journey heading toward some unknown destination that unfolds in front of them. At several moments, both the dancers and the audience appear to be "taken by surprise" as one movement leads unexpectedly into another positioning and/or movement. I see the dancers awakening, coming together, struggling over different personal and collective obstacles, experiencing moments of calm, moments of great elation, moving toward places where they are in tight synchronicity. At other times, they appear to be feeling each other out for possible new ways to be joined together for their individual and collective benefit.

My responses here are quite visceral; they arise automatically within me as I watch the performance. This improvisational dance speaks to me, a nondancer, and suggests meanings, emotions, that I find hard to ignore. But where do these interpretations come from? Are they the product of my own individual sensibilities or are they part of conventional systems of meaning that I have been exposed to, become enculturated to, over time? I believe that a significant part of how I make sense of Contact Improvisation is based on widely shared *conceptual metaphors* that have their roots in ordinary embodied experience and can be seen in everyday, as well as poetic, language.

METAPHOR IN LANGUAGE, THOUGHT, AND DANCE

Metaphor is fundamental to human thought. It is nearly impossible for us to conceive of ourselves, others, the world we live in without embracing the power of metaphor. We use metaphor not only to express our thoughts linguistically, but to make sense of our everyday experiences and to establish coherence out of an inchoate world.[9] Ask people about some aspect of their lives and metaphor will inevitably burst forth, sometimes dominating the narrative. Although no one claims that all human concepts are metaphorical, various work in cognitive science has demonstrated the prominent role of metaphor in structuring many, especially abstract, concepts.[10] Empirical studies have shown that several hundred metaphorical systems are pervasive in everyday thought and help structure a large variety of domains of human experience (for example, time, causation, spatial orientation, emotions, politics, concepts of morality). These conceptual metaphors are not isolated linguistic statements, but reflect modes of thought in which we try to understand difficult, complex, abstract, or less delineated concepts (the target domain) in terms of familiar, often embodied, ideas (the source domain), such as when we conceive of Life as a Journey, Time as Money, Emotions as Containers, and Love as a Physical Force.

Consider just a few of the other ways that people think and speak metaphorically about their experiences. Pay special attention to the spatial, embodied character of these metaphors: they suggest important links between metaphor and embodied meanings in dance, including some of the interpretations I find myself thinking about while watching Julyen and Alito's dance performance.

The conceptual metaphors Happy is Up and Sad is Down (I'm feeling up, That boosted my spirits, My spirits rose, You're in high spirits, I'm feeling down, I'm depressed, He's really low these days, My spirits sank) reflect the recurring bodily experiences that drooping posture typically goes along with sadness and depression, and erect posture with a positive emotional state.

The conceptual metaphors Consciousness is Up and Unconsciousness is Down (Get up, Wake up, I'm up already, He fell asleep, He's under hypnosis, He sank into a coma) reflect the recurring bodily truth that humans and most other mammals sleep lying down and stand up when they are awake.

The conceptual metaphors Health and Life are Up and Sickness and Death are Down (He's at the peak of health, Lazarus rose from the dead, He's in top shape, He's sinking fast, He came down with the flu, His health is declining, He dropped dead) reflect the recurring bodily experiences that serious illness forces us to lie down physically. When you are dead, you are physically down.

The conceptual metaphors Having Control or Force is Up and Being Subject to Control or Force is Down (I have control over her, I am on top of the situation, He's at the height of his power, He ranks above me, He's under my control, He fell from power, He is low man on the totem pole) reflect bodily experiences in which physical size typically correlates with physical strength, and the victor in a fight is typically on top.

The conceptual metaphors Unsteadiness is Near Failure and Falling is Failure (He stumbled through his oral exams, The government is tottering, His jokes fell flat, The scheme fell through, The government has fallen) reflect the idea that to be erect and straight represents moral qualities of straightforwardness, uprightness, and respectability. Stooping and bent body positions are associated with debasement and failure to stand erect (They hung their heads in shame, Her spirits dropped, They were weighed down with grief). To be crooked is to be dishonest (That man is crooked).

These metaphorical concepts are not arbitrary. They have a basis in our physical, embodied experience. Such spatial, embodied metaphors arise from the fact that we have bodies of the sort we have and that they function as they do in our physical environment. Many aspects of Julyen and Alito's performance make use of these body-based metaphors. For example, various body postures and movements express via metaphor different sorts of conventional meanings. Upward movements, following the conceptual metaphors of Happiness is Up, Good Health is Up, and Having Control is Up, are suggestive of positive affect, and of greater conscious control of one's body and, more generally, one's life. For instance, there are many moments in Julyen and Alito's dance when their upward movement, both while on the ground and while standing, signifies positive emotions, especially when they are in balanced positions of contact.

On the other hand, downward body postures and movements reflect the metaphors of Sadness is Down, Sickness and Death are Down, and Being Subject to Control from People is Down, suggesting negative affect when individuals are under stress, have poor health, and have little control over their movements and their lives. The opening of Julyen and Alito's performance, when Julyen lies prone with Alito on top of him, suggests, even if for a moment, Alito's control over Julyen. At the very beginning Julyen lifts his head and looks over his shoulder at Alito as if to question this control. Some of their unsteady movements and positions reflect the metaphor of Unsteadiness is Near Failure and suggests uncertainty. Falling reflects the Falling is Failure metaphor and represents lack of control, illness, and feelings of debasement. At a later moment in Julyen and Alito's dance, Alito runs toward Julyen and leaps into his arms, as if wishing to establish a more personal bond between them. But the movement fails because the dancers are immediately unbalanced and the two dancers tumble onto the stage very gracefully and start anew to establish contact. Throughout the performance, bodily movements that are balanced, when a dancer is moving, or stationed alone, or in contact with other dancers, reflect mental, emotional, and moral stability.

Beyond these brief observations about some of the embodied metaphors underlying Julyen and Alito's dance, I shall consider in more detail one conceptual metaphor that is pervasive in thought and language, and which, for me, structures many aspects of Julyen and Alito's performance. The conceptual metaphor Life is a Journey (Look how far we've come, It's been a long, bumpy road, We're at a crossroads, We may have to go our separate ways, Our marriage is on the rocks, We're spinning our wheels) emerges from our embodied experiences as we first learn to focus our eyes and track forms as they move throughout our visual field and, later on, move our bodies in the real world, from reaching for objects and other people to moving our entire bodies from one point to another. From these varied experiences, a recurring pattern becomes manifest in tracking a trajectory from point A to point B. The pattern itself may vary considerably (many objects, shapes, types of paths), but the emergent experiential gestalt can be projected onto more abstract domains of understanding and reasoning. Thus, the emergent gestalt of our many journeys starting from a source, traveling along some path, and ending up at some destination, gives rise to conceptual metaphors such as Life is a Journey.

We see the prominence of the Life is a Journey metaphor in the many conventional expressions shown above, each expression reflecting different aspects of the complex mental mapping of journeys onto the concept of life. Furthermore, the Life is a Journey metaphor demonstrates how we speak in coherent ways about aspects of our experiences that are otherwise incoherent: for example, when we embark on our careers, but along the way get sidetracked or led astray, and are diverted from our original goal. We try to "get back on the right path" and to "keep the end in view" as we "move along." Eventually we may "come a long way" and "reach our goal." It is not simply an arbitrary fact of English that we speak about our lives and careers in terms of sources, paths, and goals; rather, we metaphorically conceptualize our experiences through very basic, sensory experiences that are abstracted to form higher-level metaphoric thought.

In Julyen and Alito's dance, movements across the stage reflect aspects of the Life is a Journey metaphor with embodied experience of physical journeys as its source domain. Here the movement from point A along some path to point B expresses progress toward some concrete or abstract, sometimes personal, goal. One sees the struggle when the dancers first begin a journey (some movement from point A to point B), the obstacles they encounter along the way, how they try, and sometimes fail, to support each other, the times when they seem to be spinning their wheels (including one moment later in Julyen and Alito's performance when Alito actually walks briskly in place), until they break free and almost fly toward their long-anticipated goal. The movements Julyen and Alito perform are not interpreted by observers simply as arbitrary physical acts with no sense of purpose or communicative meaning. Instead, the basic images in their dance are movement structures that are imaginatively patterned and flexible, both in terms of their physical instantiation and their symbolic interpretation.

EMBODIED METAPHOR AND SUBJECTIVE INTERPRETATION

Many dancers and dance scholars might object that the metaphorical systems of meaning I refer to in my analysis of Julyen and Alito's performance appear far too analytic and reductive. After all, concepts like Happiness is Up, Being Subject to Control is Down, and Life is a Journey are highly abstract, clichéd ideas. One of the beauties of Contact Improvisation is the willingness of dancers to challenge tradition, to resist what is cliché about experience and thought, to break the chains of cultural prohibitions against touch and intimate interpersonal space. Contact Improvisation is much more than the physical instantiation of cliché metaphors, isn't it? Moreover, if one asks a dancer why he or she moved in some way at a particular improvisational moment, it is unlikely that any thought of metaphors or systematic patterns of embodied cognition will come to mind. Most dancers even resist trying to articulate in words what their movements mean.

I don't deny the power of Contact Improvisation to work against cliché, to resist common cultural beliefs, and to be a subversive force in the dance world. Nor do I deny the authority of dancers and dance scholars to voice their own ideas about the historical, political, and personal influences on the creation and interpretation of Contact Improvisation. But common, deeply rooted patterns of embodied metaphor have a strong role in the performance and interpretation of improvisational dance. Dancers and observers may not be aware of these metaphorical patterns, precisely because they are so much an automatic part of our ordinary existence. Our intuitions alone fail to provide us with access to these embodied metaphors, but these metaphors are nonetheless revealed when we look more closely at the systematic ways people speak about their experience and at the ways that people move both in everyday life and when creating improvisational pieces.

Cliché metaphors are not dead historical entities that have little role in contemporary thought and action. Consider the idea that Love is a Journey as reflected in the linguistic statements "It's been a long bumpy road" and "We may have to go our separate ways." Most literary theorists view these expressions as reflecting dead metaphors that were once alive but now have become conventionalized and cliché. Yet the same metaphorical concept about love is seen in great works of poetry. Consider how one poet, Pablo Neruda, offers unique, poetic statements about a love relationship in a poem titled "Ode and Burgeonings."[11]

> My wild girl, we have had
> to regain time
> and march backward, in the distance
> of our lives, kiss after kiss,
> gathering from one place what we gave
> without joy, discovering in another
> the secret road
> that gradually brought your feet
> closer to mine.

Although few individuals possess the talent to express their thoughts poetically in quite this manner, Neruda's poem illustrates how a significant part of our ability to think creatively about concepts, especially abstract ones such as those having to do with love and one's love relationships, are partly motivated by our bodily experiences in the real world. In these lines, Neruda talks about going *backward, in the distance* (that is, the path) of his love relationship with the *wild girl,* stopping at those places that *we gave without joy* to find *the secret road* that brought true unity and happiness. Providing new ways of looking at the entailments of conceptual metaphor is itself a creative act. But our ability as readers to interpret these lines stems from our shared conceptual metaphors. What is frequently seen as a creative metaphorical expression of some idea is often only a spectacular instantiation of specific metaphorical entailments that arise from a small set of conceptual metaphors (here, Love is a Journey) shared by many individuals within a culture. Thinking creatively is motivated by aspects of bodily experience in the sense that there is some tacit connection between human embodiment (our experiences of taking journeys) and how we think about different concepts (love and love relationships). The fact that we, as ordinary readers, have similar metaphorical understandings of many abstract concepts, ones that arise from our own embodied experiences, allows us to make sense of creative works.

My appreciation of Contact Improvisation is somewhat similar to my experience of reading the work of great poets. Dancers, like poets, do not necessarily create de novo conceptualizations of experience each time they make a dance.

Although poets and dancers each employ language or perform bodily movements in ways that take us by surprise, both poets and dancers are essentially elaborating in creative ways on body-based metaphorical ideas that are possibly shared by all human beings. Once again, we can acknowledge dancers such as Julyen and Alito for their creativity in moving in the moment, positioning themselves alone and in contact with others. At the same time we can (and should) recognize that in part we appreciate Contact Improvisation *not* because something entirely new has been created but because old ideas have been instantiated in new ways.

In fact, much of the creativity we see in Contact Improvisation, such as in Julyen and Alito's performance, rests on our multiple understanding of embodied metaphors. For instance, there are moments of great power and happiness as Julyen and Alito move down across the floor, struggling to find harmony between them. Being down close to the ground might seem to be the opposite of metaphorical notions that to be down is to be sad, in ill-health, unconscious, or even dead. Yet we can take joy in how even those who are down, with great burdens upon their shoulders (as when Alito climbs onto Julyen's back) actually reverse the preexisting metaphorical idea and express different emotional nuances than are traditionally assumed by such body positions. Most important, though, we may be aware, as I was, of how the new insights in an improvisational dance are rooted in established patterns of embodied meaning; at the same time, these same conventional patterns of meaning are overturned and lead to the sense of being "taken by surprise." There is much irony in Contact Improvisation, one of the reasons why it is such a subversive force in dance. Part of our sense that some movements are ironical comes from the tacit recognition that conventional, perhaps embodied meanings, have been reversed. Thus, even when our readings of Contact Improvisation appear to be the opposite of what is suggested by conceptual metaphors, these interpretations still depend on our understanding of the normative quality of certain embodied metaphors.

I am not arguing for an objective interpretation of a Contact dance performance. Instead, I am suggesting how our varied readings of Contact Improvisation in part depend on the multiple nature of recurring embodied metaphors. Many theorists contend that creativity results from the simultaneous appraisal of two opposite concepts.[12] Some of our appreciation of Contact Improvisational dance is based on our tacit recognition of the multiplicity of meanings that we construe for particular sets of movements and positions. Not all aspects of creativity are rooted in, or can be predicted by, bodily experience, but an important part of how we think, reason, and use language in creative ways is motivated by our embodied experiences. Of course, any improvisational dance performance will, in unpredictable ways, consist of many varied movements that may express a whole host of embodied meanings. What is interesting, though, is that even naive observers, those who have not participated in or observed much dance, can see an improvisational performance and come away with a sense of how the performance as a whole expresses certain themes. I like to think that dancers are communicating narratives or stories via a combination of various bodily movements that are reflective of widely shared metaphors. The movements dancers make create the impression of stories that we can understand, not just in the local sense of watching someone move across a stage, but in broader terms of relating to the human story, of our own mundane lives as we struggle to find meaning between order and chaos.

CONCLUSION

How dancers perform, how observers interpret and then talk about Contact Improvisation is strongly based on their recognition of common metaphoric concepts rooted in everyday bodily experience. Metaphor serves as one of the pillars of the creative mind, but as each of us, artists and common folk alike, act creatively, we must recognize the constraints that our common bodily experiences and the resulting abstractive metaphoric concepts place on our creative imagination. Creativity in Contact Improvisation is not merely the result of spontaneous, unconstrained, imaginative thinking (or movement) because body-based metaphoric imagination is a systematic and orderly part of human cognitive processes. Of course, it takes special people such as Julyen and Alito to create wonderful improvisations and talented individuals (that is, dance scholars and critics) to interpret all aspects of an improvisational dance. But the fact that almost any of us can move improvisationally, and can recognize meaningful elements in dance improvisation, suggests that dance and mind share many of the same elements. The foundation for that shared consciousness is the body and how it gives rise to many of the metaphorical ways we ordinarily think about our lives and the world around us. My central claim about the links between body and mind might become hypotheses for future examination by psychologists, and dance practitioners, theorists, and critics. We can also ask to what extent metaphorical concepts that are body-based get elaborated upon in personal, political, and historically constructed models of identity and meaning. Most generally, understanding human embodiment in all of its diversity should be the main arena for interdisciplinary studies of dance and mind in the years to come.

NOTES

1. René Descartes, *The Philosophical Works of Descartes,* vol. 2, trans. Elizabeth S. Haldane and G. R. T. Ross (Cambridge: Cambridge University Press, 1911–12).

2. Jerry A. Fodor, *The Language of Thought* (New York: Crowell, 1975); Zenon W. Pylyshyn, *Computation and Cognition: Toward a Foundation for Cognitive Science* (Cambridge: MIT Press, 1984).

3. Mark A. Runco, *Divergent Thinking* (Norwood, N.J.: Ablex, 1991); Thomas B. Ward, "What's Old about New Ideas?" in *The Creative Cognition Approach,* ed. Steven M. Smith, Thomas B. Ward, and Ronald A. Finke (Cambridge: MIT Press, 1995).

4. Raymond W. Gibbs, *The Poetics of Mind: Figurative Thought, Language, and Understanding* (New York: Cambridge University Press, 1994); Raymond W. Gibbs and H. Colston, "The Cognitive Psychological Reality of Image Schemas and Their Transformations," *Cognitive Linguistics* 6 (1995): 347–78; Francisco J. Varela, Evan Thomp-

son, and Eleanor Rosch, *The Embodied Mind: Cognitive Science and Human Experience* (Cambridge: MIT Press, 1991).

5. Thomas J. Csordas, ed., *Embodiment and Experience: The Existential Ground of Culture and Self* (New York: Cambridge University Press, 1994).

6. George Lakoff, *Women, Fire, and Dangerous Things: What Categories Reveal about the Mind* (Chicago: University of Chicago Press, 1987); George Lakoff and Mark Johnson, *Metaphors We Live By* (Chicago: University of Chicago Press, 1980); George Lakoff and Mark Turner, *More Than Cool Reason: A Field Guide to Poetic Metaphor* (Chicago: University of Chicago Press, 1989); Eve Sweetser, *From Etymology to Pragmatics: Metaphorical and Cultural Aspects of Semantic Structure* (Cambridge: Cambridge University Press, 1990); Mark Turner, *Reading Minds: The Study of English in the Age of Cognitive Science* (Princeton: Princeton University Press, 1991).

7. Mark Johnson, *The Body in the Mind: The Bodily Basis of Meaning, Imagination, and Reason* (Chicago: University of Chicago Press, 1987); Mark Johnson, "Knowing through the Body," *Philosophical Psychology* 4 (1991): 3–20; Mark Johnson, *Moral Imagination: Implications of Cognitive Science for Ethics* (Chicago: University of Chicago Press, 1993); Drew Leeds, *The Absent Body* (Chicago: University of Chicago Press, 1990).

8. This performance does not represent Contact Improvisation in the strictest sense. The performers are not in constant physical touch, and at one point a musical accompaniment is introduced. Both of these elements are uncharacteristic of Contact Improvisation; however, the performers are well-trained Contacters dancing under the aegis of a well-known Contact Improvisation venue.

9. Gibbs, *The Poetics of Mind*, pp. 120–207.

10. Gibbs, *The Poetics of Mind*; Johnson, *The Body in the Mind*; Lakoff, *Women, Fire, and Dangerous Things*; Lakoff and Johnson, *Metaphors We Live By*; Turner, *Reading Minds*.

11. Pablo Neruda, *The Captain's Verses*, trans. Donald D. Walsh (New York: New Directions, 1972), pp. 42.

12. Albert Rothenberg, *The Emerging Goddess: The Creative Process in Art, Science, and Other Fields* (Chicago: University of Chicago Press, 1979), pp. 121–43.

WEIGHTING METAPHORS

A Response to Raymond W. Gibbs and "Hilary"

Karen Schaffman

I sit at my laptop computer and tap, tap, tap away. Rotating to the left, I pick up the remote control and press Play. The television monitor lights up, frame after frame flowing in seamless electrical currency. I watch two men dancing together in the rustic Crewhouse of Smith College. Then I turn to the manuscript that lies adjacent to my laptop, searching for a particular phrase.

I approach this essay as a Contact Improvisation trio, as if I were partnering both the video of "Hilary," danced by Julyen Hamilton and Alito Alessi, and Raymond W. Gibbs's essay, "Embodied Meanings: Performing, Interpreting, and Talking About Dance Improvisation." The three of us are in a process of investigating the performative strategies of Contact Improvisation. I cannot ignore these others: their moves affect mine, and I could not create this dance without them provoking and stimulating my pathways. They have been dancing while I have been watching. Now it's my turn to enter, from the outside of the observational arena I step inside the dance-space.

I glance at the essay poised on the edge of the desk and flip through the pages again and again. I wonder as my head sways back and forth across the text. Capital letters declaring metaphors as manifestos of embodiment. Bold letters pronouncing intent. My speculation begins, inspired by that which is absent from Gibbs's analysis. Who is Hilary anyhow? And how does s/he operate as a metaphor? *Click.* Alessi swoons and is swooped up by Hamilton. Is Alessi some feminized persona attempting to embody Hilary? *Fast Forward.* Hamilton cradles Alessi. Is Alessi personifying a child named Hilary? *Rewind.* Alessi smacks Hamilton. Is Hilary the other woman the two men are dueling over? *Pause.* Two men embrace. Is Hamilton Hilary? Or is Alessi?

I turn back toward the manuscript and sharpen my focus. Gibbs's essay proposes to illustrate ways in which everyday bodily experience applies to the production of meaning in Contact Improvisation. Gibbs discusses how a viewer's understanding of dancing stands in relation to embedded metaphors of language. *Stands in relation to . . . I reposition myself. Upright. Vertical. Erect on two feet, as tall as I can*

Fig. Q1. Alito Alessi and Julyen Hamilton in *Hilary,* video stills from a performance at A Capella Motion, Northhampton, Massachusetts, 1993. (Printed with permission of Alito Alessi.)

be. Everyday we engage in an improvisation of spoken and physical metaphors. Metaphors create common ground for communication, serving us in getting what we need, going where we need to get, and doing what we deem necessary to do. *Pressing and locating.* Gibbs writes that "no one can participate in or observe dance without immediately recognizing meaningful patterns of movement that communicate something about how people think about aspects of their experience." I would claim instead that spectators bring to a dance performance certain expectations influenced by a set of *culturally specific* metaphors that determine their viewing experiences. By adding that these metaphors are in fact culturally specific, I differ from Gibbs, who takes a universalistic approach, believing that "body-based metaphors are possibly shared by all human beings." Contact Improvisation, according to Gibbs's understanding, "is based on widely shared *conceptual metaphors* that have their roots in ordinary embodied experience and can be seen in everyday, as well as poetic, language." Here I challenge Gibbs: What is "ordinary embodied experience?" Whose "everyday language" is Gibbs talking about? Is there anything "ordinary" about Contact Improvisation? How does Contact Improvisation operate as a metaphor for "everyday language"?

I lean into the essay. Gibbs approaches "Hilary" through the lens of his particular conception of everyday metaphors, bringing standardized notions of "up" and "down" into his interpretation of the dance. He writes that the dancers' upward movement "signifies positive emotions, especially when they are in balanced positions of contact." And, "where Julyen lies prone with Alito on top of him, suggests, even for a moment, Alito's control over Julyen." Gibbs also elaborates on his understanding of the embodiment of "failure," equating "failure" with "unsteadiness." He writes that "the movement fails because the dancers are immediately unbalanced." For Gibbs, "up" corresponds to happiness, consciousness, and having control; "down" signifies sadness, unconsciousness, and being controlled; and "falling is failure."

Perching on the edge of my seat, I exhale, recall a dancing moment from the video and then a recent dance from my own memory: We begin in an embrace. My head rests against my partner's neck, dropping into the crevice of her clavicle. I listen to her breath, heavy and winded after a long phrase of tumbling. We compress our torsos together. In the next moment, I lightly slough down the surface of her torso. Sliding swiftly past her thighs, I gather my legs into a tight ball as I sense the cool surface of the floor on my side. My partner follows the flow of forces, sequencing in her spine and deeply folding through her hips, knees and ankles. She falls gently, and I catch her weight momentarily in a delicate balance.

I press on with my objection to Gibbs's analysis. Contact Improvisation relays kinesthetic information in terms that contest and challenge culturally prevailing metaphorical associations with "up" and "down." Unsteadiness is not a sign of failure any more than up signifies the positive. Conventions concerning the notions of space and weight lose their determinacy, granting room for unconventional perceptual and sensorial experiences. In Contact Improvisation, the moving body, defined by momentum and touch, defies traditional Western codes, though not through an inversion of conceptual metaphors. Instead, as a practice, Contact Improvisation presents alternatives to these conceptual metaphors that we hold as common language. What kinds of metaphors does Contact Improvisation elaborate upon? I continue with my observation of "Hilary."

Play. Hamilton lays face down on the floor. Alessi carefully steps onto Hamilton's thighs and crouches down, his full weight on Hamilton's body. While balancing in this position, Alessi gently places his hand on Hamilton's shoulder blade. Quietly, they listen to the micromovements of each other's skeletons. *Response.* Although both Hamilton and Alessi are directed downward in space, they do not represent feelings of sadness. Nor is Alessi, by balancing his weight on top of Hamilton, able to exert control over his partner. Rather, both dancers reside in a space of uncertainty, working reflexively from their tactile senses to compose the dance. Not only do up and down exist simultaneously through ongoing negotiations between partners, but by practicing falling, dancers learn to venerate "the down" and revel in disorientation. Training in Contact Improvisation consists of learning how not to hold oneself "up" but rather to welcome perspectives from inverted spaces and deviated angles, by softening one's vision, listening to microskeletal shifts, and rolling through spherical space. These actions generate an increased sense of awareness, enabling dancers to fall safely and effortlessly. Contact Improvisation celebrates falling and in doing so proposes an embodied alternative to the metaphors of space and failure that Gibbs adheres to.

Fast Forward. Alessi jumps onto Hamilton with a surprising pounce. Just before the moment of collision, Hamilton grabs his own leg to divert predictability (perhaps even to provoke a situation that invites instability). They plunge down and tumble backward in unison. *Punch Pause and scan the essay.* Gibbs responds to this section of the dance by stating that "the movement fails because the dancers are immediately unbalanced." But Contact Improvisation blatantly refutes Gibbs's notion of failure. In a talk at the June 1997 celebration of Contact Improvisation's twenty-fifth anniversary, veteran teacher Nancy Stark Smith, a pivotal figure in the development of the form, explained that Contact Improvisation "is just as much about the misses as the hits." Thus, being on or off balance hold the same value. Moreover, the dance could not exist without the ongoing interplay of (de)stabilizing activity between two (or more) moving bodies. Judgments, therefore, regarding failure or stability prove beside the point, while attention to ongoing physical decisions becomes paramount. With skill, the handling of balance in practice and performance can be (mis)managed, confronted, and refigured to create varying degrees of tension. The question of failure in Contact Improvisation remains valid, but it is not measured in terms of stability or instability. Rather, it has to do with such issues as reluctance, manipulation, and lack of attentiveness to the moment. Unless safety is in doubt, I believe many practitioners would not frame even these points as failure, but as opportunities for dancers to learn and challenge their individual patterns and limitations.

Gibbs's essay slips out from under me. Balancing precariously on the corner of my chair, I pour my weight into my left hip as I lengthen my arm down to pick up the manuscript. In order to describe embodiment, another metaphor surfaces. And another. Beyond the two-dimensional space of video, underneath the words on the flattened paper, exist the contours and crevices of dancing bodies, dancers not only moving with definitive qualities in space and time, but with distinct consideration to weight. In Contact Improvisation, practitioners learn how to maneuver their body mass through actions that are commonly articulated by such verbal metaphors as emptying, spilling, and throwing their weight. Placement of one's mass, precisely in terms such as perching, lofting, pressing, spreading, leaning, sinking, and softening, provides the variety of possibilities for continuous weight exchange between partners.

Click. Alessi luxuriates in the middle of a lift. His body indulges in a free-flowing suspension with the support of Hamilton, who helps direct the spiraling motion. Alessi extends his limbs, allowing his torso to splay, open and unrestrained. Never passive, he participates in his aerial adventure by propelling his body upward. Hamilton and Alessi perform the principles of mutual support with extreme proficiency. They distribute and direct their weight so that, together with the forces of gravity, they collect enough momentum to send Alessi flying upward. *Resume.* Alessi sustains the extension of his body while Hamilton swirls him around. By folding his torso forward, Hamilton catches Alessi on his thighs. The audience snickers, for this appears an unlikely place for Alessi to land. Although it appears unlikely, it is exactly this type of landing that exemplifies the unpredictability of the form. Contact Improvisation, through its blending of weight, flow, momentum, and gravity, carries the dancers into moments of uncertainty and surprise.

Fast Forward. More laughter from the audience. *Rewind again to the big lift.* As Alessi balances across Hamilton's shoulders, Hamilton proudly raises one arm above his head, and the audience snickers again. What creates humor in this duet is how Hamilton and Alessi manage to mix modes of representation by dancing between different kinds of metaphors that equally inform the piece. The two dancers embody the traditions of Contact Improvisation, but add to them an ability to construct characters. They attend to weight, momentum, and gravity while investing themselves in the development of distinct personae. They compose this whimsical duet by diverging from the casual pedestrian style of traditional Contact Improvisation, coloring the dance with dramatic characterizations.

Alessi, assuming the role of a feminized boy-child, expresses his needs through emotional outbursts, hands and legs stiffening, torso thrusting into the air. His demand for attention receives support from an overrational Hamilton, who throws him into the air as he explodes. In the next moment, Hamilton soothes Alessi's hysteria as Alessi curls into Hamilton's chest looking for warmth and support. One might read Hamilton as the masculinized, gallant rogue emblematized in the moment he and Alessi separate from the point of contact. Here Hamilton stands erect with arms spread, presumably welcoming his partner back into his embrace, only to refuse Alessi, who in the next moment crawls submissively toward Hamilton on his hands and knees. With the delicate circling of an ankle, a slapping on the chest, a percussive shimmying of the head, Alessi appears sweet yet mischievous. He dances with abrupt and explosive outbursts, in contrast to the understated and suspicious character created by Hamilton, who with a swoop of the head underlines his dignity. Repeatedly, Hamilton stands with one leg off the floor, thereby establishing vocabulary to signify his "stable" character. At times, these flamboyant gestures merge with and punctuate the task-oriented principles of Contact Improvisation in order to create an amusing and arbitrary social relationship for Hamilton and Alessi. At other times the gestures signal a call-and-response chain of events. For instance, Alessi, sitting piggyback style on Hamilton's back, snaps his fingers, instigating a quick shift in Hamilton's weight. Or, when Hamilton bangs his foot on the ground, Alessi immediately changes his spatial direction. Exaggerating their expressions and finely tuning their timing, they remind me of Laurel and Hardy. One without the other just wouldn't work. Could Alessi explode without the support of Hamilton? Could Hamilton depict composure in the absence of Alessi's volatility?

And there's music too, melodic Eastern European folk music that adds to the charm and offers Hamilton and Alessi a steady rhythm to which they dance in accord. Whereas traditionally Contact Improvisation has avoided meter and rhythm as guiding structures, this duet relies in part on the accents of the music to create its effects. Using the music for support, Hamilton and Alessi slip into a complementary duet that lyrically blends waltzing, large spiraling jumps, and graceful horizontal patterns. The music guides their choices in phrasing and elicits the personalities of their characters.

And then comes the dramatic ending: Alessi reestablishes contact by sneaking his head under the crook of Hamilton's arm, managing to heave Hamilton, propelling him in low-level lifts that turn and drive through the space. Hamilton reverses the weight support by dragging Alessi downward from that very same crook of his arm. After a roughhousing moment, Alessi surrenders to Hamilton's embrace and a moment of tenderness ensues. Then, Hamilton again hoists Alessi up high above his head—but not without the help of Alessi's levering action. Poised elegantly, Alessi appears not merely a weight above Hamilton's shoulders, but a prize he has just won. Or, a burden he must carry?

We recognize these gestures through our own social production of meanings, which incorporate some of Gibbs's metaphors, but also supersede them. Placed not beside, but entwined with the alternative metaphors of Contact Improvisation, the duet becomes a complex blending of embodiments. Hamilton and Alessi cleverly play with this tension by mixing modes of representation smoothly, masking the labor of their skills. Those uninitiated in the codes of Contact Improvisation might marvel at the duet because of its recognizable comedic gestures and feats of fantastical flying, whereas a Contact Improvisation audience might appreciate Hamilton and Alessi's abilities to construct a sustaining theatrical relationship while using the techniques of the form so efficiently. In other words, both dancers and viewers engage in a complex exploration of corporeality and identity, created not as Gibbs suggests unaware "of [these] metaphorical patterns, precisely because they are so much an automatic part of our ordinary existence." Rather the clarity and precision of Hamilton and Alessi's performance suggests that they are completely aware of the images they compose. They intentionally create a playful dialogue by toying with the embodiment of familiar codes of social relationships that can be recognized by an array of spectators.

Approaching stillness, I notice the video monitor has turned to snow. As I rest in this moment, I can sense my body's discovery of yet another metaphor. I scan the moving possibilities while "weighting" in anticipation for the next dance.

PRESENT TENSE
Contact Improvisation at Twenty-Five
Ann Cooper Albright

When people ask me how CI25 went, there is one moment I love to describe: when I walked back into the main dance studio in Warner Center at 2:30 A.M. Sunday morning and saw more than sixty sweaty people dancing in the space, with another fifty-some bodies scattered around the periphery of the dance floor chatting, singing, playing music, doing bodywork, sleeping, or just lying back and observing the scene. That this many people were still dancing after twelve days of classes, jams, and various conversations about Contact Improvisation struck me as wonderful. It was a demonstration of the enduring physical and ethical values (and just plain good fun) of this particular dance form.

CI25 was a two-week celebration of Contact Improvisation's twenty-five years of existence. While a few cynics expressed a belief that this jubilee might actually be more of a wake for a form that had lost its relevancy to our fin de siècle culture, the sheer enthusiasm of the participants and their extraordinary dancing gave ample testimony to the continuing appeal of Contact. Indeed, over the course of the three central events—a three-day intensive Contact training workshop, a mixed-ability weekend, and a weeklong jam and jubilee celebration—I had the very great pleasure of witnessing the finely tuned craft of experienced Contact dancing. In addition, there was the excitement of seeing this improvisational form expand beyond the cultivation of virtuosic dancing techniques to explore what kinds of dancing can engage a wide diversity of bodies and cultural experiences.

Giving a coherent description of Contact Improvisation is a tricky business: the form has grown exponentially over time and has traveled through many countries and dance communities. Although it was developed in the seventies, Contact Improvisation has recognizable roots in the social and aesthetic revolutions of the sixties. Contact at once embraces the casual, individualistic, improvisatory ethos of social dancing and the experimentation with pedestrian and tasklike movement favored by early postmodern dance groups such as the Judson Church Dance Theater. Resisting both the idealized body of ballet as well as the

Fig. R1. Steve Paxton at CI25, Warner Center, Oberlin College, 1997. (© Ray Chung)

dramatically expressive body of modern dance, Contact seeks to create what Cynthia Novack calls a "responsive" body, one based in the physical exchange of weight.[1] The physical training of Contact emphasizes the release of the body's weight into the floor or onto a partner's body. In Contact, the experience of internal sensations and the flow of the movement between two bodies is more important than specific shapes or formal positions. Dancers learn to move with a consciousness of the physical communication implicit within the dancing. Curt Siddall, an early exponent of Contact Improvisation, describes the form as a combination of kinesthetic forces: "Contact Improvisation is a movement form, improvisational in nature, involving two bodies in contact. Impulses, weight, and momentum are communicated through a point of physical contact that continually rolls across and around the bodies of the dancers."[2]

CI25 took place at Oberlin College in June 1997. Nearly 250 dancers from nineteen different countries and five continents attended this celebration.[3] (The Sunday before the event, I answered phone calls from Germany, Japan, Canada, and Brazil—all within the space of an hour!) Some of the participants stayed for all three events, while some just passed through for a couple of days. That so many people would find their way to a small town in Ohio to honor the coming of age of this form of dance was truly extraordinary. Of course, Contact Improvisation has a strong history at Oberlin College: it was Steve Paxton's residency and workshop there during January term 1972 that provided the physical platform for some of the experiments that later took place (under the new rubric of Contact Improvisation) at the John Weber Gallery in New York City in June 1972. In addition, it was while Paxton was teaching at Oberlin that he met Nancy Stark Smith, who was then a student majoring in dance and creative writing. Smith joined Paxton in New York City later that year, embarking on a career that would make her one of the most influential figures in the development of Contact Improvisation. Smith is a widely respected teacher, dancer, as well as the coeditor of *Contact Quarterly,* a journal committed to documenting the various aspects of this contemporary dance form. Inspired by the idea of creating an anniversary celebration at Oberlin, Smith became the central coordinator of an event whose behind-the-scenes organization is as reflective of Contact's communal ethos as is the late-night dancing I described earlier in this essay.

After several preliminary discussions with the board of Contact Collaborations and other calls to check out the feasibility of hosting a dance conference at Oberlin, Smith sent out a letter to more than 150 people who taught and/or organized Contact events around the country, inviting them to participate in organizing a celebration of Contact's twenty-fifth anniversary. By November, she had over thirty cocurators who then took responsibility for organizing the teaching-intensive, mixed-ability weekend, the archive and art gallery, documentation, hospitality, the local newsletter, and many other tremendously inventive aspects of the event. Smith describes this process: "What a pleasure to work with devoted, intelligent, responsible, creative, playful, funny, dancing organizer-artists, all operating from a love and respect for the work we were there to celebrate, and who never let this fact get too far out of reach. People whose organizing was informed by their dancing: skilled at both initiating and following, listening, offering and asking for support where needed, generating creative ideas, willing to set limits on what they could and wanted to handle."[4]

Because one of the most significant tenets of Contact Improvisation is the marked absence of any hierarchical school, committee, or accreditizing association, many Contact dancers quickly become skilled at organizing classes, jams, and retreats simply in order to keep dancing themselves. This grassroots involvement (Need a dance partner? Teach it to your roommate!) and community facilitating of dance events has allowed Contact to grow in many different communities that otherwise would not have the funds to support a licensed dance school. One of the most interesting pages of Nancy Stark Smith's personal documentation of the early days of Contact was a letter, mostly unsigned, which was meant to trademark the name Contact Improvisation and certify only certain teachers of the form. Instead of becoming responsible for this kind of technical policing of the form, however, Smith, Paxton, and other early practitioners decided to create "a vehicle for communication in which to report activity and current thinking within the work, to keep the work open by inviting ourselves and others further into the dialogue."[5] The result was *Contact Newsletter,* which would later evolve into *Contact Quarterly,* a journal of contemporary dance and improvisation that encouraged dancers to write about their experiences with the form. Each issue of *Contact Quarterly* contains a "Contacts" list of teachers and facilitators in the United States and abroad. Indeed, it is not uncommon to hear of people dancing their way across the country, stopping in on jams here and there as they pass through.

The amazing diversity of regional affiliation and nationalities was marked at CI25 by a series of photographs taken on the final day of the jubilee (fondly called Pinnacle Day). Dancers were grouped according to home continents and regional connections, as well as by the number of years dancing, age, facilitator-teachers, original members of the Weber gallery collective, Oberlin alumni, and whatever other celebratory connections people chose to name. Because this dance form can trace its existence through living bodies, it was amazing to see the interconnections and to trace the various generations of teachers and students present. Many of those present had studied with either Nancy Stark Smith or Steve Paxton or their students. For instance, my first exposure to Contact came in college when I took a summer workshop with John Gamble, who had picked it up while working with Anna Halprin when Paxton was in the area. By the time I had entered a Master of Fine Arts program, Contact Improvisation had become my preferred dance form. As I became more committed to this form, I began to teach within my local community, all the while continuing my training by participating in intensive training workshops and jams. When I became an assistant professor of dance at Oberlin College in 1990, I had studied with many of the most influential Contact dancer/teachers of the 1980s. My own teaching acknowledges their influences and integrates this history with my particular interests in feminist thought and the cultural positioning of bodies in the contemporary world. This interweaving of physical sources of Contact Improvisation with one's own focus created one of the most interesting aspects of CI25. People would spontaneously create small discussion/study groups surrounding issues of spirituality, sexuality, race, disability, age, body therapies, and elitism, to mention only a few. Despite this incredible diversity of people's involvement with Contact, however, CI25 often celebrated a specific genre of Contact, one exemplified by virtuosic dancing and improvisational ease.

CI25 began with a three-day Contact Training Intensive, with classes taught by Steve Paxton, Nancy Stark Smith, Danny Lepkoff, K. J. Holmes, and Martin Keogh. These experienced Contacters gave a demonstration/performance one evening. It was tremendously satisfying to see the depth that a real history of dancing together can give to an improvisational duet; nowhere was this more evident than in the extended duet that Nancy Stark Smith and Steve Paxton did that evening. CI25 marked not only the twenty-fifth anniversary of Contact Improvisation, but also twenty-five years of Smith and Paxton dancing together. This recognition of their interconnected movement history provided a highly charged frame for their dancing, a fact recognized by the audience as well as the other performers. In fact, once Smith joined Paxton in the space, the other performers quickly pulled back to the edges, allowing them an uninterrupted space and energy. The fluidity with which these two dancers' body weight poured into and out of one another's bodies, the sensate, three-dimensionality of their physical awareness, the graceful suspensions and backward falls, the way that their contact flowed from the center of their torsos through a limb and out into space, not to mention the requisite shoulder lofts—all marked this duet as exemplifying the "classical" form of Contact Improvisation. Grounded by twenty-five years of kinesthetic communication, their dancing was exceptional, paced in a manner slow and sensitive enough to allow the audience a window into their dancing experience. A wonderful moment occurred about halfway through this duet when a spinning movement brought Smith standing about two feet in front of Paxton. As he reaches his hand toward her back, his spine begins to lean just as she arches her head and pitches sideways. Paxton catches her, and they both drop toward the floor with empathetic responsiveness.

Although their duet was improvisational and therefore unscripted in a traditional choreographic sense, Smith's and Paxton's dancing is based on a vocabulary of specific Contact skills. Some of these are the physical skills of falling and rolling, learning to use the head as an extension of the limbs, spatial disorientation, finding strength through spatial extension and lofting the pelvis. Underneath these physical skills is a whole complex of psychic skills that set up the *real* foundation for their improvisational dancing. At its best, Contact Improvisation reorders our traditional Western conceptions of the body and identity. The sense of self as an ego that goes forth to make its mark on the world (the frontier mentality) is subtly reshaped into a sense of one's own body as it exists in space and with others. While this radical reorganization of the psyche can be emotionally complicated for specific individuals, the Contact exercises that train for these kinds of awarenesses are often deceptively simple.

There is, for instance, the stand, developed by Paxton as the final section of *Magnesium,* a piece he made while at Oberlin in January 1972. The stand is just that, a stand with feet placed about hip-width apart, knees and ankles relaxed. Although each teacher will use slightly different images (my favorite is to imagine that your body is a fountain with water pushing up through your feet, legs, spine, shooting out through the top of your head into the air five feet, then washing back down over your skin and draining down into the core of the earth), the point is to feel the small internal shifts one's body necessarily makes to stand "still." It is an awareness of one's body in a space with other bodies, a relaxation of the pores of one's skin so that the world can flow through you. It is a mutual moment of interpenetration and interdependency, one that always strikes me as a potentially very transformative (and ecological) moment. Of course, I realize that not all Contact improvisers appreciate, internalize, or even understand the psychic implications of this work. Yet I have taught enough Contact classes to realize that something extraordinary can happen to a group of thirty individuals working within this form over the course of a semester. Although academic institutions are full of talk about community, Contact Improvisation is the only undergraduate course I know of at Oberlin that actually trains individuals in concrete techniques for creating a sense of community.

It is this kind of psychic (re)training of self and other that lies at the core of the work showcased in CI25's Mixed Ability Weekend. Bruce Curtis, Karen Daly, Sue Stuart, Riccardo Morrison, and Teri Carter all contributed to curating and facilitating the weekend workshop, but it was Alito Alessi, one of the most influential figures in this area, who led the opening workshop and introduced the parameters of the experience to those who were new to this work. Alessi teaches a form of Contact Improvisation that focuses on movement as a form of physical communication rather than a form of physical virtuosity. Touch becomes a window into one's partner's physical experience. In this way, Alessi replaces the dis- of disability with dance, calling his work DanceAbility. Although this Mixed Ability work makes a special effort to accommodate dancers with disabilities, Alessi is quick to assert that these dancing experiences don't just inspire or enable the disabled participants; they create a mutual physical dialogue that can empower and inspire the nondisabled participants as well.

Saturday night featured a Mixed Ability performance followed by a jam. One of the most exciting pieces on the program was a dance on wheels—roller blades, skateboard, and wheelchair—in which the signifier of disability (the wheelchair) blended in with the various technologies of mobility. The participants—Bruce Curtis, Karen Nelson, Caroline Waters, Ricarrdo Morrison, Ray Chung, and Tom Giebink—used the fluid mobility of the wheels to play with momentum and speed. Also featured was an improvisatory piece by the Brazilian Compannia 100 Habilidades. While many of these pieces were interesting, the truly extraordinary dancing came in the jam after the performance.

Unlike a structured workshop or a performance, the Contact jam setting allows for open-ended dancing, a mode particularly conducive to dancers with different abilities. For one thing, it is a lot easier to rest or stop and talk with your partner. This space to dance, talk, and experiment was very helpful in getting the nondisabled participants who had little previous experience dancing with physically challenged folks to give it a try. And vice versa. For instance, a student who was struggling physically with an enormous cast on her broken leg (not to mention psychically struggling with her first experience of having her body incapacitated in any way), went to the jam expecting only to watch; by the end of the evening, however, she had joined the forty people rolling, crawling, and spinning around the room. Even though it is a major ideological shift for many people to see disabled movers as dancers, the elements of much contemporary dance—breath, rhythm, extension, release, various effort qualities, partnering, humor—were all abundantly present within the dancing that evening.

More than any other genre of dance, Contact Improvisation has nurtured and embraced dancing that can integrate multiple abilities and limitations. In fact, many of the most renowned nondisabled Contact practitioners (including Steve Paxton), spend a lot of time teaching, facilitating, and dancing with disabled communities. Then, too, there are the Contact teachers and performers that are themselves disabled. (As Steve Paxton once remarked, "Have we previously heard of a paraplegic dance teacher? No, we have not.") As I have argued elsewhere, the Contact aesthetic does not try to create a static, "classical" representation of the ideal body; rather, it focuses on the process of the dancing communication between two bodies.[6]

Still, it would be disingenuous to pretend that all Contact situations embrace such a democratic aesthetic. It seems to me that there is, in fact, a very real tension within the larger Contact community between two kinds of dancing: one that emphasizes virtuosic movement skills and one that emphasizes movement communication that is accessible to any body. (The two are not mutually exclusive, of course.) This tension was clearly embedded in the very structure of CI25. The first three-day Contact Training Intensive was generally focused on skills only the most able bodies could do. There were no disabled teachers, nor were there classes that specifically addressed mixed-ability work. Most people who attended this performance were hungry to improve their dancing skills, and a lot of the jam dancing during these days was acrobatic and fast-paced. This beginning of the celebration set up a dancing energy and an aesthetic mind-set that had to shift gears radically for the Mixed Ability weekend to be successful. Fortunately, one of the most telling principles in Contact Improvisation (originally articulated by Nancy Stark Smith, and now ubiquitously quoted) is "replace ambition with curiosity." This openness to new experiences, combined with a willingness to be disoriented and feel awkward (two of the best lessons that Contact has to offer) helped the dancers move from one dancing situation and aesthetic into another space, one open to a new definition of Contact.

In the months since CI25, I have been wondering what it would have been like to begin this event with a mixed-ability training. Would it have immediately deflected any prioritizing of different modes of dancing? Would it have shaken up everyone's expectations? It is hard to say. It might have further marginalized the work, inadvertently positioning it as a "preconference" event. Although participants had to shift gears from the Intensive Training to the Mixed Ability workshop, this shift helped to create an inclusive atmosphere for the following week of dancing, talking, and celebrating the continuing presence of Contact Improvisation.

NOTES

1. Cynthia Novack, *Sharing the Dance: Contact Improvisation and American Culture* (Madison: University of Wisconsin Press, 1990), 186. For references to the Judson Dance Theater see Sally Banes's work on the era, especially *Terpsichore in Sneakers* and *Democracy's Body: Judson Dance Theater, 1962–1964*.
2. Curt Siddall, "Contact Improvisation," *East Bay Review,* September 1976, cited in John Gamble, "On Contact Improvisation," *Painted Bride Quarterly* 4, no. 1 (Spring 1977): 36.
3. For a more complete discussion of CI25, see *Contact Quarterly*'s CI25 anniversary issue, vol. 23, no.1 (Winter–Spring 1998).
4. Nancy Stark Smith, "Editor Note," *Contact Quarterly* 23, no. 1 (Winter–Spring 1998): 11.
5. Ibid., 35.
6. See "Dancing Across Difference" in my *Choreographing Difference: The Body and Identity in Contemporary Dance* (Middletown, Conn.: Wesleyan University Press, 1997).

*IMPROVISATION
IN EVERYDAY LIFE*

SOME TRAVELER'S TALES
Rachel Kaplan

For seven months in 1995 I traveled around the world by myself. My journey began in the Netherlands, where I lived in Arnhem and taught a class in performance art at the European Dance Development Center. I left Europe for Southeast Asia (Thailand, Indonesia, Singapore) where I traveled in a more haphazard and aimless manner for the next few months. I went "home" to San Francisco for a brief time, and then returned to Europe to teach in Germany. The stories in this piece, written the year after my return, come directly from this experience; some of the entries are taken verbatim from a journal I kept while traveling. Process comments, all.

I went to Asia for some of the reasons Westerners often go to Asia: something in my life was not quite right and I hoped an exposure to something "other" would force a change upon me. I was eager to leap, albeit imperialistically, into a different context to find something new. As my journey progressed, I was taken by its highly improvisational nature: how I never knew what would happen next; the endless coming and going of people, places, and things; the full and constant rush of adrenaline in my body; and my commerce with things known and un-known that gained meaning through context and juxtaposition. Midway through my journey, I saw how, without much planning, everything was conspiring to teach me what I needed to learn. Like the I Ching or any other wise oracle, my traveling pointed me toward insight without forcing me outside my own experi-ence. And, like Dorothy's, my quest for home led me closer to myself and fur-ther away from my known world than I imagined possible.

For a number of years, I have been working in the studio with a score called "Wandering and Arriving," which allows the dancer the options of walking and stopping, in whatever sequence and for whatever duration is warranted to derive information about these two states. Part of the game is to find wandering in still-ness, and arriving in motion. One day, as I lay down my pack for the hundredth time on a new bed, in a new place, in another country, I realized on a visceral level that I was doing this score, only on a much larger scale. I have been mildly

Fig. S1. Rachel Kaplan (*left*) and friends, Bali, Indonesia, 1995. (Cour-tesy Rachel Kaplan.)

obsessed with the way the metaphors of art are reflected in the body and then further outward onto the body of the world. In the face of fragmentation and a general breakdown of the social order, I am looking constantly for proof of the myriad ways these bodies exist as one connected whole. My enactment of "Wandering and Arriving" while traveling was a concrete manifestation of this process of reflection in art, physicality, and perception. I was impressed also with the fact that the research I had been doing in the studio for so many years had been following me, without my conscious awareness of it, and was supporting the grandeur of my trip.

From that moment on, questions of improvisation and my work as an artist expanded to include everything around me. I began to notice the serendipitous conjunctions of my experience with more excitement and equanimity. Much of my fear dropped away. My dance got smaller and larger: barely recognizable as dance, yet seeking to make contact with more of the world with more of my body. I said to my students in Arnhem, "Let the world sink into your body." My coteacher said, "You have got to be kidding," so I decided to try it myself. I dedicated the creativity usually reserved for my studio to the activity of my travels, and my awareness of everything around me deepened. I experienced improvisation not as a series of techniques I do in the studio, but as a dominant principle in this world, an essential truth. I wanted to give myself fully to its mystery, to its constant unfolding, and the deep, inarticulate wisdom I saw everywhere around me. I wanted to be that free, that open to change and the adventure of living. I started defining an improvisation simply as a moment in time unfurling, and the dance of the improviser being the small and large gestures offered to that moment.

The "Wandering and Arriving" score comes from a piece I have been doing for the last few years called *Diaspora, Stories from the Cities*. A collection of vignettes and dances for large and small groups, *Diaspora* explores wandering, homelessness, the fragmentation of the self, and questions of meaning/communication. The subtitle of this piece is "by necessity, an improvisation." As a term, the word "diaspora" means "dispersion" and has been used to describe the time when the Jews were forcibly evicted from their homeland and sent into exile. It has also been used to describe the history of the Africans and the Chinese. In most histories of the Jewish Diaspora, there is no mention of the fact that the Jews were evicted from a homeland they had stolen from the Palestinians. This is part of my history of the Diaspora, and the larger context in which my piece unfolds. Rather than researching the Diaspora from a purely Jewish (read: eternally victimized) stance, I have been exploring this state of wandering, homelessness, and drift as a late twentieth-century phenomenon, largely separate from ethnic or tribal affiliations, and affecting us all.

It seems to me that most of us live without a solid sense of home or belonging, thus with compromised ability to enter into respectful and right relation to ourselves and one another. My own brand of homelessness has engendered envy, fear, and sorrow in me. One compensatory strategy is the practice of returning to my body as a resting place, a temple, a home. Then I am neither homeless, nor displaced. Wherever I am, I am in my right place. It is a practice of self-love, and one that deepens my understanding of the utter subjectivity of perception. Such understanding is useful in a complex, fractured world where there is clearly no one truth, only our separate and unique experiences. The next step in this practice of returning is to treat the people around me as if they are also at home, worshiping in the temple of their bodies, and to extend the same respect to their perceptions as I extend to my own. There is a great work in communicating across the borders—physical, social and invisible—that separate us. This kind of physical homecoming feels important to me. I followed the main character of *Diaspora,* a fast-talking, slow-dancing storyteller, around the world to gather more stories and practice these principles. I wanted to find a way to be home wherever I was.

In the manner of that quest, I kept returning to the lessons I had been studying in the studio for so many years, and was now teaching to others. The perfect unfolding nature of my journey was grounded through many of the strategies and consequences of improvisation: the random, chaotic nature of experience; the slippage of meaning; the surprising ways in which objects, bodies, and thoughts collide to shape a new understanding; the seamless unfolding of every moment; and the work of survival. The inner listening; an acknowledgment of the tandem nature of solitude and union; a respect for other people and the environments in which they live; and the work of finding my place in relation to all that surrounds me and manifesting it through my body in expressive forms—these improvisational tactics were also implicit in my journey. All of this is recapitulated, I hope, in both the form and content of this essay.

I cannot create a narrative whole of my journey. I found a home in my body, but I am still wandering, still returning, still homeless, still improvising. I can access bits and pieces, and can report various adventures, but the essence of my trip remains private, internal, and ineffable. As my journey slips from experience into memory, I am left only with traces of its impact, rare moments of insight, and few words that really serve me. Like an improvisation that works, I saw it happen, I felt it, and then I watched it pass. I cannot always name its forms, structures, or patterns. Mystery and beauty walk hand in hand; I am glad to become small enough to interrupt my habit of human interference.

SCORE: LET THE WORLD SINK INTO YOUR BODY

> As you walk around the world, allow your eyes to sink back into your head.
> Liberate your mind from its desire to name. Let yourself know nothing. Allow
> yourself the discernment of mind, without taking action. Let whatever image
> or experience is in front of you sink into your body, as if there is no separation
> between you and it. Encourage yourself to join with what you see.

Traveling is a rare state. Most people live their daily lives, here and everywhere, appreciating and gravitating toward routine and pattern, creating a known world in the midst of chaos. The traveler invites and cultivates the unknown, the absence of routine, with the question, What do I want?

There are stairs on the way to this path, steep, steep stairs that stop me. At the bottom of the stairs today is a large pile of dirt. The women are coming down from the top of the stairs with baskets on their heads. They have small walking sticks in their hands. When they reach the pile of dirt, they will crouch in front of it, without using their hands to assist their descent, and fill the baskets on their heads with more dirt than I could possibly carry. They will stand again, without using their hands to aid their ascent, and they will then walk slowly up these stairs, the steep, steep stairs that stop me. They will do this over and over again for many hours.

We stop at a temple where the priest is blessing the food piled high in cere-monial baskets, and the women who carry them make us welcome and put rice on our foreheads and holy water in our hands. After we pray, we sit and talk among ourselves about our jewelry and our clothes, fingers pointing, mouths smiling. There is much female laughing among us, that shared language, but no words in common.

In the middle of the rice fields is an enormous tree. It looks as if its roots are growing out of the ground and alongside its trunk. The tree is old. Underneath the tree is a simple temple, a square structure of gray and red stone, a place to stop and pray along the rice-field path. As I drive past on the motorcycle, the wind on my skin, my arms around my friend, I let this tree, this shrine, this green, green field, my friend, the wind, the motorcycle, the chaotic road, become my body. I am old, wind-worn stone, brash motorcycle, green, green, green.

Outside my window is a well from which women draw dirty water and where everyone bathes. The men are kind and laugh with their children in a rare and beautiful way. A plane passes overhead. A rooster crows. The Beatles sing in the background: "You say you want a revolution." Loud, loud, loudest country I have ever visited. My body doesn't know how to sleep here. Across the way, a boy holds a moth by its wings and watches its legs shudder and twitch to escape. Men sleep on benches outside the *losmen*[1] at any time of day. On the steps of the old water palace, a man stretches, asleep on the cement. On Marlioboro Street, which is packed with the same cheap, touristy junk, row after row after row, women rest their heads on their arms for their midday nap, sleeping through this heat, this noise, this constant motion.

I sit in the temple and watch the people pray. They are dressed impeccably and kneel in front of the colorful shrines. The shrines are adorned with incense, large baskets of ceremonial food, prayer flags. The priests bless the worshipers, walking around with holy water, which the people drink three times and then splash over their heads. The offerings of rice are placed on their foreheads, their temples, and the base of their throats. When they are finished, another group of followers comes and kneels in front of the shrine, and the priest begins again. At one point, the rain starts to fall, and people get up, take shelter under the struc-tures of the temple and wait for the rain to stop. When it does, everyone goes to the center of the temple again, kneels down to pray, and rises when done, each person still meticulously clean, and dry.

Riding at night, I am one with the moon, the reflection of the water off the rice fields, the Indonesian stars, the texture of the dark. It is all so beautiful here. A stop at the small market reminds me of the market near my grandparents' house on Long Island where we used to buy candy and soda. My grandparents greeted the people there by name and were remembered. I cannot understand what is said in this Indonesian market, but I experience their language sweeping over me like a wide brush stroke to explain itself. I feel the words wash over me, their sounds and their rhythms, the gestures of the people in the store, their laughter, the slight menace that comes from knowing so little of what is going on around me. Then we are driving again and Dayu is on her bike with a cute boy she wants to kiss who wants to kiss her, who turns out to be her cousin, so they don't, but he wraps his arms around her sweetly anyway. Gusman on his motorcycle tries to pull ahead of us and Leslie and I try to keep him back, still loving his strength, his pull to lead, bursting in front of us to take us to grandma's house. She greets us old and laughing, toothless and half-naked, offering us sweet coffee and coconuts and so much love you don't need the name in any language to know it is clear and present. The men take their machetes and open coconuts dripping with juice and fruit and offer them to us. I laugh at my own unknowing, how much I am part of this moment, and how welcome I am here. Grandma reaches out to touch me and steal my cigarettes and laughs and laughs and laughs. The feeling of the dark, the wind on my face, the sound of the rice growing and the ping, ping, ping of electric circuits snapping, my prayer continuous and grateful: this moment this moment this moment; my body my body my body. Teach me something about the mysterious connection between language and gesture and meaning. The body and sound clue me in to what I need to know, and the game that is living continues.

Does the fruit taste different because I do not know its name, because it is unfamiliar to me?

At a dance conference in Solo, Java, I am touched by the talk of difference and the desire to build bridges. I am sitting in a circle with artists from all around the world, and everything is being translated into at least three languages: English, German, Indonesian. But the pace is purely Indonesian, more slow than slow. It is hot, even under the roof of the *pendopo*.[2] I am thinking about my practice of letting the world sink into my body. I am hot, I am slow, I am various, I am bridging and being bridged. Being among so many people and other languages, most of which I do not understand, I see how I do best when I remember how little I know, and how my assumptions are fully subjective, fully my own.

Each of us reflects the world through our bodies; we are or become our place. I think we need to find and tell the stories lodged in our bodies in this work of building bridges; we also need to learn to witness and listen and communicate across the borders that separate us. Some of these borders are logistical: we need to speak one another's languages, give one another simple adjectives, nouns, verbs. Some of these borders are social. We need to learn of one another's experiences. Some of these borders are illusions. We need to release the fears we hold of our differences.

I want to create this elusive thing called "community" everywhere I go. I want to know I belong. I believe that means bridging the gap between how we are the same and how we are different. We have to share this with one another in whatever languages we have; this sharing, this revelation, creates a common language with which we can begin. My task is community building, self-recognition, self-possession, artmaking, the navigation of various borders and boundaries, the complex interaction of social, historical, genetic forces. I am trying to find metaphorical ways through the phenomena of the body: the ways we displace ourselves in time and space: our wandering and arriving; our separating and joining; all the possibilities of change in terms of time, space, weight, flow; those characteristics of movement in the body which give rise to voice, emotion, sensation, narrative drift.

There are stories in our bodies, lodged there, waiting to be heard, danced, seen. I want to find them and tell them. I watch a German man struggle with his identity as an artist, his need to be seen and heard. I share his struggle. I think: I care about craft; I want to bring the fullness of my attention to my art. On a deeper human level, however, I want to say to everyone around me: I respect you as a dancer, but I want to know you as a person.

SCORE: MAKING AND BREAKING CONTACT

> Make and break contact with other dancers in the space. Use the whole space. Track your internal landscape. What feelings or images or memories or associations are triggered when you separate and unite with other people?

I have an image of myself tramping through the world with only my knapsack and the clothes I am wearing, walking into and through some kind of fire. My heart is clear, even if my mind often is not, about what it is I want. I need to engage, over and over again, in my faith. This whole trip is an act of faith, an attempt to come to terms with my solitude, my "self as the terminal abode,"[3] my separateness from others, my connection to the world. My fear of being alone is central to me every day. Like a homeopathic remedy, or an inoculation against habit, I am choosing to walk alone through that fear. If I survive, I will be different on the other side.

I meet a monk today who wants to practice his English. We sit and talk for a while in Bangkok's biggest temple. I ask him questions: "What happens if I touch you? Will you always be a monk? What is the name of that Buddha? Why are your robes saffron?" And he to me, "Where are you from? What are your ambitions?" He is twenty-two years old and has been in the monastery for ten years. He asks if I can meet him the next day to practice English, and I agree.

The next day, I go to the pier, a short walk through temple grounds with a nearly expired dog lying on its side. Narrow alleys. My monk barely acknowledges me in public when I meet him at the pier. I am, after all, a woman. What I know about Thai monks is this: They aren't supposed to speak to women. They aren't supposed to pick up anything touched by a woman. If I touch his robe, even by accident, he must go through elaborate purification rituals. I am näive, and curious. I want to see what happens.

He tries to get immediately on a boat. I say: "Where are we going? I need to know where we are going before I go anywhere with you."

He says: "To a temple."

I say: "Will you promise to get me back here?" and he promises. We wait a bit on the pier; the river a filthy, irredeemable thing. We pretend we don't know each other. I watch the boats coming and going, their faded wood, their speed, their efficiency, the people pouring on and off before they fully dock. When our boat finally arrives, my monk embarks and I follow. He gets off, and I follow at a polite distance through three or four blocks of a quieter Bangkok, with trees and places where people actually live. No Westerners. I feel some fear in my body, but I figure if you can't trust a Buddhist monk, whom can you trust?

We walk to the place where he lives. I sit on the porch. He goes inside and then invites me into his small room. It's lined with cassette tapes, a classy stereo system, a TV, a desk, some food, a small bed, and, on the wall, photos everywhere of Western people in various states of undress, making love with one another: on top of Potrero Hill, the neighborhood where I live, or rolling around in the sand, in their half-opened Calvin Kleins. There are quotes in English on the walls: "Marriage is either the greatest blessing or the most dreadful curse," and the words to an American love song adorn a bulletin board across the room.

Returning to the pretense of the visit, he asks me to help him with his English. He has me show him the answers to a fill-in-the-blanks exercise about the evolution of the word "cocktail." Once this is done, the conversation shifts more and more to who we are, what we care about. What is our point of contact? It is not clear, but we are together in this small room, talking. He is young and sweet and I give him so much leeway for being different from me. He starts touching me more and more, in what feels mostly playful, if not somewhat incongruous. I am curious, watchful, not fully afraid.

I ask him if he plays the stringed instrument hanging on his wall. He says, "Not very well," but he gets out his guitar and starts playing a Bruce Springsteen tune. I cannot parse this image: young monk in a saffron robe playing a Bruce Springsteen tune on the guitar in the middle of Bangkok, on his walls, Western people fucking.

At one point, one of the other monks comes to the room, notices me, and says something in Thai. My monk gets him to leave and then locks the door of the room. I am now locked in a room with a hormonal monk on the outskirts of

Bangkok. I have no idea where I am or what's going to happen next. A friend's warning comes to me, "You're going to get into some difficult situations out there," and I think: "Here I am."

The conversation turns more and more to love. This guy's been penned up in the monastery for ten years. Meanwhile, he's touching me more and more, in a sort of boyish, friendly way. No more English lesson, that's for sure. He asks me how old I am. Thirty-two surprises him and then he starts telling me how it would be better if I were younger, then we could, you know, get married and I could take care of his children. I am getting more and more uncomfortable.

"I thought you weren't allowed to touch women," I say.

"Right, you are untouchable for me," he says.

"Why are you touching me?"

"Because you're a foreigner."

I tell him I am a stranger in the house of Thailand and need to know what's allowed and what's not. He confesses that it wouldn't be so good if the other monks knew I was there. I tell him I am getting scared. He doesn't know the word, so I take out the dictionary.

"Scared of *me?*" he asked. "Have I made a mistake?"

I tell him that he has, and that English is okay, but marriage is out of the question. I am uncomfortable, angry at my persistent naïveté, and I want to leave. I ask him to get me back to the boat. He hedges and doesn't want to let me go. He starts again with the "it's too bad you're not younger, too bad we didn't meet sooner, too bad you're not staying longer" frenzy of the earlier conversation. I tell him to be a good Buddhist and just accept the situation. This doesn't go over too well. He's still reluctant to take me to the pier, and my fear has turned to anger, as it so easily does. I stand up and look down at him. I say, "I want to go *now.*"

After an absurd bit of cross-cultural processing in which it becomes clear that the expression of my anger is both futile and dangerous, I convince him to walk me back to the pier. As we're leaving, he says, "I guess I have some things to learn about women," and I say, "I guess you do." I follow five feet behind him as we leave his place. He never looks back at me. When we arrive at the pier, he sits down and speaks to a man, which is, of course, perfectly permissible. When the boat comes, he gets on and I follow. He stands in the saffron sea of monks, I stand with the people. At my stop, I wave to him, in a small way, and get off the boat. He acknowledges me with his eyes but makes no public gesture. I never see him again.

When I travel to Solo, Java, I sit with some Germans because I am getting tired of the "Are you traveling alone? Are you married?" harassment of Indonesia. They are more than happy to offer me the protection of their union, and then a young Indonesian girl comes and sits next to me. On top of me, really, in that charming way Indonesians have with people they have never met. We spend much of our train ride looking at the dictionary and trying to speak to one another; when we get to Solo, which is where she lives, she takes me and her mother and herself and my knapsack onto a small *becak,* a three-foot-wide conveyance powered by a man on a bicycle. We go to her house, where she changes her clothes, introduces me to her grandmother who is making batiks in the yard, quickly climbs a tree and picks me some *rambutan,*[4] then gets me into a cab and takes me to my homestay. She sits with me while I shower (even then I am up-tight and take my passport with me into the bathroom). I give her my coins from Singapore and Thailand because she has a collection. We say, "I hope I see you again soon," and then we say goodbye.

I meet other travelers everywhere I go. I ride elephants in Thailand with a German woman and her Balinese boyfriend. I take a long walk and a nauseating ride up a hill to a lavish temple with a Jewish couple from New York State. She vomits all the way down the hill, and he sits and watches, ineffectual. I meet a British man on a small island off the coast of Thailand and we talk about books and the possible existence of God. I meet another man on this same small island who grew up ten miles from me, and who watched the same televi-sion shows as a child. I sit with some foreign exchange students and shock them with tales of bisexuality and political activism. I meet a Dutch man in Chaing Mai and talk to him briefly, then accidentally run into him when I arrive in Bangkok. He goes with me to watch the international trade in young Thai boys and girls at Pat Pong, Bangkok's red-light district. A Burmese woman on the flight from Amsterdam to Bangkok worries that I will not find my way in Thai-land. She tells me to call her when I arrive. I can't figure out how to make the phones work, much less find my way to where she lives. Even though people everywhere say this same thing to me, "Find me later on, down the road," I never reach out this way, preferring to let the moment that unfolds without effort be enough. I am free of the need to make anything happen; everything is happening all around me.

Improvisation devotes itself to this randomness of experience. It revels in the mystery of creativity, in desire pushing against its own walls to be free. At its best, it is a practice of embodied expression which is not about making something hap-pen, but about the experience of experience. I don't make contact to alter some-one's experience, or to intervene with force. All of the people I meet are part of me. I am glad to need nothing beyond the moments that arise between us.

I stand up and decide absolutely that I am going to leave the dance confer-ence in Solo when a woman I had met briefly comes up to speak to me. With no prompting she says, "Some of us had mothers who didn't love us the way we needed to be loved. I wanted you to know, just remember, you can always find the mothering you need from other people at any time. Sometimes just for a little while, and sometimes for a longer time, but it's there for you if you need it. I had a bad mother, so I know." I look at her and say, "How did you know?" And she says, "I can just tell." She smiles, kisses me softly on the cheek, and then I leave.

I think I have believed in some sort of grandeur I could possess that sets me apart from other people, that makes me different or bigger or exempt from the laws that govern this life. I see now that this is not, could not, be true. How could it be? The more I sink into the details of living, details both significant and insignificant, the more fully connected I am to the stream of what is human, to what life is. What am I saying? There is no grand destiny, no fame, no fate that sets me apart from others, either in affect or luck or position or talent. I am like others. I live the way others have lived before and will live again and there is nothing grand, but something very true, about it. I have set myself apart in so many small and large ways. I am beginning to see the center of who I am as part of everything else, and not separate, my body in constant harmonic adjustment to all other surrounding bodies. There is no isolation, no lack; it is only the mind, the mind, the desert of my mind that tells me this is so.

The cumulative dance of all of these meetings and leavings feels like a rush of energy around a strong center pole, which is me. I've grown thrilled by the question: What do you want? The point of intimacy, the point of contact, the shifting fulcrum of weight. What do you want? is a heavy question. The answer separates me from my childhood and from you. Any practice that supports finding the answer to the question catapults me toward responsibility, spirit, truth. Improvisation is one of these practices, but I don't care any more about its form: dancing, writing, loving, sitting. The answer is the grail. When I let myself answer to this, my dance is wild and free.

SCORE: RETURNING

> In whatever action you do, encourage your consciousness to return to a perception and experience of the vast internal landscape of your body. Feel the small parts of your body in motion and stillness. Enter your body as if entering a home, or a temple. Bow to your perceptions and sensations and emotions and associations and images and memories, and allow them to inform you about your desires, your motivations, your location in time and space.

I see myself on stage, sitting in total stillness, dressed in white. I want to color my body red and blue—I'm so mad, I'm so blue, I am such an American—and tell stories of the places where I have been, and the familiar world to which I return.

I dream of sitting in total stillness. I dream of many people in a circle sitting in total stillness. I go to my studio with this image in my head. But in my dance, I can't find the perfect stillness of my dream. I am not brave enough, or quiet enough, this morning. I stretch and my mind starts to unwind. I give myself the task of dancing, without speaking, for the next twenty minutes, or until the music on the tape deck gives way to silence. As I dance, rolling and unrolling on the floor, eyes still closed, the street outside a constant assault of people, poverty, and road construction, I am reminded of that Indonesian word I loved: *pelehanlehan*. More slow than slow. In America, we feel the need, the need, the need for speed.

I am breaking into a thousand million pieces. Some part of me got left behind on my journey around the world. I cherish my experiences in Asia as invitations to do less, to slow down, to let nothing be something. This is my revolt against the world outside my window today. But it leaves me lost, unintegrated with my American present, dreaming of a return to a place where I really do not belong.

I am consumed by an understanding of opposites that threatens to silence me. If everything is both true and false, slipping away from itself even as it comes into being, West turning into East, yin turning into yang, dying turning into living, of what use is it to try to pin it down with language, which rarely shifts shapes, just sits here on the page, waiting to be read?

I plan a class called "Creating Change, Breaking Habits." Seven people are kind enough to come. We dance and talk and write and dance again. I say, "Change, change, change" when they write; I notice their movement patterns and habits. Midway through the class, I see through my own bluff. Three hours on a quiet Sunday morning isn't enough to even identify a habit, much less change it. I laugh at how I am teaching what I need to learn. I apologize to my students. I say, "I can't give you what I promised." They remain enthusiastic about the bold enterprise of looking at our unconscious behaviors. No one is angry with me for not having the answer to the questions we are all asking.

More and more, I see how there is less and less to do, how activity and reaching out teach me something, but do not necessarily facilitate the kind of inner listening or strength I need or want. There is so much I don't know, and the more I remember that disappearing truth, the clearer I become. It is so much easier to do than not to do. I don't imagine there will come a time when I cease acting. That is not even a goal, but rather to be clear, crystalline, in my intention to act, and not motivate out of habit, addiction, or fear. For this, I need to grow even more still, even more slow, even closer to the center of my heart. I question the futility of action, and the desire to create change. Change is clearly happening all the time, all around me. I apply this to my art as an invitation to make only the necessary gestures, to say only what really needs to be said.

I say to my friend, "I want to dance with you." She answers by saying, "So many hopes, so many fears," and walks away from me. She acknowledges a feeling of anxiety that my desire creates in her. Later, as we pass each other on the dance floor, I ask out loud, "How can I express desire without creating pressure?" As she drifts by me, wrapped and rolling in someone's arms, she says, "Desire *is* pressure." I rest my body against hers and ask what the Buddhists have to say about desire; she says, "It is the root of all suffering."

I teach my students the returning score. They are willing to come into contact with one another, and themselves. As the teacher, I go in and out of dancing with them and watching them. At one point, I question the relevance of the score as "art." They are, after all, nothing more than eight bodies in a pile on the floor, laughing sensuously, rolling around, touching one another, listening. I do not ask them to stop but let the score continue for many more minutes. I release my judgment of this process that I cultivate in this room. I sense something about improvisation in times like these, as I give way to my faith in the uprisings of any given moment. I dig inside myself for what I call my "faith" in this process of returning. I know the answers are in my body. I know that I was not taught to listen to this wise guide. I sense this as part of our cultural dilemma. I teach this score in all of my classes, practicing this faith and this listening, not knowing the outcome or the weight of the teaching.

I am identifying loneliness as habit, pattern, mind, body, truth, fiction. In this quest for true love I am undoubtedly and unequivocally on, it is clear that the only quarry worth pursuing is myself. And I am gaining on her.

If life is in the details, in all the small acts of living and loving and making a home, the small dances of eating and sleeping and drinking tea and speaking to the ones you love, it seems crucial to locate myself in a place with people I trust and love who trust and love me. This is where life unfolds, where life is: this small, daily dance that people everywhere do, because they must, because it is this that keeps us alive and well. The heart is the center of the world.

I see the simultaneous and random absurdity of things conspiring to make this world what it is. There is no bigger picture. There is only this moment, this action. And then the next.

If I believe even a little bit in the metaphors and practices I have been gathering all these years, I can't help finding something outrageous on this journey. I can't help finding another route into the work to which I have committed myself. Perhaps it is this I fear, this deepening intimacy with myself? Perhaps, but I believe what I still fear is being exposed before I am ready, before I feel prepared or have said a true yes. This is why improvisation is a challenge for me: it is the real possibility of being exposed at any time, seen and revealed in that state of being off balance and unknown. And here I am, on the edge of all my planning, setting off toward the possibility of that revelation.

NOTES

This essay is adapted slightly from the version originally published in *Contact Quarterly* 22, no. 2 (Summer–Fall 1997).

1. Another word for hostel. Also referred to as a "homestay."
2. A templelike structure with a roof, floor, and no walls.
3. Natalie Goldberg, *Long Quiet Highway: Waking Up in America* (New York: Bantam Books, 1993), 71.
4. A small hairy red fruit with white meat that grows in Southeast Asia. Somewhat resembles a lychee nut.

WHAT'S THE SCORE?

Structured Improvisation as National Pastime

Maura Keefe

Here I present a score for a structured improvisation to be performed for a large audience. It may be danced by professionals and amateurs together, but it works best if the skill level of the performers is roughly on equal footing. I offer this score for everyone's use, to be set on and used by anyone. In the interest of full disclosure, however, I should say that I am not the creator of the improvisation. I am a frequent viewer of, and rare participant in, the improvisation. The structure itself has been shaped over time by the participants in collaboration.

The action begins with eighteen dancers divided into two groups of nine, with the possibility of understudies filling in as replacements throughout the piece. Despite the large number of performers and the collaborative aspect of the piece, there are ample opportunities for solos built into the structure, as will be explained below. The score requires quite a bit of room, so I would suggest that it be performed outside, preferably in an open field. It does not matter whether you choose an urban or rural setting, but the piece works best on grass and dirt. What's more, it is most successfully performed in the round in order to give the audience the opportunity to observe the action from many different perspectives. Speaking of the audience, while certain types of audience participation—mostly of a spontaneous verbal nature—are encouraged in the event, no audience member may enter the performance space. The performers, meanwhile, must remain within the confines of the designated space, which is in the shape of a fat ice-cream cone. While the outside edges of this shape must be clearly defined, and the triangular part of the shape must be exact, the rounded edge may be irregular. All of the participants, however, must agree on what the boundaries of the space are prior to the beginning of the improvisation. The strict use of space is a fundamental aspect of this improvisation. Performers stay in. The audience stays out.

The first group of nine players enters the space from one side of the triangular edge of the space, spreading out around it in a regulated and symmetrical fashion. The first dancer, as the one who begins the independent action in the improvisation, has a leading role throughout the improvisation. She walks with

Fig. T1. Chicago Cubs, 1948: Andy Patko. (*Los Angeles Daily News* Photographic Archive, Department of Special Collections, Charles E. Young Research Library, UCLA.)

authority to the center of the space. Her eight fellow dancers then enter and situate themselves in relationship to the first dancer. One sets herself immediately opposite the first dancer at a distance of about sixty feet and then crouches down, facing the first dancer. Four others spread themselves out equally on diagonals radiating away from the crouching person, and behind the first dancer. A final trio runs into the space to assume widely spaced positions in the widest part of the cone, dividing the space equally among them. This completes the entry of the first group of improvisers, who wait in a state of supreme readiness. The audience typically encourages the entrance of these dancers with verbal support and applause.

It must be noted at this point that the manner in which the first set of dancers takes their positions is a lively part of the improvisation. For example, the first dancer and the croucher may choose to stroll into the space slowly, talking and laughing. Others might enter pensively, assuming a theatrical internalized focus. One improviser might hurry to her place and lean over, bending and stretching, while another enters slowly, as if attending to a muscle overstretched during a dress rehearsal. The last three, because they have the farthest to travel, are encouraged to hurry so that all the dancers arrive at their positions at roughly the same time. While waiting for the second group of dancers to join the improvisation, the three dancers in the wide part of the cone occasionally, and at their own timing, sprint in fast bursts. These bursts serve to heighten a sense of excitement and expectation in the audience, making this section particularly beautiful to watch.

Now, unlike the first group of improvisers, who enter en masse, the members of the second group of nine enter the space one by one, taking their turns as soloists. Before entering the space, they wait on the sidelines opposite the first group. Because each solo must begin in the same location, at the narrow end of the cone and adjacent to the crouching person from the first group of improvisers, the second soloist cannot begin until the first has moved out of her starting position. Furthermore, in some cases, determined by complicated rules of the structured improvisation, the first soloist may continue her dance while the second begins hers. Thus, this section—the most substantial in the piece—could be described as a long string of solos, serially linked in a variable additive structure. This portion begins thus: the first soloist strides confidently to stand directly next to the crouching dancer. Simultaneously, the second soloist moves into the space beside the edge of the cone, poised to replace the first soloist when her time comes. The second soloist need not stand still while waiting; she has the option to mark her solo in full view of the audience. When the first soloist has finished her brief solo, she either moves out into the midst of the first group of dancers or returns to join the other waiting soloists. The second takes her place while the third soloist marks her material nearby. And so on.

As I said, the first dancer from the first group spawns the action of the event. No one from the second group may begin her solo until the first dancer performs her movement task. While the actual phrasing of her task is up to the leading dancer, she may get suggestions from the crouching dancer, among others. No matter who is the lead dancer, and how she chooses to move, the rules indicate that she must always perform a repeatable movement of the arms in a wide circle followed immediately by a momentous step forward. Audience members who watch closely may see that the first dancer, having improvised this initial movement, attempts to duplicate it as exactly as possible on subsequent iterations. This takes great concentration. Meanwhile, the soloists of the second group begin their individualistic and idiosyncratic phrases in response to the circular action, taking it as a kind of cue. The rhythm of this section moves back and forth between taut readiness and large fast-movement outbursts of arm action and solo. The exchange builds tension and can be quite satisfying to watch for the audience.

The manner in which the solos accrue depends on factors that are best learned and intuited subtly over time. I cannot go into all the details here. But this must be said: neither improvisers nor audience members should be deterred if at first this interaction seems too complicated to fathom. In good time, all will make sense. This section might typically proceed like this: Depending on the action of the lead dancer from the first group, the first soloist runs to stand near dancer 3 of the first group. The second soloist comes to stand beside the crouching dancer, while the third soloist enters the waiting area. This time, the action between the first dancer, performing the arm actions, and the croucher prevents the solo from continuing. The second soloist returns to the group. Meanwhile, the third soloist comes on, begins her solo, and runs to stand near dancer 3. This forces the first soloist to move out of the way of the new soloist, so she runs to stand near dancer 4. Another soloist strides out. This soloist embarks on an extended trio with the first dancer and the croucher, then runs to stand by dancer 3, at the same time as the first soloist moves to stand with dancer 5. Thus the soloists are dancing their way around a diamond shape that is encased within the ice-cream cone. Dancer 5 now refuses to share her space with the first soloist who, as a result, is forced to exit the space. That decision inspires dancer 3 also to refuse to share her space. And so on. This section requires subtle interaction, but you will surely be able to catch on from watching the other dancers, learning from their choices. After as few as three dancers take their solos the two groups switch roles, with the second group distributing itself evenly around the space while the first group prepares for the series of solos.

While each dancer has his or her own task to accomplish, a particular feature of this improvisation is that one dancer wields a large effect on the actions and tasks of other dancers. In fact, many of the dancers' activities are dependent on the overall action of the event, with activities only triggered by the outcome of choices or actions of others. The nuances of this triggering activity are sufficiently interesting to support nine full cycles of the improvisation, with unflagging audience interest. (At least in most cases: occasionally the improvisation falls flat and fails to ignite interest in the audience. In such cases, viewers may choose to leave before the score is completed, which is often taken as implicit criticism of the performance.) Nonetheless, in accordance with the dictates of the score, the improvisation continues, with the dancers returning again and again to the solo position. Soloists may repeat their preferred movements or invent new ones each time. While the overall duration of the event is not set, it should be noted that there is a built-in conclusion. Much is foreordained by the rules of the structure. Still, once the structure is clear, an infinite number of variations can be seen to be possible, which may explain the tremendous audience interest in this particular score. Despite everyone in the audience and in the performance space knowing the rules, unexpected decisions made by one group of dancers may surprise and further inspire the other group. Audiences often number in the tens of thousands.

And for good reason. The piece calls for tremendous collaboration and focus. Many things happen simultaneously. There is much to engage the audience's attention. Often times, audience members may make notes about the course of the action to review and verbally reconstruct after the performance. And, when the action is especially complicated or nuanced, audience members may find themselves in deep conversation about the structure, sharing knowledge of the event and guiding less skilled observers. The same may be true from the side of the performers. To keep track of and regulate all the action, it often works best to designate two dancers to serve as directors. If possible, two other dancers may serve as assistants to the directors, thus increasing the number of dancers who can take part as well as smoothing the flow of communication. The directors, whose job it is to guide the action of the improvisation, need to be completely familiar with the structure in order to anticipate the greatest number of variations possible for the improvisation—which makes it the most exciting and compelling for participants and observers alike.

Does this score sound impossibly complicated? Too unwieldy to be organizationally feasible? It needn't be. Just remember that, like any improvisation, this one requires thorough knowledge of the structure and the rules that govern it. While those rules may be arbitrary, the participants must agree to participate within the designated structure. Of course, there are limits on where you can be in the space and where you can't be. There are limits on how far you can travel through space and when you can travel. There is a limit on the number of people who can participate at any one time. And, like all structured improvisation, there is the challenge of staying within the rules while simultaneously testing their limits. This is all part of the experience. Obviously, the version of the dance that I described above is simply an example. I begin with it to illustrate my point that the structure of this improvisation is quite complex. What makes this exciting, however, is that once the structure is understood, it may be danced by anyone, of any skill level. Further, just think of the endless variety of ways in which the dancers may move.

I originally began thinking about the connections between dance and baseball several years ago, when I was at a minor league game played by the Hagerstown Suns in Hagerstown, Maryland. I was watching the batter, Mel Waring, in the batter's box. Waring is a big man, his stats in the program said he was 6′3″ and 230 pounds. He lumbered up to the plate, and stood there, ready for his solo

moment, facing the pitcher (dancer 1). I did not anticipate that I would be struck by this man's grace. Yet there was something about his stance, the way he dropped his weight way back onto his back leg, until he swung. As he did so, he would launch forward and upward, lifting himself up to meet the ball with his arms. It struck me at the time that the fall backward and the recovery upward carved by his body, driven by the arc of his pelvis, could have been from a Doris Humphrey reconstruction. As it turns out, Mel Waring has not gone on to be a famous ball-player. But the smoothness and strength of his swing, the unexpected harmony of his motion, and the elongated time of an afternoon ball game, set me thinking about the choreography of baseball. Since that summer's admiration of Waring, over the past several baseball seasons, I have come to further define the choreography of baseball as a structured improvisation. The rules for this improvisation are absolutely set, but as with any other improvisation, there is an infinite variety of ways to travel from beginning to end of the game. Baseball's structure seems impenetrable to the uninitiated but simple, perfect, almost holy to those in the know.

The rules of baseball, while exact and well defined, have parallels in the very structured mathematical kinds of improvisations that Trisha Brown and Lucinda

Fig. T2. Players with the Hollywood Stars, 1953: Jim Walsh, Larry Shepard, Mel Queen, and George O'Donnell. (*Los Angeles Daily News* Photographic Archive, Department of Special Collections, Charles E. Young Research Library, UCLA.)

Childs, among others, performed in the 1960s and 1970s. Further, the notion of improvisation itself suggests a kind of play. In 1965, *Village Voice* critic Jill Johnston wrote about Judson choreographers infusing dance with a sense of play. She commented: "The demonstration of play as a mode of action central to dance is a significant regression. Central to play is improvisation."[1] Where dance critic Johnston sees the play as invoking a sense of freedom to dance, sports theorist Karl B. Raitz ties play to rules in his essay "Theater of Sport." Play in sport gives it a structure, a set of guidelines. "People play games according to rules. . . . [T]o engage in a sport is to be rule-bound by it. Many rules that control how the games are played are intended to create an artificial space within which those rules apply. Outside that space, the rules have very little meaning other than as symbols."[2] The arbitrary nature of a structured improvisation is familiar to most dancers. The boundaries we set for ourselves, limiting space, time, sequence, or body parts, provide challenges that inspire invention. Outside of the improvisation, those limits fall away.

Why sully the art of dance with the pop culture of baseball? Inversely, why burden the sport of baseball with yet another metaphoric celebration? To what advantage do baseball and dance enter into the same ballpark of discussion? Most often, people think about improvisation as it applies to music and dance. But in fact, improvisation happens everywhere. Applying concepts about improvisation that have been theorized about dance can be expanded to examine other physical practices to broaden our definitions of both dance and improvisation.

Baseball's structure is understood, certainly, but every game is different. If people were taught the kinds of analytic tools for understanding structures of choreographic improvisation as they are baseball, we could finally put to rest the notion that dance can't be discussed. Given the same kind of education, improvisation and dance could be discussed with as much ardor and intelligence as baseball by the general audience. But this begs the question: does the general audience have any interest in discussing dance with the attention to nuance and detail that baseball fans pay to baseball? Despite the ranking of dance as a high art and baseball as popular culture, there is a level of sophistication held by the average U.S. spectator of sports coupled with a relative lack of sophistication about dance. Sophistication may well be a loaded term: people uninitiated into a world of appreciating and understanding and analyzing dance assume that in order to appreciate dance one needs to be sophisticated. However, the sophistication about sports in general and baseball in particular stems from experience. One of the big differences between spectatorship of dance and of sports is that, in the United States, people grow up playing sports because of mandatory physical education. They come to the spectacle of baseball having grown up with the rules of the game, and a kinesthetic appreciation for the effort on the part of the athletes. I would argue that it could be useful to encourage people to bring what they already know about physical culture to viewing dance.

That might explain what dance improvisation gains from being considered akin to baseball. But what about the inverse? What does baseball gain from being considered a form of dance improvisation? In 1997, I participated in the panel discussion "Dance and Sports" at Jacob's Pillow Dance Festival, where I first publicly declared that baseball is a structured improvisation. On the panel, among others, was former Yankee pitcher Jim Bouton.[3] Bouton was performing that week at the Pillow as a community dancer in David Dorfman's *The Athletes Project*. (Dorfman is both a postmodern choreographer and former college baseball catcher.) Bouton scoffed at my theory because of the difference in the goals of the two projects. He argued that there is always a winner and loser in a baseball game, and that's the point. True, there is no similar measure of success or failure in a typical dance improvisation. However, this is where removing baseball from its accepted place, denaturalizing it from its identity and cultural context as a sport, as a game, and considering it dance makes it possible to see more within the movement of the players and game itself. More than any other sport, baseball is already celebrated in the poetry and essays of great American writers. The beauty, grace, athleticism, and agility of the players and the game are already recorded. Every day, during baseball season, there are vivid descriptions in the sports pages about baseball that we long for about dance performances. But what about looking deeper? I suggest that it is possible to examine the movement of the players not just for the risk of the great diving save or the courage of the long pull that sends one out of the park, but for the ways in which dance theory has taught us to decode underlying meanings in movement.

I now turn to a specific example of a perhaps more familiar structured improvisation to show the similarities between it and the one I have described above. To illustrate my point, I have selected a group work from 1976 choreographed by Trisha Brown, called *Solo Olos*. Brown, a founding member of Judson Dance Theater and Grand Union, is known for her improvisational structures. Some of them are complicated, mathematical, and seemingly impenetrable to the audience. Others are simple and tasklike in their precision. *Solo Olos,* part of the series known as *Structured Pieces,* falls somewhere in between. Sally Banes reports that "the piece was originally choreographed as a single phrase to be performed as a palindrome."[4] This initial concept remains in the title of the piece, but the piece reveals itself as more complicated than a dance that is the same forward and backward.

Certainly an audience member would need an acutely trained visual sense to decode Brown's original structure. Just as not everyone would discern that "sit on a potato pan, Otis" is palindromic, not everyone would recognize a phrase of movement being retrograded. Even without our understanding the structure, the first version of the dance still would have had the potential to be quite satisfying, kinesthetically and aesthetically. The structure that emerged similarly invites the audience to notice the rules, but does not keep them from enjoying the improvisation without an understanding of it. Just as a novice baseball fan can begin to appreciate the action of a game without understanding the finer details of a ground-rule double or the infield fly rule, an audience can appreciate the action of *Solo Olos*. The piece is for five dancers, four distributed around the performing space and one sitting on the edge of the space, watching the action. This dancer, whom I refer to as the caller, is most like the director of the action in the first improvisation. She dictates a series of commands that the dancers execute. The caller watches the action, reacts to what she sees, and changes the course of the action. She makes decisions based on her observations and on what she imagines she would like to see happen next. The other four dancers, like the bulk of the eighteen dancers in the first improvisation, each have a particular task to do. They share a phrase of movement that they know implicitly, with any facing, going from beginning to end, or end to beginning, from any point in the phrase in any direction.

The structure of *Solo Olos* limits the caller to a few simple instructions: branch, reverse, spill. From those instructions, an array of variations can transpire. The relationship between the words and the actions is not readily apparent. While the commands are simple and direct, the words in and of themselves do not provide an indication of what exactly the action will be. Commands like "walk," "run," and "stop" would be easier to relate to the action of the dance. Further, it is not apparent who reacts to what command as the caller gives the instructions by addressing the dancers by name and audience members may not know anyone's name.[5] Unlike the score for the first improvisation, the structure of *Solo Olos* provides no space for the four dancers to interact with one another or to make independent decisions based on the actions of other dancers.

Initially, one might think that the talking dictates the action of *Solo Olos*. That interpretation ignores the inspiration the caller gets from the physical manifestation of the words. The caller watches the action of the dancing, choosing where in the phrases to alter the path of a performer. The caller watches *Solo Olos* just as the director from the first improvisation makes decisions based on the movement of the dancers and directs that course of action. In *Solo Olos,* the structure of giving the commands makes the audience and all of the participants privy to the changes in action: everyone can hear, "Judith, spill." Despite that transparency, the audience does not know what to expect. Even once the audience defines the structure, the verbs cause different things to happen depending on where in the movement sequence a dancer is. Because variations occur with each of the different words, Brown resisted creating a one-to-one correspondence between a word and an action. The performance does not fulfill expectations.

In contrast, one facet of the structure of the first improvisation hides the direction of the course of action. Each director makes choices to guide the action for the group of nine dancers she supervises, but attempts to communicate the instructions to her group without allowing the other group or other director to know what those commands are. Each director works with her group to develop a secret and silent language of gestures to be read for direction in the midst of the action of the improvisation. The gestures can include things like touching the chin and nose, clapping hands, shrugging shoulders, and the brushing of hands down forearms. Although Martha Graham said that movement never lies, some of the gestures are intentionally calculated to mislead. Typically, the director will go through a long series of gestures, each one having a different meaning. One of them is called the "indicator," the purpose of which is to silently say, "Disregard all of the signs I called before. Do the next one." In this case, despite the mystery of the call, the action that emerges comes from within a range of expectations of the other group and the audience.

Solo Olos and a baseball game share a variety of aspects: solo actions occurring simultaneously, directions for the action coming from an external viewer who responds to the visual and kinesthetic events occurring in the moment, and a structure that is set up to limit and challenge the performers. Obviously there are differences between them. On the level of structure of the dances, there is a variation in how the structures are revealed to the audience, how transparent the instructions are made, and the interaction among the performers. Because the two improvisations differ vastly on the level of their value as cultural commodities, they are only possible to compare when they enter the same field of view. Using an understanding of structured improvisation, we can move beyond the familiar frame of dance and consider the embodiment of other improvisational practices. By using baseball, which has deep cultural resonance in the United States, as an example, I have demonstrated that improvisation is present in our everyday life. Further, this acknowledgment of the improvisation that occurs all around us suggests that it is possible to denaturalize familiar events, providing alternate perspectives for viewing familiar embodied practices.

NOTES

1. Jill Johnston, "Dance Journal: Play," *Village Voice,* November 18, 1965, pp. 15, 22.
2. Karl B. Raitz, "The Theater of Sport," in *The Theater of Sport,* ed. Karl B. Raitz (Baltimore: Johns Hopkins University Press, 1995), 11.
3. "Pillow Talk: Dance and Sports; A Conversation with David Dorfman, Susan Marshall, Elizabeth Streb, Jim Bouton, and Maura Keefe, moderated by David Gere." Jacob's Pillow Dance Festival, Becket, Massachusetts, July 25, 1997.
4. Sally Banes, *Terpsichore in Sneakers: Post-modern Dance* (Middletown, Conn.: Wesleyan University Press, 1987), 89.
5. In the version of the dance that is most readily seen, the excerpt in the film *Beyond the Mainstream,* the caller addresses the commands to the dancers by the color of the costumes. The relationship between the command and the mover is more apparent, but it is still quite difficult to define what exactly "branch," "spill," and "reverse" mean.

FOR THE TASTE OF AN APPLE
Why I Practice Zen
Ellen Webb

I started to practice Zen Buddhism after my dad died eight years ago. At that
time I was performing frequently, directing a dance company, and raising two
small children. As I sat in my father's room on his last day, listening to him
breathe, I understood clearly that one day I was going to die too. Maybe not for
many years, but I could see my turn coming. Meanwhile, my life seemed to be
going by in a blur. Right then I thought that if I was going to die, whether in
one year or forty, I wanted to experience more of my life, not more blur. I decided to learn to meditate.

Zen practice has been a way for me to step outside the pattern of thoughts
and emotions, actions and reactions that dominate my everyday life. It has given
me the feeling, at times, that I have landed on another planet, one where my
idea of life as linear has given way to the horizontal, an experience of the present
so full I hardly recognize it. Meditation has allowed me to stop planning my life
so definitively, to risk more, and to respond more spontaneously to events as
they occur. My post-Zen life has become a little less predictable, which can provoke anxiety, but I like noticing the white flesh against the red skin of the apple
I am eating.

When I started looking for a place to meditate in the early 1990s there were
probably one hundred meditation centers within a fifty-mile radius of my home
in Oakland, California. I guess I was not alone. Because I was uncomfortable
with the idea of religion and was generally nervous about being asked to believe
in anything, it took some searching to find a place that felt right to me. I ended
up at a small Zen center in Oakland, with a teacher named Joko Beck. She didn't
talk about religion, and she assured me that I didn't have to believe in anything.
(Many Zen teachers welcome students to maintain their prior religious practices,
such as Christianity and Judaism, while adding Zen as a meditative tool.) Her
instructions seemed simple: find a quiet place away from the swirl of your daily
life, sit still, and observe. Pay attention to whatever comes up: the busy thoughts

in your head, the feelings in your body, the sounds you are hearing. Just quiet down and witness what transpires. Even five minutes is enough to start.

I did not take to Zen practice easily. I had a million good reasons not to sit still, even for those five minutes. During my first, excruciating four-day sitting retreat I remember thinking that everyone in the room with me was completely crazy. I vehemently told Joko exactly what I thought. Unfazed, she encouraged me to keep sitting.

I did keep sitting and gradually I learned to pay closer attention to what was going on in- and outside of me. And, as I had hoped, I really did begin to experience more of my life: more sound, more color, more sensation. Slowly, slowly I learned to notice the feeling of my breath whether it was quiet or rampaging in my chest. I felt discomfort, uneasiness, tensions that in all my years as a dancer I'd barely ever noticed. I began to open myself up to clenched feelings—anger, fear, envy—that I'd felt before but resisted to the best of my ability. I noticed my constant nagging judgments aimed at myself and everyone else. And I began to see my thoughts as slightly separate from myself. Rather than being linked together in the endless river that fills the mind during waking hours, thoughts and self began to seem distinct from one another, a distinction that arrived as a momentous, if quiet, revelation.

This aspect of Zen practice—being fully awake to the present moment— relates very directly to my years as a dance improviser. In both, the focus is on paying attention, to noticing what is going on. Poetry, painting, music, dance— all these art forms represent, at their most basic level, an effort to capture the moment and a plea to wake up. See all the colors of the forest, stop and hear this tune, share this moment of contact I am having with another dancer. Framing the moment as it slips by, dance improvisation in particular says: Notice! Notice! Wake up to the arch of my spine.

I am driving down a busy city street. Out of the corner of my eye I see an old man maneuvering the sidewalk. Just as I pass by he trips and falls prone, his body partly in the street. My blinker is on and before I know it I am changing lanes, making one U-turn, then a second, changing some more lanes. I pull up at an angle, using my car to shield the body of the old man from oncoming traffic. In an instant I find myself out of my car, talking to him. Other people have gathered and two of us help him as he struggles to get up.

This encounter, though it took place a couple of years ago, has stayed unusually clear in my memory. The man fell as I drove past and I must have gotten back to him in less than a minute, yet I felt I was doing everything slowly. For those few seconds my actions were entirely a response to the situation at hand. While I saw the man fall in my peripheral vision, I started to turn before I started to think. In fact, I can't remember thinking at all until I got back to him. In those moments of pure response, uncertainty vanished. Intuition, awareness, and action were aligned.

I have heard other people—mothers, athletes, LSD-users, Everest-climbers, astronauts, artists—describe such instances. In times of risk, crisis, or extreme exertion, we find ourselves unexpectedly shaken out of our fixed reactions and responding in a new way. Described as "a moment of disappearing when the ego is absent," "being completely open," "knowing without question what to do next," such an experience may seem unpredictable, even inscrutable. In my own life, I've treasured such experiences and have secretly wanted more, yet I haven't intentionally sought out risk, crisis, or extreme exertion in order to replicate the clarity of the adrenaline rush. In fact, years ago I discovered that I could at least taste this experience without climbing Mount Everest, running a marathon, or having a baby. I could taste it in improvisation.

Even for someone who has practiced improvisation for a long time, improvisational performance is a risky endeavor. Whether working with a score, a structure, or no plan at all, the outcome is by design unpredictable. For the performer, this can be heart-stopping. Like a skydiver who doesn't know whether or not her parachute will open, you don't know whether you will ever really connect to the other performers or to your own best resources. More to the point, how can you be sure what movement comes next?

That's where the thrill of improvisation comes in. Not that I am against choreography. I've choreographed many dances in my life. For periods of time choreography has seemed like a safer bet, with an outcome that is not only more certain but more crafted and thought out. So why take the risk to improvise? For me the answer is simple: movement that is crafted and thought out in advance is by its very nature predictable and designed; it can lose its subtlety and spontaneity. Choreography, on account of its predesigned specificity, goes on regardless of what is really happening in the room. If a dancer falls down, or makes a mistake, she gets up and continues as if nothing happened. By choosing to perform without a set plan, however, we allow something unexpected to intrude: a movement, an interaction, a random choice about space or speed that occurs in response to the present moment. This element of unpredictability changes everything. For the better.

In improvisation, as in Zen practice, I can be aware and changed by what goes on at each moment. A response is called forth from me when I pay enough attention to the situation at hand (other dancers, space, sound, light). What's especially interesting to me is that, regardless of whether that response is judged brilliant, pedestrian, inspired, or funny, it doesn't feel like mine. It is simply the response needed for that moment. In fact, when I choose to improvise, I find that one of the greatest challenges is to give up my drive to strategize, and instead to stay in the open-ended situation in which I have placed myself. I counter the urge to reproduce what is safe and familiar. It is not that I plan nothing, but that I am willing to surrender my plans to the exigencies of the situation at hand.

I began improvising in my creative dance class when I was nine years old, and I fell in love. It was a high. I felt powerful and possessed. In contrast to the rest of my life, I seemed always to know what to do next. I was absorbed by the image or structure of the dance. And when we were encouraged to think of ourselves as snakes or birds, I felt freed of myself, able to be completely new—squirmy, slimy, feathery—in ways I didn't know as me.

As I grew older and experimented with many kinds of dances, I came back to improvisation again and again to experience this flow of creativity and connection. Having an audience helped. People could share the discovery. They paid attention and heightened my attention. They upped the ante by witnessing this alchemy of attention and response. I felt as though complete strangers could share in what was flowing through me. The channels between human beings seemed clear and unobstructed.

Now, as a mature dancer, I realize that the channels may not always be so open. My friend Christina Svane ascribes the faltering improvisation to what she calls the "Chihuahuas of the mind." These are the nagging judgments that dog our choices at the instant we make them. Some days the barking makes one doubt every step one takes. Midstream in a movement along comes a thought— "this is clumsy" or "you can't dance this long with your back to the audience" or "this must be getting boring"—and the next thing you know you feel lost. It can seem almost impossible not to be thrown off course by such yapping. Christina suggests teaching these little beasts to Sit! and Stay! For myself, I prefer to attend to the Chihuahuas as I would to a cough in the audience, respectfully taking note of their noisy voices and simply continuing to dance.

There is much talk in Zen about the need to practice and, given the fact that not every improvised dance flows like water, practice is essential to dance improvisation as well. Some students of mine with very little technique or experience nonetheless move remarkably. I love to watch them. But their palette is limited. Their range of available choices is narrow. When I am improvising, and I sense what should happen next, I want to be able to do it, to have access to a wide array of choices. It helps to know my instrument well and to be in tune with my body. Practice lets me know what I can count on. To rehearse the process of improvising might seem a conundrum, but practice opens up a wider range of possibilities when the moment of performance arrives. As Mark Salzman writes in his novel *The Soloist,* "you cannot make great music happen; you can only *prepare* yourself for it to happen."[1]

Eight years into my practice, I am finding that Zen offers me the one simple thing I said I wanted: to be present for more of my life. But as it turns out, that is only part of the package. As I become more attentive (again slowly, slowly) my thoughts become simply thoughts rather than the truth. I observe them but am not so attached, possessive, and identified with them. At times my feelings are just feelings, pain instead of *my* pain, anger rather than *my* anger. My old sense of self—a complex matrix of thoughts and feelings—becomes less solid. Sometimes I experience my breath, tension, and anger as who I am, but sometimes I experience those feelings as simply free-floating sensations, nothing more.

I begin to observe the feelings in my body and the thoughts in my mind as I might observe the color of the trees and the sounds in a room. These experiences don't always come to me as self and other or as internal and external. As my experience of self becomes less fixed, I become less attached to what I create. I don't feel such a strong need to protect it or myself. The outcome of every situation isn't so urgent; I don't always have to win, look good, or gain acknowledgement. I don't have to strategize all the time to make things work out for myself or to shore up my self-image. I can tolerate a little more failure, discomfort, and embarrassment, which opens up a huge arena of possibility. I can play around, try new things and ways of being. As when I came upon the old man who fell in the street, I am free to respond to the situation at hand rather than stick to a strategy that will look after my own well-being.

To me this realm in which I am not so identified with what I create, or as protective of it, gives me freedom. I notice it in my improvisation and in my daily life. I can be more open to what is going on around me and responsive in new ways not bound by my usual self-definition. I surprise myself. Improvising, I can dance the hollow in my bones, or a leaf blowing in the wind, or the feeling of my partner's weight resting on my body. I can become all of these things. I feel more fluid and undefined, and part of my surroundings. At the very best of times I feel that I don't create the dance: the dance dances me.

I fall onto my partner's back and she shifts to assist my rolling and to slightly increase its momentum. I tumble diagonally across the stage and she runs in a circle, sliding to within an inch of my knees as I unfurl to sit up. I feel her breath on my cheek and someone in the audience laughs. We stand up facing each other. I turn away from her, then fall backward, caught in a perfect "spoon" of her body. We walk forward, knees bent, two left feet, two right feet. We stop midstep and start backward. I think, "How are we going to get out of this?" We hesitate, then walk forward again. Midway she falls to the floor backward. I stand center stage, frozen, alone, off balance. My back is cold. The music is louder.

NOTE

1. (New York: Random House, 1994), 274.

LIFE SCORES

Nancy Stark Smith

I am sitting here in the middle of Warner Main Space, a beautiful old wooden gymnasium turned dance studio at Oberlin College. This is where Steve Paxton created *Magnesium* in 1972, one of the early pieces leading up to what we now know as Contact Improvisation. This is also the space in which Nancy Stark Smith set off on her life of dancing and writing. I cast myself off from this island of writing — this haphazard spread of Xeroxed pages, scribbled notes, and yellow paper — into a sea of dancing space around me. Rolling, spinning, spiraling down to and away from the floor, I search for the right gesture, the right tone, the right entry into my introduction of Nancy Stark Smith's short and pithy writings. My own editor's note.

Over the past two decades I have come to know Nancy Stark Smith as a teacher, a performer, a writer, and an editor. Almost as seamlessly as she moves from partner to partner in a jam, Nancy travels between words and movement, language and dancing. As founder and coeditor of *Contact Quarterly* dance journal, she has helped shape a body of work that weaves together the multiple threads of physical experience and intellectual rumination and that helps us make sense of what we are doing in our dancing. Her commitment to reflect on bodily practices and cultural issues that inform and support contemporary dancing has fueled several generations of dancers and encouraged artists from many different fields to discuss the ramifications of their own work. She is willing to engage the places of friction, to confront the contradictions and the awkward moments as well as to explore the euphoric experiences in her dancing life. Nowhere is this more clearly demonstrated than in her Editor Notes at the beginning of each journal. In these, her approach to the dual crafts of dancing and writing is informed by improvisation. She balances issues of physical skill and improvisational strategies with a willingness to look at, and write about, the often overlooked moments or forgotten places within a dance, or within a life.

The unchronological writings that follow, selected for inclusion here by their author, span the years 1987 to 2000 and are chosen to reflect Nancy's interest in the point where dance and life coincide. This compilation includes some of my favorites — short

Fig. V1. Photo: Bill Arnold. Printed with permission.

pieces that I often share with my Contact students simply because they are so right on. They are like mini-dharma talks that highlight the resonant truths behind our dancing and living. Playing across the mysteries of open/shut, speed/stillness, moving/talking, self/other, individual/community, play/work, rest/restlessness, and even war/peace, Smith has written statements that inspire both reflection and new insights into the complicated movements of our lives.

Ann Cooper Albright
Oberlin College

TAKING NO FOR AN ANSWER

Contact Quarterly 12, no. 2 (Spring–Summer 1987) (Improvisation Issue 1)

Today is my birthday and I'm sitting in my car, parked, with the engine running, outside our building, watching the shadow of the building rise on a high pile of snow as the sun goes down behind the building. Maybe sitting here facing this blank page is the closest I'll be able to get in writing to the feeling of improvising. Because how can you describe something that isn't there yet? I want to be able to write from inside the movements of an improvisation and tell from there how things look, how they feel, how they're going. But I keep finding myself back here walking the line, on the page, trying to make pens pirouette, words walk, and ideas bounce and split open, like dancing can do. I'm impressed and informed by all the efforts evident in this issue of people putting a finger on what isn't there. It's like talking about a hole. In this issue, we're trying to say what shapes the hole from within.

In the early 1970s, when I was first getting immersed in the world of practicing and performing dance improvisation, I spent a lot of time watching the Grand Union[1] perform. For hours, I would see material surface on shaky ground, get nourished, worked, referred to, developed, and I'd see it begin to strengthen, come into its own, and become the ground for what would happen next. I saw material be given life or death (which in itself could become the next material), and I learned that there was, in practice, no inherent hierarchy of material. Every move had equal potential to unify, clarify, destroy, or transform what was going on. It was not just the material itself but how and when it was delivered that gave it depth and power.

Where you are when you don't know where you are is one of the most precious spots offered by improvisation. It is a place from which more directions are possible than anywhere else. I call this place the Gap. The more I improvise, the more I'm convinced that it is through the medium of these gaps—this momentary suspension of reference point—that comes the unexpected and much sought after "original" material. It's "original" because its origin is in the current moment and because it comes from outside our usual frame of reference.

When Katie Duck teaches improvisation, as she has many times as a guest teacher at the Theaterschool in Amsterdam, she often tells people not to use their first impulse, but instead to wait for maybe the second or third before taking action. This ability to wait and not follow the impulse is a lot like learning how to break a habit. Holding the moment open a few seconds longer widens the gap where the old behavior/idea/movement/thought/feeling would have gone. And maybe you have nothing to put in its stead. So you put in nothing.

On January 28th, it was a year since I stopped smoking (and, coincidentally, a year since the space shuttle Challenger exploded). I never stopped before and the change feels enormous. Every time I want a cigarette and don't have one I'm creating a gap. Moments that once were easily and automatically filled have become uneasily and consciously unfilled. By leaving them unfilled, I'm not only breaking a "momentum of being," a pattern of behavior, but I'm bringing attention and charge to a moment that would have passed without remark. One of the things that improvising and stopping smoking have in common is that they both require an appetite for learning. Both have the capacity to take you to new ground. Both are about unconscious pulls and conscious choices, and about reckoning with habitual perspectives and behaviors.

Being in a gap is like being in a fall before you touch bottom. You're suspended—in time as well as space—and you don't really know how long it'll take to get "back." And then, when you *do* finally get back, no one even noticed you were gone.

RIDING THE WILD BEAST BACK TO ITS DEN [EXCERPT]
Contact Quarterly **21**, no. 1 (Winter–Spring 1996) (Sexuality and Identity Issue 2)
Moving fast has always been one of my passions. As a child, I would race with my sister to see who could get their pajamas on first. As a Contact Improviser, I've been a reflex junkie, a momentum freak; loving to feel the adrenaline rush, test and take to the turbulent waters with a partner, seeking our limits: of body, mind, and communication. Speed can be irresistible to me. I like to think fast, talk fast, and enjoy the challenge of racing to meet the force of a speeding volleyball in exactly the right spot at the perfect angle with the exact power to send it where I want it to go. Thrilling, funny, fun.

Dancing in the speed of my reflexes, disciplining myself to stay open in the midst of intensity, ready, available for information and for action, makes me feel alive—and the kinship with fellow movers, with whom I am sharing these magical milliseconds of reflex and response, grows easily intimate. They can "hear" my weight shift in that last moment of falling, feel just what force is necessary to balance the kooky flow of my weight, suggesting through a tiny shift of their touch a solution to our movement puzzle, a next chapter to our story. Through touch and movement, we love, cherish, challenge, and rail on each other as long as it lasts. This continues to be a great part of my pleasure in dancing.

But passions change. Mine were changed, or rather forced open, by a broken heart. A simple heartbreak, as they go, but for me, total. I had suffered disappointments before, but this time I let the wild beast have me. Exhilarating, raw, intense. The heat burned though my body like lava, travelling out in thin hot lines under

Fig. V2. Nancy Stark
Smith. (Photo: Bill Arnold.
Printed with permission.)

my skin, out through my limbs, down into and through my core. Something was happening to me. An initiation of sorts.

The heat made me move differently. Cut my speed, and created a new intensity. It was slow, delicate, deep. This molten lava moved almost imperceptibly, directing me to open the way for its passage through my body. Turn this way, extend your arm, release weight into left hip, twist to the right, open eyes and stretch focus to that corner of the window sill. After awhile, the organization of limbs and tensions would be complete and there would be no more desire to move. Just to stay. Inside the position, energy raged, flew, circulated throughout my shape, energizing and soothing me, both at a stillpoint and the peak of fire. Sooner or later, this inner circulation would come to rest, and the impulse to move would return. . . . The heat and heart of this dance created a new movement practice for me. One that nearly always makes me weep, it's so painful and sweet.

MEASURES OF REST
Contact Quarterly 20, no. 1 (Winter–Spring 1995)

Yellow leaves dangle from the tall linden tree like earrings. This issue's production has taken us from summer's end and the first show of color on the trees in northern Vermont, through New England's awesome display, to the first delicate

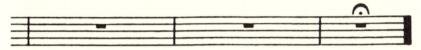

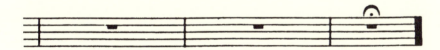

and daring days of leaflessness. There is something particularly fragile yet fierce about this newly exposed, though waning, light.

Fig. V3. Photo: Bill Arnold. Printed with permission.

Week before last, during one of the heaviest weeks of production on this issue, I took a twenty-minute drive through the back roads of western Massachusetts at the peak of autumn splendor, to a renovated schoolhouse where two hundred people were attending a weeklong retreat with a Tibetan Buddhist Dzogchen teacher. I was visiting for the morning and had gotten up especially early to squeeze in a few hours of work before I left.

After the talk I lingered in the field by the schoolhouse, smelling the sweet wet hay, the decomposing leaves, watching a cluster of kittens climb and tumble all over a station wagon parked in the middle of the field. As I strolled to my car with a friend and her baby, I felt how time had finally slowed down, and space opened up—I could not only see where I was but actually absorb the nutrition from it.

On the drive back to the office, my heart swelling with the beauty of the glowing landscape, intoxicated by the earthy smells, I felt simply glad, relaxed, open to what was in front of me, and deeply satisfied, excited. And then it occurred to me: this is how I feel when I'm dancing.

Snow falls on the open field. Here, for you to play, are a few found measures of rest. To play, and to repeat, as you like.

COMING TO MEET THE OTHER
Contact Quarterly 19, no. 2 (Summer–Fall 1994)

> The sun was setting; it was getting late.
> He walked her to the garden gate.
> He wanted to thank her, but he didn't know how.
> 'Cause he was the farmer, and she was the cow.
> *Sixth- grade autograph book inscription*
>
> Opposition is true friendship.
> *William Blake*

It was by chance that I happened to see Israel's Prime Minister Yitzhak Rabin and P.L.O. Chairman Yassir Arafat shake hands on the White House lawn last September. I was stopping home midday and flicked the TV on for a quick weather report and found, instead, the ceremony about to begin. I stood, then sat, spellbound, watching their movements: every shift of weight, turn of head, direction of gaze, the reach, hesitation, grasp, shaking it, the hand, firmly, finally, and letting it go. When the ceremony was over, I cried, feeling slightly embarrassed, slightly proud, and surprised at the force of my reaction.

I think what moved me most was the movement and how it spoke of what was inside it. As much as the teams of experts tried to choreograph this handshake—having Clinton step back and open his arms, leaving the space in front of him empty, a powerful vacuum into which the magic handshake might (be made to) suddenly appear—it wasn't going to be that easy. Though diplomats, skilled in the art of shake and smile, these two men were, for a long moment, much more than political symbols; their movements couldn't hide the enormous personal investment, the hope, reservation, courage, pride, fear, and discipline that brought them all the way to the touch of each other's hands.

When I went into the studio up in Vermont last year for a "studio visit" with my friend Simone Forti, a dancer whose work I respect and enjoy, I wasn't sure what would happen. All I knew was what I had asked for: that the two of us be in the space together, working alone on whatever was most compelling for us at the time, and that we wouldn't, unless irresistibly drawn to it, interact with each other directly.

I began moving as I had been for some months, slowly, deeply, on the floor, finding my way through a satisfying terrain of micro-stretches and weight releases, full of feeling, sensation, and image—private, personal—when I began to hear Simone warming up. She was light on her feet, moving this way and that, sometimes going to the floor, then hopping up, talking in a high animated voice: "Yes, yes, I *really did* like that book. . . . It really is a good book," etc. As she continued her work, I began to feel increasingly uncomfortable, irritated, bothered. I can't relate to this, I thought to myself. I don't *want* to relate to this. And then I realized I didn't exactly have to. I had made the rules and the rules said to stay with what I was doing, not worry about meeting or trying to adapt to the other. The point was not to try to *block out* her presence, but to accept and appreciate it while continuing on my own way. This makes its own kind of relationship. After twenty years of meeting partners through Contact Improvisation, I find this kind of meeting extraordinary, a tremendous relief and a demanding discipline.

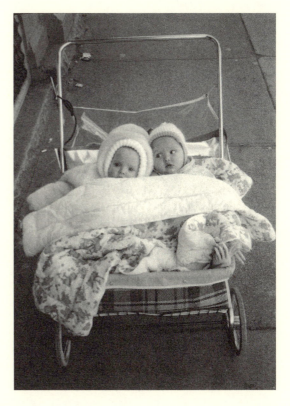

Fig. V4. Photo: Bill Arnold. Printed with permission.

So I continued, aware and not aware of Simone's whereabouts, following the thread of my sensation further through the maze of images that it provoked. An hour or so later, I noticed that we were very close to each other in the room, she still on her feet dancing and talking, me moving slowly on the floor. At that moment I experienced us in the same image—she as a slightly crazed, dehydrated woman dancing lightly through the desert telling her tale, and I, below, was the desert under her feet—geologically slow, compressed layers of time and earth, moving imperceptibly out in all directions, going nowhere. I had arrived at our meeting.

Perhaps what really moved me in the Rabin-Arafat handshake was realizing that their extreme differences would not be dissolved by the touch of their hands. That they would remain fiercely opposed and at the same time deeply united. I hope to support this stance in my own work and life within the dance community. How can we share in the creation and development of work—the collective work and the particular works? How do we, as individuals, stand alone with our experience, and how do we shift in and out of synch with our peers without losing contact? How can we respect the integrity of the individual's contribution and at the same time share freely in the collective bounty of the work?

FORCING THE ISSUE
Contact Quarterly 25, no. 1 (Winter–Spring 2000) (To Dance or Not to Dance Issue)

First, gotta slow it, way, way, down.
More, down.
Almost to sleep.
To find, what there is, to say.

Ask the body—why dance
Go to the cells, deeper, the soul;
take the body's reason.
Not about logic
justification
not an idea
Not either about "deciding" anything.

Take the inroad,
the path that leads to why bother,
why must.

To dance or not to dance—is this a question? For me it wasn't, until we asked. I've never seriously contemplated stopping dancing. But then again, I never seriously contemplated starting. My passion for moving was channeled early on into sports and gymnastics, which I adored. But by the time I got to college, though my love for movement had not flagged, my lack of interest in the increasingly competitive nature of my sports experience left me in movement limbo. By luck, I found myself in a monthlong college dance workshop with Twyla Tharp in the early 1970s, just when the dance revolution of the 1960s was making its way onto college campuses. I found in this dancing a perfect synthesis of my love for physical rigor, and the creativity, wit, and poetry I had found lacking in competitive sports.

Later in college, as a dance and writing major, both my dance and writing advisers told me I would have to stop doing the other thing if I wanted to "get anywhere" in my career. I gave this serious thought, for a few minutes, and realized I wasn't going to be able to choose to stop doing either. It was like being asked to choose between eating and breathing. I needed both to survive. (I didn't think that either one would likely be my livelihood [was I still thinking I'd end up being a doctor?] but giving either up, or for that matter calling one a "hobby" and the other a "career," seemed arbitrary and impossible.)

Moving and writing are two ways I stay balanced and alive on this planet. They are the ways I make sense of loss, express joy, share with others, pursue the mysteries, and try to articulate what I find.

Dancing is where I put everything I've ever learned and loved into practice—whether it's leverage, composition, or compassion. It's where I try to practice what I preach, and where I go to feel for the next handhold.

Fig. V5. Photo: Bill Arnold. Printed with permission.

Dancing is also where I detect the grain of sand in the oyster shell, the pea under the princess's mattress, the irritation that leads me to some microscopically new corner of my awareness, a new piece of the world revealed through the dancing lens. Dancing not only allows, it *forces* me down into the richness, the muck, the fertile emptiness, forces me down into the essential questions, unaskable and unanswerable, about living, in this body, on this land, in this life, at this time. And then it gives me a language with which to "read the book," so to speak, and ask the next question.

There are too many minds in my body trying to write this Note about dancing (or not). There's the athlete invigorated after a full-out match; the poet high on a word choice; the scholar studying; the human looking to love and be loved; the artist admiring the power and beauty of what's just out of sight and struggling to make it visible; the fool happily letting it all fly out of hand. And there are others.

I dance to attempt a single expression of these Minds—one that can flicker between them, that can layer, reveal, embrace, isolate, research, synthesize, and play them, in one body at one time. I may be of several minds when it comes to dancing. But when I am doing it, I am of only one. I do T'ai Chi everyday, and playing league volleyball is good, great even, but neither is a substitute for dancing. They don't speak with as many minds, don't touch me in as many places at once. It is indeed a miracle. Who invented dancing anyway? What was the big idea?

All I know is that I feel better after I've been dancing. To bring the myriad minds together momentarily, to keep my body, this precious vehicle, humming, willing, to be somewhere, here, in it, in the dancing, knowing there's nowhere else I'd rather be. Illusory though it may be, when I'm dancing, I feel free.

Talking and writing about dancing is dangerous, though. It can give us the impression that we know what we're doing.

I've been lucky. I continue not to have a reason to stop. "The word 'gratitude' comes to mind," Bebe Miller said this summer after a satisfying afternoon of dancing. Yeah.

NOTE

1. The Grand Union dance theater collective performed improvisationally from 1970 to 1976. The members of the group included Trisha Brown, Barbara Dilley, Douglas Dunn, David Gordon, Nancy Lewis (Green), Steve Paxton, Yvonne Rainer.

EPILOGUE

DWELLING IN POSSIBILITY

Ann Cooper Albright

It is October 11, 2001, a month after the terrorist attacks on New York City and Washington, D.C., and a few days after America started bombing Afghanistan in retaliation. The world as Americans have known it for the last several decades is falling apart. In the midst of this cataclysm, I want to talk about why I think improvisation matters. About why, in the midst of our rude awakening to the meaning of global antagonism, and a subsequent reevaluation of national priorities, I still believe that the practice of opening one's physical and psychic being to the unknown can be both personally useful and politically profound. Because improvisation leads us to imagine other ways of being-with-one-another-in-the-world. Because improvisation is one of the few experiences that cultivates a self open to possibility. Because improvisation can teach us how to dwell in our bodies and live in an unpredictable world. Because improvisation provides a perspective that allows us to see the emptiness in Lower Manhattan not as a failure of national security, but rather as an open field in which to imagine a different future.

It is the day after the attacks. Most of my improvisation class has spent the last twenty-four hours watching video footage of the towers falling. Many of my Oberlin College students are from the New York City area. By now, most of us present know that our immediate friends or relatives are okay—shaken, of course, but nonetheless alive. Still, we are left with a desire to do something, to create a response to an event at once close and far away from the reality of this midwestern campus. I gather the students together and ask them to trust in our usual practice of centering and expanding, of releasing and opening our bodies in order to be prepared for whatever might arise. As we finish a vigorous warm-up, I am gripped by a vision of us all outside on the town square, standing tall in the sunlight and then slowly curling to the ground, rolling, and then unfolding to stand again. All of us gradually moving together, yet each person working in his own time. A simple, but profound score. I wonder if, with only a week of classes under their belt, the students will be ready for it?

Fig. W1. Contact Jam, Oberlin College, 1999. (Photo: John Seyfried. Courtesy Ann Cooper Albright.)

257

Walking in silence out to Tappan Square, we focus our energy, acknowledging the uncertainty inside while attending to the external sensations prompted by a shift in our environment. We feel the difference between pavement and grass, light and shade, taking a moment to focus on the light breeze on our skin. This physical mindfulness prepares us for the public performance. Arriving at our destination, we spread out across the field, each person facing a different direction. Slowly, each in his or her own time, we sink to the ground, roll, and then rise up into a standing position, playing with the soft balance of muscles and bones that makes maintaining a most simple position into an intricate dance. Sink, rise and stand, sink, rise and stand. Eventually, we move closer to one another until we are in a tight clump, close enough to feel the heat from one another's bodies. We smile as we end the score, aware that even in the midst of this national crisis, improvisation has become an act of creative defiance. It has become an opportunity to transform our grief into an offering—at once a physical act of prayer and a healing gesture grounded in our bodies. Later, at a local café, someone tells me how watching us gave them a sense of peace, a sense of being part of a ritual, a response that allowed them to breathe more easily.

In the weeks following the collapse of the World Trade Center, the newspapers were full of speculation about what, when, and how the towers would be rebuilt. These discussions struck me as frantic and anxious responses to the situation, born out of a desire to refuse the position of underdog and reassert U.S. power by erecting another monument to cover over the emptiness. Improvisation can teach us to be patient, to see a future in the hole. It can help us resist our first response (fear, the urge to get them back), therefore allowing the empty space of lower Manhattan to guide us into another kind of responsibility, literally giving us the *ability to respond differently.*

In an Editor Note for *Contact Quarterly* in which she connects the practice of improvisation with quitting smoking, veteran improviser Nancy Stark Smith writes:

> Where you are when you don't know where you are is one of the most precious spots offered by improvisation. It is a place from which more directions are possible than anywhere else. I call this place the Gap. . . . Every time I want a cigarette and don't have one I'm creating a gap. Moments that once were easily and automatically filled have become uneasily and consciously unfilled. By leaving them unfilled, I'm not only breaking a "momentum of being," a pattern of behavior, but I'm bringing attention and charge to a moment that would have passed without remark. . . . Being in a gap is like being in a fall before you touch bottom. You're suspended—in time as well as space—and you don't really know how long it'll take to get "back."[1]

This "gap" or moment of possibility is an existential state, a suspension of reference points in which new experiences become possible. Smith's use of the metaphor of falling is only partially literary. In fact, the state of falling is quite real in Contact Improvisation. In order to embrace those moments of falling, in order to experience that state of suspension, however, one needs to train the body (and, by extension, the psyche) away from one's conditioned fear of losing control. Being suspended between up and down, stretching one's awareness to attend to the split-second experience of falling—these are all physical moments that point to an existential openness (which includes a suspension of the self as we have come to think of the self/ego in contemporary Western society). Nancy Stark Smith's gap constitutes what I think of as a space in which to change our habitual responses, thereby expanding the possibility of dwelling in the world.

Certainly the earth-shattering "gap" of the World Trade Center has created just such a moment. Locally, this deep loss of civic iconography and human lives has galvanized an outpouring of concern, generosity, and community spirit unusual for that urban environment. The physical reality of being close to that vacant space has made many people reevaluate their priorities. Just recently there were a series of articles in the national press about how this tragic event has, in fact, served to bridge various racial divides as many communities embrace and praise their police, fire, and emergency medical civil servants regardless of their skin color. The official government response (complete with the rhetoric of retaliation and vanquishing evil), however, seems much less inventive and much more concerned with covering over that "gap," rather than dwelling within it.

Improvisation can be both a physical and a metaphysical practice, one that has kept me dancing through pain and joy, made me hungry for new physical experiences, and allowed me to be happy with the changing abilities of my body for more than twenty years. During this time, I have explored many approaches to improvisation, including those found in Contact Improvisation, social dancing, and contemporary performance work, as well as several related somatic practices such as Body-Mind Centering and Authentic Movement. More recently, I have added to my improvisational repertoire the movement exchanges in Capoeira, an Afro-Brazilian martial/dance form. Like many forms of martial art, Capoeira has a codified series of moves, but the strategic combination and timing of those moves is entirely improvisational, as is the need to be present and responsive in the moment. Although I have performed solo improvisations, I find myself most intrigued by improvisational forms that specialize in crossover between two or more people. There is something so satisfying to me in meeting an "other" in the space of movement such that traditional separations between us can become fluid and mobile. Recently, I have come to realize just how much the physical state of launching into the unknown has deeply influenced not only my dancing and thinking, but also my being-in-the-world. Improvisation is a philosophy of life, although not one based on a specific doctrine, or system of beliefs. Rather, it is a way of relating to movement and experience: a willingness to explore the realm of possibility, not in order to find the correct solution, but simply to find *out*.

I believe the potency of improvisational practices today lies less in the opening up of more movement options (locomoting across a space, say, on three or four limbs instead of the usual two), but rather in understanding how to encourage a willingness to cross over into uncomfortable territories, to move in the face of fear, of what is unknown. This willingness is made possible by the paradoxically simple and yet quite sophisticated ability to be at once external and internal—both open to the world and intensely grounded in an awareness of one's ongoing experience. "Dwelling in Possibility" refers to this dual experience of being present "here" in order to be able to imagine what could happen out "there." (I am employing the term "dwelling" in the Heideggerian sense of a space consciously constructed to provide not only the necessary type of shelter, but also an equally essential sense of place.)[2] Dwelling is a heightened experience of inhabiting—fully and consciously—such that a space becomes more than the sum of its parts, such that that space *makes things happen.* This conception of dwelling is similar, I believe, to what Simone Forti describes as a "dancing state," where sensations juice the body, encouraging imaginative connections that might otherwise be impossible. These textual phrases describe the kind of solid physical awareness and subtle mindfulness that must be engaged as the corporeal foundation for improvising across our own experience.

Taking the risk of sounding overevangelistic, I claim that improvisation can give us the skills we need to deal with many of the social and aesthetic issues of the twenty-first century. Although we have all become adept at talking about aesthetic hybridity, cultural alterity, crossing borders (both earthly and cyber), and global fusion, few of us have really studied what physical and intellectual practices will make our bodies and our minds ready for this brave new world. My improvisational experience has been based on the combination of training in disorientation (falling, being upside down, moving through fear and with a great deal of momentum, being out of control) and somatic study in subtle bodily awarenesses. Improvisation can lead us out of our habitual responses by opening up alternative experiences—new physical sensations and movement appetites, encouraging dancers to explore new positionings and desires. Although this practice begins with an attentiveness to corporeal experience, it also develops a mental flexibility that can provide a sort of intellectual map with which to chart new pathways for negotiating awkward or difficult cultural crossings.

Oddly enough, even though I am a dancer and a scholar interested in the ideas embedded in a variety of movement practices and choreographies, I have only recently begun to reflect on the larger implications of my work in improvisation. Like many improvisers, I have been reluctant to move beyond the articulation of the embodied experience into an exploration of the ideological structures within my practice. As the essays in this volume amply attest, however, there is an amazing amount of physical and intellectual material to be mined within different approaches to improvisation. Indeed, this collection represents the possibility marked by the intersection of dancing and writing. Each essay is, in fact, an improvisation in itself, helping us to uncover new strategies for engaging dancing and thinking bodies.

As a textual practice, however, improvisation is very slippery. It also fits uneasily with certain kinds of academic discourses. I have found it difficult to find the right frame, the right tone with which to theorize about improvisation. Clearly it takes a leap of faith to articulate the nuances of a state of physical and meta-physical flux. It is delicate work, and there is the omnipresent fear of bruising the form of improvisation, pinning it down to static meanings, dissecting it for the sake of epistemological stability. But the alternatives are equally deadly; by keeping improvisational work outside of current intellectual discussions we limit its influence. Sure, my experience of improvisation will change as I write about it, but then again, my experience of writing and thinking will also change as I engage with my embodied knowledge from an intellectual perspective.

I remember a conversation I had a decade ago with a member of my feminist study group (fondly referred to as "the flaming bitches"), who remarked that my approach to scholarship seemed deeply informed by my dancing. I agreed, thinking she meant it was marked by a sort of general physicality, or emphasis on corporeality. I failed to realize at that moment that improvisation—that act of launching oneself (with or without music, props, or other people) across the open space of the studio, field or stage—had been my primary movement experience for most of my adult life. Fortunately for me, this collection has provided an opportunity (a textual space for improvisation) to pursue the theoretical implications of my work in improvisation. In this essay, I am beginning to elucidate the continuum of knowledges that support my commitment to this movement practice in order to engage with their ramifications in my daily life.

Generally speaking, improvisation is a misunderstood phenomenon, especially within the dance world. Figured as the opposite of choreography, improvisation is often seen as free, spontaneous, nontechnical, wild, or childlike, as if one can simply erase years of physical and aesthetic training to become a blank slate onto which one's imagination can project anything. Of course, as seasoned improvisers know, improvisation requires training to open the body to new awarenesses and sensations, and the imagination to new narrative possibilities. Most improvisational training works to release the body from habitual responses, whetting one's curiosity about "what if's." Improvisation often crafts an awareness of aesthetic priorities, compositional strategies, and physical experiences that may, at first, be less visible or less easily discernible.

One of the earliest exercises that I give in my improvisation classes is referred to as "the small dance" or "the stand." First developed by Steve Paxton in the early seventies as he explored the physical skills that would lead toward defining the form of Contact Improvisation, the stand allows one to focus on the small dance created by the shifts of bones, muscles, and breath required to stand "still." After they have been warming up, moving through the space with big, vigorous movements, I ask the students to choose a spot and stand in a relaxed, but active manner. At first, I call their attention to the multiple rhythms contributed by their heartbeat, pulses, and breathing. This is a moment when they are suspended between sky and earth, a moment at once grounded through the feet and opening through the top of the head. Later, after they have focused on the internal sensations of their bodies, I ask them to play with shifting their balance to the point of almost falling in many different directions. Eventually, this exercise will develop into one that encourages them to play with a gentle falling off balance, which moves them through the space of the studio.

Sometimes, while they are in the stand, I ask the dancers to focus on allowing sounds, light, and space to enter their bodies. Engaging one's peripheral vision is crucial to this process, and I tell the dancers to release the fronts of their eyes, allowing images and colors to come into their heads instead of straining their eyes in order to go out and grab the visual image. Then, I ask them to concentrate on opening the pores of their skin so that the world can penetrate their physical awareness. This image helps us feel our bodies as part and parcel of a whole landscape, rather than the instrument that views, arranges, or destroys that landscape. I have, at times, described this somatic moment as facilitating an ecological consciousness: in this dialogue between the self and the world one becomes aware of the intriguing possibilities of interdependence. With this comes a deeper sense of responsibility, not as an oppressive duty toward others, but rather as an ability to respond, an ability to be present with the world as a way of being present with oneself. This is the fruit of attention, a mindfulness that prepares one for improvisation.

This dialogue is also a kind of somatic engagement that leads to a profound psychic reorganization as well. If the world is already inside one's body, then the separation between self and other is much less distinct. The skin is no longer the boundary between the world and myself, but rather the sensing organ that brings the world into my awareness. In this intersubjective space in which one can be penetrated by sensations both external and internal, the heretofore unquestioned separation of individual and the world (or me and you) becomes more fluid. What I am talking about here is the possibility of reconceptualizing the physical borders of bodies through attention to sensation. This reimagining, it seems to me, is a very different model than the popularized Buddhist notion of being "one" with the world. I am not suggesting we lose all sense of personal boundaries, such that any distinctions between self and other melt into homogeneous goop. In fact, most improvisation, whether it is based on an interaction with music, props, stories, or other people, works well when the participants play off one another's differences (in aesthetic priorities, variety of technical training, approach to syncopation, rhythm and tempo, energy, performative demeanor, or narrative structure, to mention only a few).

Interestingly enough, most improvisational practices, while they may celebrate points of difference as a meeting place for the dance, also insist on the mobility of those differences. Certainly much of the improvisation within forms such as Contact Improvisation and Capoeira plays with the joy of physical moments of synchrony as well as the very real pleasure of interrupting that connectedness. There are times of mutual suspension or fall, places in which one move is gracefully countered by another, equally beautiful, gesture. It is magical, this dwelling in which a fluid exchange and intuitive meshing of energies is possible. At any point, however, one can break the point of connection to lead the improvisation into a specific direction. Part of the work (and play) then is learning how to deal with these situations openly, with curiosity and not determination. Improvisation trains one to react without ever being reactionary, to regard a change of rules as an opportunity rather than a disappointment (or failure).

In forms that use partners, such as Contact and Capoeira, this ability to release expectations about the direction of the duet is crucial. In order for the play of forces to develop, the partners must be able to shift what they are doing in response to how their partner (in dancing or sparring) moves and shifts. In his fascinating essay linking the thinking of Levinas to the practice of Contact Improvisation, David Williams explains this meeting of self and other: as an "in-between or go-between, [it] is another space in which the 'I' is both implicated and (re)conceived; it is the articulation of meeting-in-difference."[3] Williams continues to stake out the existential possibilities of the form when he claims that:

> For each of the partners, con()tact constitutes the possible coexistence of form and spontaneity, rules-of-the-game and dance, cause and effect, center and margin, proximity and distance. It is the "play" within the obdurate fixity of corporeal identities, its "give," its supple-ment, its différance: the unstable borderlands where an ethics of alterity occurs.[4]

Williams's words describe the effects of a somatic experience in which the usual boundaries between bodies, the sense of fixed identities, is suspended. Although he is writing about Contact Improvisation in particular, I believe that this suspension of fixed identities is at the core of many different kinds of improvisational practices. Nevertheless, Contact takes this very play between self and other as the basis for much of the work.

One of the first themes introduced to beginning students of Contact Improvisation is the articulation of the point of contact. Facing a partner, one presses a forefinger against that of their partner. Attending to how the energy of their whole bodies can move through their spines out their arms and into their fingers, the partners wait. They wait and listen to that point of contact that will eventually begin to move. The point created by the joining of two energies is sometimes referred to as a "third mind," and it is that which becomes the focus of their mutual attention. The two partners endeavor to follow its spatial and rhythmic journey. At first, it may seem clear who is leading and who is following; eventually, however, with time and practice, the shifting back and forth evolves into such a rapid and subtle exchange that the categories of leader and follower begin to lose their oppositional meaning. The binary is subverted as the attention shifts onto the play of space and touch between the two movers. David Williams describes this intellectual idea in terms that easily translate into the improvisational dynamic of this partnership. "The crucial factor here is not how many ways two different units can relate to each other, but recognition that this 'third element' is not a unit but an axis, not an entity but a state of being, *less a relationship than an act of relating*" (emphasis mine).[5]

Embedded in this "act of relating" (improvisationally) is a fluidity of experience that can change our perceptions of relationships. It is the verb that mobilizes the noun, the *act* of relating that refigures the very significance of the relationship. This claim is extravagant, I realize. Nevertheless, once again I insist that we return to the studio, to our physical practice, to the somatic dwelling that creates possibility in the world. One of the most amazing experiences in my improvisational practice is that of shifting back and forth between active and passive, between letting go and taking charge, between being influenced and deciding which way to turn. This situation is not simply one in which roles are exchanged. Rather, the experience changes the roles, changes the very "act of relating." Here is the dance score I am talking about:

> This is a duet, not an exercise. A dance, not an activity. To begin, the A partners lie down, completely passive, allowing their weight to sink fully into the floor. The B partners begin to move their bodies with attention to giving the passive A partners an experience of the weight of their bones and the mobility of their joints. As any one who has ever done any kind of body work or physical therapy knows, a passive body allows one to feel sensations unavailable to a body that is self-engaged, even the most released one. Focusing on their breaths, the A and B partners together establish a vibration of energetic exchange. Bit by bit, percentage point by percentage point, the passive partners become increasingly active, engaging first the core of the body's structure and working outward to mobilize their limbs—arms, legs, head, and tailbone. Then, both partners dance together in a fully active state. Eventually, the originally active partners become progressively passive until they are lying on the floor, enjoying the sensations of their own bodies through their newly active partners' manipulations.

Over the course of this duet one experiences the continuum of possibilities in being active or passive. Normally in our culture, these various positions of active and passive are pathologized into power dynamics, where the passive figure is seen as powerless, as not having control over her own body, as being either infantile or lazy. But my experience and that of many of my students is that the experience of being passive, rather than feeling powerless, actually opens up a great deal of sensation. This grounded somatic experience is, in fact, quite empowering. Of course, the reason that it is pleasurable comes from a place of trust and a willingness to witness one's own process that has already been set up within the group, class, or community. I would never give this particular score to a group of beginning improvisers. Nor could I have ever imagined myself doing such a score before I became an improviser. More than anything else, improvisation has taught me how to survive just such unimaginable moments.

While I have tried to make a case for the transformative potential of improvisation to help us meet many of the cultural challenges of the twenty-first century, I want to finish with a much more specific discussion of my personal transformation from dancer to invalid back to dancer, a cyclical journey that would never have been possible without the grounded somatic wisdom and spontaneous joy at the core of my dance practice. Because I had experienced how to move and feel within the passive as well as the active state, I understood (in some deep fiber of my spinal cord) how to convert an ending (my doctor suggested I retire from dancing) into a beginning.

A little more than a month after the birth of my son, as I was training to get back in shape to teach dance again, two discs in my lumbar region herniated into my spinal cord, causing intense pain, some nerve damage, and temporary loss of movement in my lower limbs. The shock of a sudden and profound disability is traumatic for everyone, but for a dancer in her mid-thirties, it is devastating. Add to this the stress of a newborn baby (in addition to a toddler) and the fact that I was going up for tenure at the same time, and it becomes pretty easy to imagine the scope of the physical and psychic identity crisis I was experiencing at the time. There was, of course, a desperate moment in which I thought I would never be able to dance again in the same physically vigorous manner which I adored. Fortunately, in situations such as the Breitenbush Contact Jam, I had had some experience dancing with dancers with a variety of abilities and physical limitations. Having jammed with dancers who were differently abled helped me to believe in the possibility of continuing somehow. But beyond the actual empowerment of role models, it was my improvisational training in disorientation and somatic mindfulness that provided the foundation for reenvisioning my life. By having who and what I thought I was so radically fractured, I had to revise not only the details of my identity (how could I call myself a dancer as I hobbled around with a cane), but also the very act of identification. Not simply the title, but rather the entire process of entitlement. I had to reclaim my body and thus my dancerhood from the inside out.

Six months later, when I began to teach again, I realized what an extraordinary opportunity this injury had been for me. In the gap created by limited function and relentless pain, I was able to move small, but still teach big. Like many dance teachers, I use my body to demonstrate and instruct. In the absence of my usually strong body, I had to change how I taught, substituting verbal descriptions and group scores for the skill-building exercises with which I usually launched my class. Instead of my body, I relied on my eyes, language, and my imagination. Ironically, that class was one of the best I have ever taught. Somehow, I managed to move beyond a catalogue of my limitations into new pedagogical territory. The students met my challenged state with an open generosity of spirit and a willingness to accept me as I was. In retrospect, it is clear to me that without my training in improvisation, I would never have dared to attempt teaching movement again.

I began this essay by exploring how improvisation might help us respond to one of the most politically sensitive events in recent years. The terrorist attacks on New York City and Washington, D.C. have elicited worldwide responses. I end locally, with a discussion of how dance improvisation helped me imagine other options for dancing in the midst of a devastating personal injury. I shall not attempt to draw any parallels between these two radically different ruptures of the fabric of daily life. Sometimes it is difficult to understand the implications of the local on the global. Nor shall I suggest (although it is an amusing fantasy) that heads of state might very well employ movement improvisation as a negotiating strategy (I am envisioning something somewhere in-between Capoeira and Contact Improvisation). Nonetheless, I want to echo Nancy Stark Smith's discussion of that famous late twentieth-century handshake between Israeli Prime Minister Yitzhak Rabin and Palestine Liberation Organization Chairman Yassir Arafat in recognizing the importance of small, physical gestures toward peace. The significance of their touch—like the significance of any gesture to connect with another—lies in a willingness to begin an exchange, the outcome of which is unknown.

NOTES

1. *Contact Quarterly* 12, no. 2 (Spring–Summer 1987): 3.
2. For a discussion of dwelling, see the chapter "Building Dwelling Thinking" in Martin Heidegger, *Poetry, Language, Thought*, trans. Albert Hofstader (New York: Harper and Row, 1975). Here Heidegger discusses the ecological character of dwelling as a form of living in which being in the world is an awareness of living as "sparing and preserving" (149).
3. David Williams, "(In) the In-Between," in the Australian journal *Writings on Dance* (Winter 1996): 26.
4. Ibid.
5. Ibid., 25.

ABOUT THE EDITORS AND CONTRIBUTORS

Editors

ANN COOPER ALBRIGHT is the author of *Choreographing Difference: The Body and Identity in Contemporary Dance* (Wesleyan, 1997) and co-editor with Ann Dils of *Moving History/ Dancing Cultures: A Dance History Reader* (Wesleyan, 2001). Albright earned her B.A. from Bryn Mawr College, her M.F.A. from Temple University, and her Ph.D. from New York University. She is currently Associate Professor of Dance at Oberlin College.

DAVID GERE is currently writing a book on dance and AIDS. He earned his B.A. from Oberlin College, his M.M. from the University of Hawai'i at Manoa, and his Ph.D. from the University of California at Riverside. Gere is currently Associate Professor at UCLA's Department of World Arts and Cultures.

Contributors

SALLY BANES is Marian Hannah Winter Professor of Theatre History and Dance Studies and director of the Institute for Research in the Humanities at the University of Wisconsin–Madison. Her books include *Terpsichore in Sneakers: Post–modern Dance; Democracy's Body: Judson Dance Theater, 1962–1964; Greenwich Village 1963: Avant–Garde Performance and the Effervescent Body; Writing Dancing in the Age of Postmodernism; Dancing Women: Female Bodies on Stage;* and *Subversive Expectations: Performance Art and Paratheater in New York, 1976–85.* She also directed the video *The Last Conversation: Eisenstein's Carmen Ballet.* She has written dance criticism for the *Village Voice,* the *Soho Weekly News,* and *Dance Magazine.* Banes is a past president of the Society of Dance History Scholars and the Dance Critics Association, and a past editor of *Dance Research Journal.*

BRUCE CURTIS is a pioneer in the emerging field of disability performance art, with a strong commitment to the belief that disabled and nondisabled persons, through mutual exploration and collaboration in the arts, can challenge stereotypes and prejudice while making significant contributions to the legacy of human artistic expression. In 1987,

Curtis began producing a series of annual events in San Francisco featuring disabled performance artists that helped propel the current national debate within the disability community about the existence of disability culture. He has taught Contact Improvisation in mixed classes of disabled and nondisabled students since 1986 and has also performed as a dancer in the United States, Brazil, Russia, Denmark, Finland, Australia, Canada, Iceland, Ireland, and Germany.

KENT DE SPAIN is a dance and multidisciplinary artist who holds a doctorate in dance studies from Temple University. He has taught and toured throughout the United States, has been the recipient of several major choreographic awards (including the Pew Fellowship in the Arts and an Established Choreographers Fellowship from the Pennsylvania Council on the Arts), and has been a visiting artist/professor in dance at Oberlin College, the University of Georgia, Ohio State University, UCLA, and the University of North Carolina at Greensboro. He has presented his research at numerous international conferences and symposia, and is particularly known for his work on the interface between dance and technology, and for his lectures, workshops, and writings on improvisational process. He also serves on the advisory board for *Dance Research Journal.*

MARGARET THOMPSON DREWAL is associate professor and director of graduate studies in the Department of Performance Studies at Northwestern University. She is the author of *Yoruba Ritual: Performers, Play, Agency* (Indiana University Press, 1992) and coauthor with Henry John Drewal of *Gelede: Art and Female Power Among the Yoruba* (Indiana University Press, 1983). In addition to research in West Africa, she has also published numerous articles on American dance and popular entertainments and dance in the African diaspora. Her current research interest is the history of the global circulation and transnational flows of performance practices.

SIMONE FORTI began dancing in 1955 with Anna Halprin, who was doing pioneering work in improvisation. She went on to study composition with musicologist/dance educator Robert Dunn, who was introducing dancers to the scores of John Cage at the Merce Cunningham Studio. Thus she began her association with the Judson Dance Theater group. Her work spans from early minimalist dance-constructions, through animal movement studies, news animations, land portraits, and, most recently, Logomotion, an improvisational form based on the resonance between movement and the spoken word. Jennifer Dunning writes in her 1991 *New York Times* review, "Simone Forti presented her first dance program in [1961] and has since then had a steadily increasing influence on post-modernist choreographers interested in exploring 'natural' or nonformalist movement and dance." Forti's *Handbook in Motion* was published in 1974 by the Nova Scotia College of Art and Design Press and appeared in French translation as the fall/winter 2002 issue of the Belgian dance journal *Nouvelles de Danse,* a publication of Contradanse. Now in her sixties, Forti continues to perform and teach worldwide.

SUSAN LEIGH FOSTER, choreographer, dancer, writer, is professor in the Department of World Arts and Cultures at the University of California, Los Angeles. She is the author of *Reading Dancing: Bodies and Subjects in Contemporary American Dance* (1986), *Choreography and Narrative: Ballet's Staging of Story and Desire* (1996), and *Dances that Describe Themselves: The Improvised Choreography of Richard Bull* (2002).

RAYMOND W. GIBBS, JR. is professor of psychology at the University of California, Santa Cruz. He is the author of *The Poetics of Mind: Figurative Thought, Language, and Understanding* (Cambridge University Press, 1999); and with A. Katz, C. Cacciari, and M. Turner, *Figurative Language and Thought* (Oxford University Press, 1998). He is co-editor with Gerard Steen of *Metaphor in Cognitive Linguistics* (Amsterdam: John Benjamins, 1999) and editor of the multidisciplinary journal *Metaphor & Symbol.*

MICHELLE HEFFNER HAYES, executive director of cultural affairs at Miami-Dade Community College, holds a Ph.D. in dance history and theory from the University of California, Riverside. A former dancer and choreographer, she has performed with the flamenco company of Armando Neri and the postmodern companies of Stephanie Gilliland and Susan Rose. Publications by Heffner Hayes include scholarly reviews of contemporary flamenco studies (*Dance Research Journal*, 1996), issues in cultural identity and dance (*Encyclopedia of Homosexuality*, 1998), and discussions of contemporary flamenco on film (*Dancing Bodies Living Histories: New Writings on Dance and Cultures*, 2001). As the artistic director of the Colorado Dance Festival (1997–99), she became an aficionado of tango, flamenco, and *baile popular*. She is a member of the board of directors of Dance/USA.

CARMELA HERMANN, M.F.A., creates choreographed and improvised dances. She has appeared in such venues as Highways Performance Space, Sushi Performance and Visual Art, The J. Paul Getty Center, and Judson Church, performing her own work and in the works of artists such as Simone Forti, Victoria Marks, Tom Young, Lower Left Dance, and Luke Johnson. Hermann is the founder of *Making Dances Workshop* in Los Angeles, a workshop that provides a forum for artists of various backgrounds to create and perform dances with the supportive feedback of fellow artists. In addition she has spent the last ten years studying and teaching the Feldenkrais Method, the Dance Alive Method, and other forms of movement that bring deeper awareness into the connection between the mind and the body. She maintains a private bodywork practice and is a certified Applied Feldenkrais Instructor and Dance Alive Instructor.

CONSTANCE VALIS HILL is a jazz dancer, choreographer, and dance historian who has taught at the Alvin Ailey School of American Dance, Conservatoire d'arts dramatique in Paris, New York University's Tisch School of the Arts, and is currently Five College visiting associate professor of dance at Hampshire College in Amherst, Massachusetts. She received an M.A. in dance research and reconstruction from City College of the City University of New York, and a Ph.D. in performance studies from New York University. Her articles and reviews have appeared in such publications as *Dance Magazine, Village Voice, Dance Research Journal, Studies in Dance History;* and in Gay Morris's edited anthology, *Moving Words: Re-Writing Dance* (Routledge, 1999), and *Dancing Many Drums: Excavations in African-American Dance* (University of Wisconsin Press, 2001), edited by Thomas DeFrantz. Her book *Brotherhood in Rhythm: The Jazz Tap Dancing of the Nicholas Brothers* was published by Oxford University Press in 2000.

RACHEL KAPLAN is a writer, director, and teacher based in Northern California. Her work is concerned with the creation of community and the possibilities of intimate spectacle. She creates large-scale theatrical and cultural events with professional artists, lay-people, and teenagers.

MAURA KEEFE is a choreographer, dancer, and historian. She is a scholar-in-residence at Jacob's Pillow Dance Festival, and she has led audience programs at UCLA; University of California, Riverside; the Kitchen Performance Space in New York; and the Goethe-Institut in Los Angeles. Her work has been published in *Salmagundi, The International Dictionary of Modern Dance,* and *The Encyclopedia of Gay History and Sexuality.* She holds an M.F.A. in dance from Smith College and a Ph.D. in dance history and theory from the University of California, Riverside. Keefe is an assistant professor of dance at Ohio University.

VICTORIA MARKS received the 1997 Alpert Award for Outstanding Achievement in Choreography and has been the recipient of grants and fellowships from the National Endowment for the Arts, the New York State Council on the Arts, the New York Founda-tion for the Arts, and the London Arts Board, among others. She has received a Fulbright Fellowship in choreography and numerous awards for her dance films, including the Grand Prix in the Video Danse Festival (1996 and 1995), the Golden Antennae Award from Bulgaria, the IMZ Award for best screen choreography, and the Best of Show in the Dance Film Association's Dance and the Camera Festival. Marks is an associate pro-fessor of choreography and performance in the Department of World Arts and Cultures at UCLA.

AVANTHI MEDURI is a scholar, dancer, playwright, and professor of South Asian cul-ture, history, and the performing arts. She received her Ph.D. from the Department of Performance Studies, Tisch School of the Arts, New York University, and held a three-year visiting appointment in the Department of Performance Studies, Northwestern Uni-versity. Recipient of several national and international awards, Meduri curated the Ruk-mini Devi traveling exhibition, built around a photo-archive, and presented it as part of the Rukmini Devi Centenary Celebrations in New Delhi, Calcutta, Singapore, Malaysia, and Penang. The exhibitions, scheduled for Sri Lanka, Bangladesh, United Kingdom, and Japan in 2003, are the product of Meduri's commitment to coalition building in the South Asian Diaspora. Meduri's book on Rukmini Devi, including a play dealing with her life, is forthcoming.

STEVE PAXTON teaches, performs, and choreographs mainly in Europe and the United States. His technical background includes the study of modern dance, classical dance, yoga, Aikido, T'ai Chi Chuan, and Vipassana meditation. He was an early member of the Merce Cunningham Dance Company, one of the founders of the Judson Church Dance Theater, Grand Union (both in the United States), and Touchdown Dance (for the visu-ally disabled, in the United Kingdom), and he instigated Contact Improvisation. He has used grants from Change, Inc., the Foundation for the Performance Arts, the John D. Rockefeller Foundation, and the award from a Guggenheim Fellowship to support this research. He has received two Bessie Awards and is a contributing editor for *Contact Quarterly* movement journal, a vehicle for moving ideas. During 2000–2001, Mikhail Baryshnikov's White Oak Dance Project performed two of Paxton's works from the 1960s, *Flat* and *Satisfyin Lover,* in the program titled *Past Forward.*

JANICE ROSS, Ph.D., teaches in the Department of Drama at Stanford University. Prior to that, for ten years, she was staff dance and performance art critic for the *Oakland Tribune.* She wrote for *Dancemagazine* from 1976–1996 and her articles have also appeared in the *New York Times* and the *Los Angeles Times,* among other publications. Her book, *Moving Lessons: Margaret H'Doubler and the Beginning of Dance in American Education,* was published by the University of Wisconsin Press in 2000. She is completing a biography of Anna Halprin to be published by the University of California Press. She is a member of the board of directors of the Society of Dance History Scholars and is past president of the Dance Critics Association. She is the recipient of a 2001 Guggenheim Fellowship.

KAREN SCHAFFMAN is assistant professor of dance at California State University, San Marcos. Her research currently focuses on Contact Improvisation in relation to globalization, theories of transgression, feminist studies, and choreographic analysis. She attributes her knowledge of the form to numerous dance partners and extensive studies with notable teachers including Nina Martin, Karen Nelson, Lisa Nelson, Steve Paxton, and Nancy Stark Smith. She is also cofounder and comember of Lower Left, a teaching and performance collaborative and company-in-residence at Sushi Performance and Visual Art in San Diego.

NANCY STARK SMITH first trained as an athlete and gymnast, leading her to dance in the early 1970s, greatly influenced by the work of The Grand Union. She danced in the first performances of Contact Improvisation in 1972 and has since been central to its development as dancer, teacher, performer, writer/publisher, and organizer. She travels worldwide teaching and performing Contact and other improvised dance work, collaborating with many favorite dance partners and performance makers over the years including Steve Paxton, Karen Nelson, Andrew Harwood, Julyen Hamilton, and musician Mike Vargas. In 1975 she cofounded *Contact Quarterly* dance journal, which she continues to coedit and produce. She lives in western Massachusetts.

ELLEN WEBB studied dance at Bennington College, then performed with Anna Halprin in San Francisco in 1969. Soon after, she moved to New York to perform with both Carolyn Brown and Douglas Dunn. Webb began choreographing and performing her own work in 1979. She has created more than forty pieces—everything from brief solos to evening-length pieces to experimental dawn-to-dusk performances. Most of these pieces have included improvisation. Webb's work has been presented throughout Europe and America, under the aegis of such presenters as the American Center in Paris, the Kitchen in New York, and Cal Performances in the Bay Area.

RUTH ZAPORAH is a teacher, performer, and director. She travels widely in the United States and abroad, performing and teaching Action Theater, her particular form of physical-theater improvisation. Zaporah has twice been the recipient of a National Endowment for the Arts Choreographer's Fellowship. She received a Lifetime Achievement Award from the San Francisco Dance Coalition. Her essays appear frequently in *Contact Quarterly* and her book, *Action Theater: The Improvisation of Presence* (North Atlantic, 1995), is in its second printing.

INDEX

body/mind connection *(continued)*
    unknown, 6–7; meaning as embodied
        experience, 185; power of mind in relation
        to, 71–72; necessity of in improvisation,
        xiv, 114–15; Cynthia Novack's attempt to
        heal, 109; observing, 242; sensation located
        in, 172; as soma, 34; in Western theater
        practice, 21–23, 129; cessation of thought
        on account of, 22. *See also* consciousness;
        Descartes, René; known/unknown
Body-Mind Centering, 259
Bourdeiu, Pierre, 130n.1
Bouton, Jim, 235, 237n.3
Bradshaw, David, 173
Brazil, 123; challenge singing in, 101n.7. *See
    also* Capoeira
Bread to the Bone at the Knitting Factory (New
    York City), 82
Breitenbush Contact Jam (Oregon), 265
Bring in 'Da Noise, Bring in 'Da Funk
    (Glover/Wolfe), 98–100
Brown, James "Buster," 93
Brown, Trisha, xv, 50, 79–80, 233, 235–37,
    254n.1
Bryant, Becky, *134*
Bryant, Steve, *134*
Bubbles, John, 89
Buck and Bubbles, 94
Buddhism, 262; and desire, 225; in Thailand,
    220–22; Tibetan, 249. *See also* Zen
    Buddhism
Bull, Richard, xviii, 5–6
Burt, Ramsay, 79, 85nn.5, 6

Cage, John, 107, 183n.
Calloway, Cab, 96
cancer, 50
Candomblé, 123
CandoCo, 137. *See also* disability
capitalism, 8
Capoeira, 259, 262–63, 266
Caribbean, 92
Carter, Teri, 209
Ceremony of Us (Halprin), 41
Chicago Cubs, 229
children, Anna Halprin's classes for, 41–51;
    as "natural" movers, 42; women's roles in
    relation to, 43
Childs, Lucinda, 233–34
choreography: Anna Halprin's goals in, 43;
    argument for, vs. improvisation, xix, 55,
    241; baseball as, 233; improvisation as
    source for, xiv, 65; indeterminate or "open,"
    78. *See also* composition
Chremos, Asimina, 28, 30–32
Christiansen, Steve, 180
Chuck and Chuckles, 94

Chung, Ray, 209
CI25, xviii–xix, 171–73, 205–11. *See also*
    Contact Improvisation, 25th anniversary of
Clinton, Bill, 250
cognitive science, 185
Coleman, Ornette, 97
collective unconscious. *See* C. G. Jung
Compannia 100 Habilidades, 209
composition: assignments by Simone Forti,
    65; improvisation as spontaneous version of,
    3; necessity of familiarity with rules of, 7;
    situation-response or "in situ," 78, 81–82.
    See also choreography
consciousness, xiv, xviii, 37; in Contact Impro-
    visation, 176–77, 181–82; definition of,
    36; ecological, 262; embodied, 8–9; as
    metaphor, 188, 198. *See also* attention;
    awareness; body/mind connection
Contact Collaborations, 206
Contact Improvisation, xviii–xix; aesthetic
    pleasure in, 186; as aid in other forms of
    improvisation, 67; classical form of, 208;
    and current events, 266; definitions of, 156,
    159; and disability, 13, 15–17, 209–11;
    disorientation in, 154, 162–63, 180, 199,
    210, 260, 265; duets, 80, 166; exercises for,
    176, 179, 209; falling in, 157, 162, 199,
    258–60, 262; concept of "the gap" in, xx,
    177–78, 180; and gender, 79, 85n.5; gravity
    in, 155–56, 172, 200; history of, 153–73,
    205–6, 245; identity in, 263; images used
    in, 176, 182–83; and improvisation in
    other forms, 67, 259; jams, 156, 205, 207,
    209–10, *256*; as common language, 167;
    and Logomotion, 71; name of, 154, 179;
    concept of "nature" in, 108–9; observation
    in, 176; partnering in, 263; Steve Paxton's
    role in development of, 182, 261; pedagogy,
    261–62, 263–65; as performance, 78–79;
    physical dynamics of, 83; as practice, 78;
    precursors of, 107; and prejudice, 170; rela-
    tionships in, 251; and Release Technique,
    182–83; relevance to other fields, 158–59;
    sexuality in, 170–71, 176; and the sixties,
    78; speed in, 247–48; and sports, 78–79,
    157–59, 175, 179–80; telescoping aware-
    ness in, 154; tenth anniversary of, 159;
    training for, 166, 206; 25th anniversary of,
    154, 171, 173, 199; attitude of witnessing
    in, 182. *See also* attention; awareness; CI25;
    consciousness; Paxton, Steve; the stand;
    small dance; Smith, Nancy Stark
Contact Newsletter, 153, 159, 163, 207
Contact Quarterly, xix–xx, 18n., 78; attempts
    to define Contact Improvisation in, 175;
    excerpts from, 153–73, 246–54; history
    of, 207; Steve Paxton quoted in, 108;

Kaplan, Rachel, xx, 63n.1, 83, *214*, 215–26, 270

Karou, Mariane, 68

Kawai, Roko, 28, 31–32

Keefe, Maura, xx, 229–37, 237n.3, 270

Keogh, Martin, 208

King, Kelli, 105–6, 111–12

known/unknown, xviii, 3–4, 6–7, 226, 257, 259–60, 266

Krishna ne begane baro (T. Balasaraswati), 141–42, 145, 147–49

Laban, Rudolf, xx n.1

Lacy, Steve, 97

Lafayette Theatre (New York City), 93

Landor, Jo, 46, 54

Lane, William Henry ("Master Juba"), 93

language: speaking while improvising, 9–10, 23; dancing as not a literary, 170; dance as, 253; limits of in description of improvisation, 36; concept of middle voice in relation to dance, 7–9; poetic, 145, 187; state beyond, xiii; in teaching improvisation, 265; as translation of experience while improvising, 28–30. *See also* speaking; words; writing

Lathrop, Welland, 43, 53

Lauterer, Arch, 49

Leath, A. A., 53

Leistiko, Norma, 46

Lepkoff, Daniel, 169, 208

Lesbian Avengers, 83

Levinas, 263

Lewis, Nancy, 79, 254n.1

Lincoln, Abbey, 89

lindy-hop, 97

Little, Nita, *152*

Logomotion, 57, 62, 68–71, 73. *See also* Simone Forti

Lorca, Federico García, 113

Lunceford, Jimmie, 96

MacAloon, John, 121

Magnesium (Paxton), 153–54, 182, 209, 245. *See also* Contact Improvisation; Paxton, Steve

Making and Doing (Bull), 5–6

Mali, 92

Mangrove, 79

Manning, Susan A., xx n.1

Marin Children's Dance Cooperative, 42–46, 48, 51nn.9, 19

Marks, Victoria, xix, 135–39, 270

Marshall, Susan, 237n.3

Martin, Nina, 71

Matheson, Katy, xx n.2

Matteo, 108

McIntyre, Dianne, 82

Meduri, Avanthi, xix, 141–50, 270

memory: as source for improvisation, 53; as information, 224; as trace, 217; types of, 32–33, 38n.9

Men Working, 79

Menon, Narayana, 142

metaphor, 72, 216, 220, 234; conceptual, 186–89; in Contact Improvisation, 197–202; cultural specificity of, 198; embodied, 190–93; in everyday life, 185; falling as, 258; use in pedagogy, 226

Middlebrook, Diane, 46, 51n.11

Miller, Bebe, 254

mixed ability. *See* DanceAbility; disability

modern dance, xiii, 6, 49, 53, 206

Monk, Meredith, xx n.5

Monson, Jennifer, 32, 82

Morris, Robert, 54

Morrison, Riccardo, 209

Movement Rituals One, Two, and Three (Halprin), 47

Murray, Albert, 97

music: in Africa and West Africa, 91, 119, 122–23; for *Bharatanatyam*, xiv, 143–46, 148–49; for Richard Bull's work, 5; collaborations with, 4, 57; for Contact Improvisation, 201; for flamenco, 110; as habit, 16–17; as used by Anna Halprin, 54; heavy metal, for Jasperse, 83; improvisation in, xv; in improvisational performance, 23; jazz, 82, 94; Latin, 95; response of improviser to, 13, 15; similarity to dance, 185; in tap dance challenge, 89–90

Nagel, Lauri, 59

Natural History of the American Dancer, 78

Nelson, Karen, 209

Nelson, Lisa, 154, 156

Neruda, Pablo, 191, 194n.11

Netherlands, 215–16

New York Improvisation Festival, 82

News Animations (Forti), 58–59

Nicholas Brothers (Fayard and Harold), 95–96

Nigeria: Yoruba people of, 120, 124. *See also* Yoruba

Niles, Doris, 113

Northwestern University, 130n.1

Novack, Cynthia, xviii, 5–6, 84n.3, 85n.5, 153; concept of "responsive body," 109, 206

Novack, Yani, 46

O'Donnell, George, *233*

Ogren, Kathy, 91, 101n.4